An Infinite God and a Father-Son God

An Infinite God and a Father-Son God

The Theology of God for a Contemporary World

KENAN OSBORNE, OFM

WIPF *&* STOCK · Eugene, Oregon

AN INFINITE GOD AND A FATHER-SON GOD
The Theology of God for a Contemporary World

Copyright © 2019 Kenan Osborne, OFM. All rights reserved. Except for brief quotations in critical publications or reviews, no part of this book may be reproduced in any manner without prior written permission from the publisher. Write: Permissions, Wipf and Stock Publishers, 199 W. 8th Ave., Suite 3, Eugene, OR 97401.

Wipf & Stock
An Imprint of Wipf and Stock Publishers
199 W. 8th Ave., Suite 3
Eugene, OR 97401

www.wipfandstock.com

PAPERBACK ISBN: 978-1-5326-7111-1
HARDCOVER ISBN: 978-1-5326-7112-8
EBOOK ISBN: 978-1-5326-7113-5

Manufactured in the U.S.A.   MAY 24, 2019

Contents

In Memoriam | vii

Introduction | ix

1   Questions Surrounding the Theology of the Triune God | 1

2   Contemporary Theologians and Their Tentative Theologies of God | 16

3   The Presentation of the Term Father—אָב—in the *Tanakh* and in Early Rabbinical Texts | 37

4   The Use of the Term Father for YHWH in the Writings of Paul, Mark, Luke, and Matthew | 71

5   The Beginning of Trinitarian Theology (100 to 300 CE) | 96

6   Trinitarian Theologies from the Beginning of the Fourth Century to the End of the Eighth Century | 132

7   An Infinite God: A Name Which Transcends All Other Names for God | 150

Bibliography | 175

In Memoriam

KENAN BERNARD OSBORNE, OFM (1930–2019) made his transition to life with God and with his friends on Good Friday, April 19, 2019. A few months before his passing he arranged with Wipf & Stock to publish his last work. While the manuscript was nearly complete it also required some editing in the introduction, chapter 1, and chapter 7. I am very grateful to the publishers and their staff and to Fr. John Hardin, OFM, Kenan's business manager, for making this book available. *An Infinite God and a Father-Son God* may be read in conjunction with the author's 2015 study, *The Infinity of God and a Finite World: A Franciscan Approach*. While the present study examines the issue of infinity in the biblical and patristic eras, the former study plumbs the medieval scholastic inheritance. Father Osborne's Scotistic Franciscan inheritance and its contemporary importance in a multireligious and multicultural world is highlighted in both books. "Well done, good and faithful servant."

JOSEPH P. CHINNICI, OFM
Franciscan School of Theology
Oceanside, California

Introduction
The Fatherhood of God and the Sonship of Jesus

Two major issues in today's Christian theology are the following: first of all, there is a growing interconnection of contemporary Christian theological issues by Anglican, Orthodox, Protestant, and Roman Catholic Christians. Second, there are positive theological interconnections among today's world religions. These inter-religion conferences, however, are only in their initial stage.

Scholarly men and women from almost all major religions have begun to meet with each other and share their theological positions on the presence of God in our human world. At times, this interrelationship has been called "ecumenical." For instance, the World Council of Churches, which began in 1948, has become a major union of Christian communities. The Roman Catholic Church, however, is not a member of these gatherings, though it has been an "observer" at their regular meetings.

The second major religious group, namely Interfaith Dialogue, has brought different religions together.[1] In this volume, I am more interested in this latter group, since my focus is on the theology of "one God" and the presence of the "one and the same God" in every human being. There are still boundaries for most major religions, especially the Christian, Jewish, Hindu, Islamic, and Buddhist religions. Nonetheless, many contemporary books and articles on interreligious dialogue, written by members of these religions, have become not only more frequent but also more united. In today's world, there is as yet no theology of one and the

---

1. See Wikipedia.org, s.v. "Interfaith Dialogue." There are many groups in this category, and the number of these groups indicates that something new is happening in the area of religion. The WCC is an international union of Christians which began in 1948. Its membership is worldwide, whereas the interfaith groups, though numerous, are still within a beginner's framework.

same God for all of these religions, but there is a growing interest in interreligious discussions. This is the issue I wish to pursue in this volume. Here in the introduction I will simply indicate six parts of the problem I am addressing.

PART ONE: CONTEMPORARY INTERRELIGIOUS DIALOGUES AND THE HISTORY OF MANKIND

In 2002, John Bowker published a book entitled *God: A Brief History*. In this volume of four hundred pages, Bowker considers the theological meaning of God in a historical and theological way for almost all world religions from the earliest centuries down to the present. He also brings in the atheistic stance in which God is not an existent being. I will not present the theology of God from these hundreds of religious communities, but Bowker's book shows us that God has been an issue from very prehistoric times down to today in almost all historical cultures. In my final chapter, I will center on the issue of "one God" and "hundreds of religions." I will do this under the title of an "Infinite God." Three particular questions arise.

First, there are questions related to the naming of God. In Hebrew, the major word for God is Yahweh, יחוה, and the meaning of this word is uncertain. For some scholars the term YHWH means "One is" or "He is," or as many Hebrew scholars state "I am who I am." We have no knowledge at all of the original meaning of YHWH, and we have no detailed history of the "theology" of YHWH nor is there any history of the "philosophy" of YHWH. To say that the term means either essence or existence is deceptive. John McKenzie writes:

> The usage of the name Yahweh in the bible shows no evidence in the OT of any etymology, and there is no evidence in the OT of a theology being built around the meaning of the name.[2]

In the history of Christianity, from the second century down to the ninth century, the major theological dispute was the divinization of Jesus. During all these centuries, there were numerous debates on the divinity of Jesus. These debates involved theologians, bishops, and even Christian communities. All of the early ecumenical councils of the church were

---

2. McKenzie, "Aspects of Old Testament Thought," 1286.

significantly focused on the divinization of Jesus.³ However, during these early centuries there were significant Christian scholars who did not accept the divinization of Jesus, and there were significant Christian scholars who accepted the divinization of Jesus. Generally speaking, the language in these councils and in the writings of these scholars was Greek. However, it was not simply the use of Greek terms, but as Lateran IV states: "Between Creator and creature no similitude can be expressed without implying an even greater dissimilitude."⁴

In today's world the usage of Greek philosophical terms in the naming of God renders these terms themselves problematic, namely the languages such as Chinese,⁵ Japanese, Hindi,⁶ etc. Greek key words such as person, nature, etc., have one meaning in Greek, but in other languages there are totally different frameworks for philosophical issues such as person and nature.⁷ For example, John Wippel, in his volume *The Metaphysical Thought of Thomas Aquinas*, frequently states that the nature of God is a unified essence-existence nature.⁸ These two issues are not divided in God. The very nature of God is the union of esse and essentia. My view is this: in the human world, there are several meanings of the word "nature." For instance, Kwong-Loi Shun has written an excellent book entitled *Mencius and Early Chinese Thought*. Shun devotes fifty-one pages on the Asian meanings of nature in the Chinese world. The Chinese meaning of nature is totally different from Western descriptions of "nature." As in many Chinese words, the same word can have several meanings, and none of them explain the nature of God. I have found this book extremely helpful.⁹ Hajime Nakamura, in his lengthy volume *Ways*

---

3. See the material on the First Council of Nicea in 325 CE, the First Council of Constantinople in 381 CE, the Council of Ephesus in 431 CE, the Council of Chalcedon in 451 CE, the Second Council of Constantinople in 553 CE, the Third Council of Constantinople in 681 CE, the Second Council of Nicea in 787 CE, and the Fourth Council of Constantinople in 869–870 CE, in which Photius was condemned because of his rejection of the phrase "Filioque."

4. Lateran Council IV, n. 6, Denz, p. 262.

5. Yu-lan, *History of Chinese Philosophy*.

6. Dubois, *Hindu Manners, Customs, and Ceremonies*, 482ff.

7. The traditional Christian theology on the divinization of Jesus remains to some degree a contemporary theological issue since today's descriptions of both "person" and "nature" are quite different from the meaning of person-nature in the early centuries mentioned above.

8. See Wippel, *Metaphysical Thought of Thomas Aquinas*, 150–57.

9. Shun's book requires some understanding of Chinese characters, for "hsing"

of Thinking of Eastern Peoples, expresses in detail the issues of disunion and not simply a comparison between Euro-American philosophy and Asian philosophy.[10] Nakamura's lengthy section on the Chinese way of thinking presents a totally different way of thinking and speaking. Nakamura points out on several pages the major and foundational way of writing and speaking. Chapters 16 and 17 indicate how foreign Greek philosophy is from the Chinese "philosophical" way of understanding. He writes: "This meant that they were little interested in universals which comprehend or transcend instances."[11] Chinese philosophy is profoundly different from Western philosophies. Can we Westerners today see that a majority of human men and women do not understand Greek philosophical terminology and they see the physical world in a very different way than the terms substance, essence, nature, person, etc.?

A second major issue today is the scientific presentation of *Homo sapiens sapiens* and the impact of this knowledge on our understanding of "salvation." In the history of human life, contemporary scientists have found the beginnings of *Homo sapiens sapiens* in a startling way. Until 3000 BCE, there are no written records of human life. However, there are many contemporary scientists who state that human life began long before humans had developed writing. The first written documents by human beings are the texts found in Sumeria Tanakh (ca. 3500–3000 BCE) and those found in Egypt (slightly later than the Sumerian texts). Contemporary scientists generally refer to our first human beings as either *Homo sapiens* or *Homo sapiens sapiens*. F. Clark Howell in his book *Early Man* states that the first true human beings appeared some ten thousand years ago.[12] In other words, there are ten thousand years between our present date and the emergence of human life. Or one can state that from

---

indicates several diverse meanings. None of them correspond to the Greek word Φύσις, which is central to a Triune God, understood as three persons in one nature. Shun opens our minds to the "One Nature" of God.

10. See the English translation of Nakamura's book, *Ways of Thinking of Eastern Peoples*. One should first read Nakamura's lengthy introduction (3–43) before moving into his analyses of India, China, Tibet, and Japan. The revised English translation of this volume is by Philip Wiener.

11. See Nakamura, *Ways of Thinking of Eastern Peoples*, 185. Chapters 16 and 17 indicate that the Chinese ways of thinking and writing are radically different from Greek philosophy, which in many ways still govern Western languages. Christian theology yesterday and today is highly expressed by Greek philosophy. Can it also be expressed by Asian philosophy? The answer is no.

12. See Howell, *Early Man*. Ten thousand years from 2018 CE is 8000 BCE.

ten thousand years ago down to the appearance of human writing in 3500 or 3000 BCE there are 4,500 or 4,000 years in which human life existed, but during those years there are no written documents. Contemporary scientists generally state that the ten-thousand mark eliminates for the most part Neanderthal and Australopithecus people. These first truly human men and women (from 8000 BCE to 3500 BCE) had no religion that we know of. There are relics of buildings, ovens, food, etc., but there are no written documents in whatsoever language, nor are there any clear "religious" relics.

Third, one of my major issues, which will be analyzed in chapter 7, is this: strangely, no theological texts by contemporary religious scholars take the earliest centuries of human life into account, that is, from the beginning of *Homo sapiens sapiens*. The scientific dating of the first *Homo sapiens sapiens* is highly divided by contemporary scientists. Roughly, one can say: around 100,000 BCE down to 10,000 BCE. These people lived prior to any of today's major religions: Hinduism, Judaism, Christianity, Islam, etc. On the basis of the contemporary scientific and historical data on the origins of human life, it would seem that the "infinity of God" might be the better way to describe God. I do not mean that one simply states that God is infinite. Other adjectives for God are wise, holy, everlasting, etc. However, in this volume I am stating that God's very being is itself infinite, and therefore all religions can speak of God only in a descriptive way and not in an essentialist way. This book will attempt to explain this position and refer to it throughout the text.

PART TWO: THE HISTORICAL UNDERSTANDING OF THE TERM "GOD"

One might ask: "Is there only one God?" Contemporary leaders and scholars of various religions might answer this question in a positive way, but the meanings of their affirmations might be: "There is only one God and that one God is our denominational God."

In the opening paragraphs of the new *Catechism of the Catholic Church*, one finds a surprising statement on the "one God" issue. This citation refers to the one God who encompasses and surpasses any and every "denominational God." We read:

xiv   Introduction

> The desire for God is written in the human heart, because man [and woman] is created by God and for God: and God never ceases to draw man [and woman] to himself.¹³

The above citation from the *Catechism of the Catholic Church*, namely that "the creator God has been written in the heart of every human being" is a remarkable statement. There is no "Roman Catholic God," since one and the same God has written his name in the heart of every human being, regardless of any religion or even non-religion. Moreover, the authors of the *Catechism* immediately add a statement from the Vatican II document *Gaudium et Spes*:

> The dignity of man [and woman] rests above all on the fact that he [she] is called to communion with God. This invitation to converse with God is addressed to man [and woman] as soon as he [she] comes into being.¹⁴

A few pages later, however, the authors of the *Catechism* present a different approach to one's knowledge of God. Instead of our knowing of God because God has written his name in our hearts at the very beginning of our life, the authors turn to a divine revelation of God which is totally beyond our human understanding. In this citation, the authors offer little to no explanation regarding the interconnection of one's natural knowledge of God with a divinely-revealed knowledge of God.

> By natural reason man can know God with certainty, on the basis of his works. But there is another order of knowledge, which man cannot possibly arrive at by his own powers: namely the order of divine Revelation. Through an utterly free decision, God has revealed himself, and [he has] given himself to man. This he does by revealing the mystery, his plan of loving goodness, formed from all eternity in Christ, for the benefit of all men. God has fully revealed this plan by sending us his beloved Son, our Lord Jesus Christ, and the Holy Spirit.¹⁵

If all men and women have a "desire for God written in their human hearts," and if "by natural reason" every man and woman can know God

---

13. See the official English text of Catholic Church, *Catechism of the Catholic Church*, 2nd ed., n. 27 p. 13. The authors refer the reader to other passages in the *Catechism*, namely n. 355, p. 91, and n. 1718, p. 427.

14. Vatican II document, *Gaudium et Spes*, n. 27. Original Latin text: *Vaticanum II: Constitutiones, Decreta, Declarationes* (Typis Polyglottis Vaticanis, 1966), 681–835.

15. Catholic Church, *Catechism*, n. 50, p. 19.

with certainty," there cannot be a divide in one religion with any other religion. Everyone is included. Two other questions arise in this context.

First, long before Judaism, long before Christianity, and long before Islam, men and women already believed in God. However, we have only some knowledge of the early stages of 3000 BCE, as there are no written records of human life. There are many contemporary scientists who state that human life began long before humans had developed writing.[16] The first written documents by human beings are those texts found in Sumeria (ca. 3500–3000 BCE) and those found in Egypt (ca. 3000–2800 BCE). Since writing was not part of human life until 5,000 years ago, our knowledge of the earliest Hinduism and Buddhism, which began in Nepal and India, is limited. Scholars differ on the historical origins of Indian religions. Some contemporary scholars find these religious origins in areas of northern India dating back to the sixth or fifth centuries BCE. Prior to Buddhism and Hinduism, there were localized religions throughout northern India and Nepal, but the data on these possible religions is extremely meager.[17]

In the history of human life, contemporary scientists have presented the beginnings of *Homo sapiens sapiens* in a startling way. They have come to the conclusion that human life—*Homo sapiens sapiens*—had its beginning between 200,000 years ago down to 50,000 or even 10,000 years ago. In these early years, there is little to no data on religion, which may have existed during these thousands of years. Thus, a major issue today is the scientific presentation of *Homo sapiens sapiens*.

Second, the names for God in world religions have been and still are numerous. For instance, in Africa, the Yorubas believe in *Ologun*, and the Ibos believe in *Chekwa* or *Chineke*.[18] The Akans in Ghana be-

16. One of these earliest Neanderthal communities has been found in Banpo, India, which is just west of Xian. It has provided us with major implements. See Osborne and Min, *Science and Religion*. There are nine pages of bibliography (179–87) which contain both articles and books on the issues of today's science and religion. Roughly speaking, one could ask: how old is the universe? Many contemporary scientists indicate an age of twelve billion years, others indicate an age of fifteen billion years, and still others indicate seventeen billion years and even beyond. See Osborne and Min, *Science and Religion*, 25–36.

17. The beginnings of both Hinduism and Buddhism are difficult to explain. The name "Hinduism" became acceptable only when India was under British rule. A more ancient name, "Santana Dharma," means "the eternal spiritual path." The earliest forms of this complex religion have been dated about four thousand years ago, and in Hinduism there are many different names and formats. Similar dates can refer to Buddhism.

18. Adewale, "Names and Concepts of Deity," 67–76. See also Lee, "Bonaventure

lieve in *Nyame*.¹⁹ These African names for God were not borrowed from Christian missionaries; rather, the names for God were present in these various tribes long before any Christian contacts had occurred. In *Naming God*, John Ansah gives the details in these religions as regards their belief in God and their naming of God.

In the writings of major Chinese scholars, there is little to no mention of God. For instance, Wing-tsit Chan in his *Source Book in Chinese Philosophy* provides us in English with some of the writings of Chung Tzu (ca. 399 and 295 BCE), who wrote: "It seems there is a True Lord . . . but there is no indication of his existence." Chan continues: "Any personal God or one that directs the movement of things is clearly out of harmony with Chung Tzu's philosophy."²⁰

Almost a thousand years later, Chu Hsi (ca. 1130–1200 CE) continued this rejection of a personal God. In his volume *The Great Ultimate*, Chu Hsi states: "The Great ultimate is nothing other than a principle." "The Great Ultimate is not a thing existing in a chaotic state before the formation of heaven and earth." And "the Great Ultimate is merely the principle of heaven and earth and the myriad things."²¹ Chan begins his chapter on "The Great Synthesis in Chu Hsi" in these words:

> No one has exercised greater influence on Chinese thought than Chu Hsi except Confucius, Mencius, Lao Tzu, and Chuang Tzu. He [Chu Hsi] gave Confucianism a new meaning and for centuries his views dominated not only Chinese thought but the thought of Korea and Japan as well.²²

In his writings, Chu Hsi gave the views of Confucius a new complexion, especially in his understanding of *Jen* as "the character of man's mind and the principle of love."²³

---

and Chinul."

19. Ansah, "Names and Concepts of God," 86–97.

20. For an English translation of the citation from Chung Tzu's volume, see Chan, *Source Book in Chinese Philosophy*, 181.

21. See Chan, *Source Book in Chinese Philosophy*, 638. On 640–41, Chan notes that contemporary scholars, such as Fung Yu-Lan, state that Chan is similar to Plato and Aristotle. Chan, however, states: "Chu Hsi is neither Platonic nor Aristotelian" (641). Chuang Tzu (between 399 and 295 BCE) wrote: "It seems there is a True Lord . . . but there is no indication of his existence." Chan remarks: "Any personal God or one that directs the movement of things is clearly out of harmony with Chung Tzu's philosophy" (181). See also Lee, "'Oriental' View of Nature and God," 98–105.

22. Chan, *Source Book in Chinese Philosophy*, 588.

23. Chan, *Source Book in Chinese Philosophy*, 591.

In various religions, such as Judaism and Christianity, scholars have translated some of their religious books, and in doing so the authors used one or the other word to signify a deity. However, there are no Chinese words which translate Allah, Yahweh, and the names for the Christian God. In the *Catechism of the Catholic Church*, as we have seen above, the authors state: "The desire for God is written in the human heart, because man [and woman] is created by God and for God." Asian scholars, for the most part, would disagree with this statement. For the Bahai, the name for God is *Bahá*. For Islam, the name for God is *Allah*. For Hinduism the main name for God is *Brahma*. For Sikhism, the primary name for God is *Ik Onkar*. The desire for God may be written in the human heart, but the naming of God has been multiple. The historical diversity of these names is overwhelming.

In some religions, God is called "Father," but the term "Father" is not used in a physical way. Rather, it is generally used in a descriptive way. In the Jewish religious world, YHWH has often been called Father, but this title is only poetic, descriptive, and metaphorical. In the Jewish religion, Yahweh is the most important name for God, but the meaning of the name Yahweh is simply "I am who I am."[24] For the Jewish people, Yahweh eventually became the major name for the one and only God. Albrecht Alt, in his lengthy and thought-provoking essay "The God of the Fathers," presents a detailed history of the Jewish gods in their earliest years.[25] With the acceptance of YHWH, all other so-called gods were, in the Jewish mindset, "false gods."[26] Alt, however, traces the history of the God of Israel in detail. Prior to Moses, the Jewish use of the names for God was multiple, and it is difficult to determine their origins.[27]

---

24. Most scholars say that from the time of Moses onward, the Jewish name for God has been YHWH. In the patriarchal period prior to Moses, many Jewish authors had stated that the Jewish God was El, and only at the time of Moses was El changed to Yahweh. The history of the Jewish names for God is a divided history: some authors unite the God of the fathers (Abraham, Isaac, and Jacob) with YHWH, while other scholars use a different time frame, namely YHWH, begins with Moses. For details of these positions, see Kaufmann, *History of Israelite Religion*, 60–78. Helmer Ringgren in *Israelite Religions* provides us with a very detailed explanation of the Jewish meaning of God, i.e., Yahweh. See ch. 1, pp. 32–33, and ch. 2, pp. 66–88.

25. See Alt, *Essays on Old Testament History*, 1–66.

26. I will return to this issue in chapter 3, in which I cite at some length both Albrecht Alt and Yehezkel Kaufmann.

27. See the conclusion of Alt's volume, beginning on p. 45, but especially 57ff.

PART THREE: THE THREE FOUNDATIONAL ISSUES FOR OUR BELIEF IN ONE GOD

For each of the three foundational issues for our belief in God as presented by Peter Phan (see ch. 2 below) I will indicate in detail how and why the current Christian approach to Trinitarian theology needs to be reinterpreted more clearly.

The First Foundational Issue

> The historical use of the term "Father" for God is found abundantly in both Judaism and Christianity. In Judaism, the use of the word "Father" has been and still is a poetic name for God. In Christianity, from the second century CE onward, the use of the word "Father" for God gradually ceased to be poetic. This took place when Christians began to divinize Jesus as the Son of God.

Today, there are serious questions regarding the title "Father God." The name "Father," when used for God, can be poetic, descriptive, and metaphorical. A poetic use of the term Father for God has been frequently used in Judaism from its earliest beginnings down to today. However, at the very end of the first century and into the early decades of the second century CE, a few Christian leaders began to call Jesus the "divine" Son of God. In their view, the human Jesus remained human but Jesus was also divine since he was the Son of God.

The Second Foundational Issue

> The historical use of the phrase "Jesus is the Son of God the Father" has been used in two ways. In the writings of Paul and the three synoptic authors, only YHWH is called "Father." In these writings Jesus is called "Son of God," but only in a poetic, descriptive, and metaphorical way. From the last two years of the first century CE down to the beginning of the ninth century CE, the divinity of Jesus was the major issue which divided Christian bishops, theologians, and Christian men and women.

From the second century CE down to the ninth century CE, there was a major division in Christian theology. There were Christian scholars who upheld the two natures of Jesus, but they also upheld that there was only one person in Jesus, namely the second person of the Holy Trinity.

During these same centuries, there were also well-educated Christians who believed that there was only one God, namely God the Father. These Christian scholars stated that Jesus might be called "God's Son," but his sonship was not divine in the sense that it was equally one and the same nature as that of the Father.[28]

The Third Foundational Issue

> If Christians use the term "infinite" as an essential aspect of their God, then the Christian church can call their God: "The One and Only God." All other so-called gods are not infinite, and therefore they are not truly divine. My question is: what does the word infinity mean and how has it been used by Christians as a description of God? If God is infinite, no human person can truly "know" God. The infinity of God challenges any and all religions which claim that their God is the only legitimate God. My question is: can any human person have a clear idea about the reality of an infinite God?

The issue of infinity was first referred to by two Greek philosophers, Anaximander (ca. 609–547 BCE) and Anaxagoras (ca. 500–437 BCE). Historically, the issue of infinity has had many different meanings. Today, the word is used in mathematics, physics, metaphysics, psychology, religion, and the arts. In religious writings, many theologians state that God is infinite, but then they begin to describe God or even define the infinite essence of God. Let us consider each of these issues in a detailed way.

PART FOUR: CONTEMPORARY QUESTIONS REGARDING THE NAMING OF GOD

The above foundational issues are important today, since the writings of Karl Barth and Karl Rahner from 1940 onward have brought about a major reconsideration of Trinitarian theology.[29] This renewal will be covered in chapter 2. In the contemporary renewal of Trinitarian theol-

---

28. In the second century CE, the divinity of the Holy Spirit was mentioned here and there, but a theology of the Holy Spirit as the third person of the Trinity began in the late decades of the third century. The ecumenical council of Nicea held in 325 CE simply mentions the Holy Spirit—καὶ εἰς τὸ ἅγιον πνεῦμα—at the very end of the main statement.

29. See Phan, *Cambridge Companion to the Trinity*, parts 4–5, 173–362.

ogy, issues can be raised with respect to the names "Father" and "Son" in relationship to God; and the infinity of God.

First, there are serious questions regarding the title "Father God." Can the name "Father" be used as an essential name for God, or can it be used only in a poetic, descriptive, and metaphorical way? A poetic use of the term Father would imply that Jesus is only human. Christian doctrine, however, says that Jesus was essentially divine since he was the Son of God. The divinization of Jesus as Son of God also divinizes the phrase "God the Father." My question is this: can the words "Father" and "Son" be used in defining God in an essential way or can they be used only in a poetic way? Let me give just two examples, one related to the early councils of the church, the other to scholarship on the New Testament.

The bishops who attended the second ecumenical council in Constantinople (381 CE) were for the most part Eastern bishops. They accepted a new creed for the entire church, namely the Nicene-Constantinopolitan Creed. At a later date, Pope Benedict VIII added a phrase to this creed, namely that the Holy Spirit was of one substance with the Father: ὁμοούσιος τῷ πατρί. Because this Greek terminological phrase was not part of the Orthodox Church, the Orthodox bishops began to separate themselves from the Roman Church. Some of the leaders of the Eastern Churches held together with the episcopal leaders of the Roman Church at a Council in Constantinople in 879–880 CE, in which they annulled the use of the term filioque. My question remains: How can one call the Christian God both a "Father God" and at the same time call the human Jesus a "Son God?"

In 1996, Raymond Brown published a book entitled *An Introduction to the New Testament*.[30] In this volume, Brown has presented an explanation of every New Testament statement on the preexistence of Jesus. In his explanations, he cites author after author who either argue for the preexistence of Jesus or who question the preexistence of Jesus. In these citations, the reader can see that in the New Testament the issue of the preexistence of Jesus is both affirmed by some scholars and dismissed by other scholars.[31] Brown claims that no NT passages state precisely that the Son coexisted from all eternity with the Father.[32]

---

30. Brown, *Introduction to the New Testament*. See also Moloney, "Johannine Theology," 1422n35.

31. See Brown, *Introduction to the New Testament*, 337–38, 347, 364, 371, 374, 391, 492–93, 683, 686, 717, 826, and 835.

32. Brown, "Aspects of New Testament Thought," 1359n22.

The Jewish gospel writers, Paul, Mark, and Matthew, refer to God—Θεός—many times. However, one might rightfully ask: who is the God in these citations? Since all three New Testament writers were Jewish, they would have called God, in Hebrew, YHWH, or in Aramaic, אבא ('abba). When they became followers of Jesus, one might ask: did the "God" whom they mention in their New Testament presentations continue to be the "YHWH God" or in their writings are they referring to a "non-Jewish Trinitarian God" of the Christians? In the writings of Paul and in the three Synoptic Gospels, the authors use the Greek word for God, namely Θεός, but which Θεός are the authors referring to?[33] At the time of their writings, the divinization of Jesus had not yet taken place.

Second, the issue of infinity. As mentioned above the issue of infinity was first referred to by the two Greek philosophers Anaximander and Anaxagoras. Anaximander was fairly negative in his description of "infinity" insofar as the universe itself would disappear. He stated in a clear way that the ἀρχή was not ἄπειρον. Anaxagoras was more positive in his analysis. André Laks presents in a detailed way that Anaxagoras argued that everything which now exists will continually survive.[34] Historically, the issue of infinity has had many differing meanings. Today the word is used in mathematics, physics, metaphysics, psychology, religion, and the arts. In religious writings, many theologians state that God is infinite, but only some scholars begin to define the infinite essence of God. Most contemporary scholars consider "infinite" as an attribute of God, not as a major description of God's nature. In the final chapter, I will present the meaning of infinite and the ways in which it is defined in science and also the only way in which it can be defined in a theology of God. My position on this issue is the following: referring to God as infinite cannot be considered as a physical definition or an attribute of God. Rather, the infinity of God is a matter of faith. We *believe* in an infinite God; we do not reason that God is infinite. Moreover, an infinite God cannot be defined by a finite human being.

---

33. Since Luke was not Jewish, he did not grow up believing in YHWH. When he became a follower of Paul or Jesus, did he become a believer in YHWH? There is no answer to this question since the historical material on Luke's early life is not very clear.

34. See Laks, "Anaxagoras."

PART FIVE: IS THERE AN ACCEPTABLE THEOLOGY OF THE FATHERHOOD OF GOD AND THE DIVINIZATION OF JESUS?

A central contemporary issue, mentioned above, is the divinization of Jesus. This will be covered more directly in chapter 1 and again in chapter 5. Biblically and theologically, this theme is closely allied to the preexistence of Jesus. My own focus is on the Christian naming of God both as "Father" and as "Son." These two words differ from language to language, e.g., Padre, Père, Πατήρ, etc., and Hijo, Fil, υἱός, etc., but the meaning of father and son is common to all members of human life. In the Scriptures, the terms father and son have absolutely two different meanings. The first meaning centers on human beings who describe God as "Father" in a poetical way. In the second century CE a second meaning of Father began to develop. In this change, God is no longer only a poetical Father; rather God is a divine Father God who has a Divine Son-God. One can rightfully ask if there are not some better terms which might have been used instead of God the Father and God the Son.

PART SIX: THE INFINITE GOD—A NAME WHICH TRANSCENDS ALL OTHER NAMES FOR GOD

Two other words which describe God are infinite and infinity. In both the Old Testament and the New Testament, the words infinite and infinity are not used at all. The question will be covered in chapter 1 and returned to in chapter 7. It should be noted in passing that medieval theologians like Thomas Aquinas and Bonaventure stated in an affirmative way that God was infinite. However, for Thomas and Bonaventure—as well as other medieval theologians—divine infinity was not presented as the major aspect of God's being. Rather, these scholars presented infinity as simply an "attribute" of God.[35] In *De Primo Principio*, John Duns Scotus writes: "Nona Conclusio: Te esse infinitum et incomprehensibilem a finito" (Ninth conclusion: You are infinite and incomprehensible for a finite mind). In chapter 7 of this present volume, I will suggest—and only suggest—that for all religions there must be just one God. All other names for God focus on something finite, for example, God is all-powerful, God

---

35. See my volume *The Infinity of God and a Finite World*, ch. 5, "The Theology of the Existence and Infinity of God in the Writings of Bonaventure," 83–121; also ch. 6, "The Theology of the Existence and Infinity of God in the Writings of Thomas Aquinas," 123–68.

is all-knowing, and God is all-merciful; secondary names for God are extremely important, but these secondary divine names reveal, only to some degree, one or another major aspect of the infinite God.

CONCLUDING SUMMARY

In summary, there are two major issues which contemporary Christian theologians might begin to reconsider in an in-depth way, namely:

1. Do the terms "Father" and "Son" have any essential meaning which might explain the relationship between God the Father and God the Son? From a human standpoint, God is essentially neither a "Father" nor a "Son." Nor do these two words have some exclusive meaning when they refer to divinity. They are human words which define a human father and a human son.

2. The meaning of the term "infinite" when used as a major aspect of God has several meanings in the theological textbooks. Most often the term infinite is considered only as another attribute of God. Infinity is in no way an attribute, even a divine attribute. If, in religious thinking, God is called infinite, the meaning of infinite is not the same as mathematical infinity, philosophical infinity, metaphysical infinity, physical infinity, etc. Divine infinity has no affiliation with any and all other infinities. We believe in the infinity of God; we do not rationally understand the infinity of God.

   In the chapters which follow, I begin by addressing a few contemporary questions in chapter 1. This is followed by a review of contemporary theologians in their "tentative theologies of God" (chapter 2) and then several chapters in which I present in a detailed way the religious history in which the Jewish religion and subsequently the Christian religion referred to God as "Father" as used in the Bible for God (chapters 2–6). Finally, in chapter 7, I offer a naming of God which includes all religions, namely the one and only Infinite God.

A NOTE ON TEXTS AND TRANSLATIONS

The following diagram lists some of the major Greek words and their meaning in early Trinitarian writings which I have used. In the first section, I have listed three books; two books are biblically oriented, while the third is a dictionary. There are three letters which are abbreviations for the three books, S, B, and O. In the second section, I have listed four Greek words used by these authors. These four Greek words are found abundantly in the early Greek Christian writers.

However, in today's English translations of the New Testament, the authors do not always use the same English translations. For instance, the Greek word φύσις appears in Romans 2:27 and in Ephesians 2:3. The Greek word οὐσία appears in Luke 15:11. The Greek word ὑπόστασις appears in 2 Corinthians 9:4. The Greek word συγγένεια appears in Acts 7:3.

There are two highly accepted books which translate the biblical Greek into English, and there are standard Greek dictionaries which translate Greek words into English. In the following outline, I am using three very acceptable Greek-English and English-Greek translations of key passages, two in the Bible and one in a dictionary.

ABBREVIATIONS	
The words connected to S (Strong) are taken from *The New Strong's Exhaustive Concordance of the Bible*	ουσια—translated as substance (S) property, wealth (B) essence, substance (O)
The words connected to B (Bauer) are taken from *The Greek-English Lexicon of the New Testament*	φύσια—translated as nature, kind (S) essence, substance, nature (B) nature (O)
The words connected to O (Oxford) are taken from *The Oxford New Greek Dictionary*	υποστασις—translated as essence (S) foundation, nature, reality (B) foundation (O)
	συγγένεια—translated as relatives, kindred (S) relationship, kinship (B) blood relationship, affinity (O)

In today's English Christian literature regarding Jesus, the above translations of the Greek words are very common not only in theology but also in philosophy. The above Greek and English words, however, are not universally accepted as the only philosophical terms which can describe all reality. As I have noted above, Asian languages have quite different names for substance, essence, person, and relationship. The Euro-Americans do not think in a yin and yang manner, but the Chinese have understood the universe in and through their own philosophical terms, yin and yang, for centuries.

I

Questions Surrounding the Theology of the Triune God

As yet, there is no theology of one and the same God for all contemporary religions, but there is, however, a growing interest in interreligious discussions, in which the issue of "one God" is only at a beginning stage.[1] In both Judaism and Christianity, the one God is called "Father." In most other religions, God may be referred to as Father, but only in a rather minimal and poetic way. In this chapter there are two issues which I focus on in depth: the first issue focuses on the name "Father," as used in the Bible for God. The second issue focuses on the infinity of God.

PART ONE: THE NAMING OF GOD

In the history of Christianity, from the second century down to the eighth century, the major theological dispute was the divinization of Jesus. It was only during these centuries that the debate on the divinity of Jesus came to end. In both the Latin and Greek Churches, the divinity of Jesus was a major belief even though the theologies of East and West were different.

In the history of human life, contemporary scientists have presented the beginnings of *Homo sapiens sapiens* in a startling way. Until 3500

---

1. The following books and articles are only a sampling of interreligious studies: Knitter, *Introducing Theologies of Religions*; Dupuis, *Il christianesimo e le religioni*; Phan, *Being Religious Interreligiously*; Fredericks, *Buddhists and Christians*; and Kloppenburg, *A Ecclesiologia do Vaticano II*.

BCE, there are no written records of human life. However, contemporary scientists state that human life began sometime between ca. 100,000 years ago down to ca. 40,000 or 50,000 years ago, or for some scientists 20,000 to 15,000 years ago.

These early men and women had no religion that we know of, and today's theological texts by religious scholars do not take into account these centuries of human life. Earliest men and women had no knowledge of Jesus, Moses, or the leaders and writers who were Hindu, Buddhist, Islamist, etc. Given the scientific and historical data of human life, it would seem that the infinity of God might be the best issue to describe God. I do not mean one simply states that God is infinite, just as God is wise, holy, everlasting, etc. Rather, I am stating that God's very essence is infinite. If this position has any human acceptance, all religions can speak of God but only in a descriptive way not in an essentialist way. Let me explain this position in a more detailed way.

In the Jewish *Tanakh*, YHWH is referred to as "Father," either directly or indirectly, only twenty-one times. In the same sacred book, YHWH—אהוה—is referred to 6,828 times. In the later history of Judaism, namely from around 400 BCE, the Pentateuch was officially completed, and by the end of the second century BCE and into the first century BCE the remainder of the *Tanakh* was completed. Around the beginning of the second century BCE, Jewish scholars and Jewish people began to call YHWH "Father" in a more abundant way. However, the term Father, when used by the Jewish population for YHWH, was used only in a poetic, descriptive, and metaphorical way.

Aramaic slowly became the major language in Israel and by 135 CE the Hebrew language had become a dead language. In the lifetime of Jesus, the common language was Aramaic, and therefore the frequent naming of God was called "Abba"—אבבא'. YHWH means "One is" or "He is" or as many Hebrew scholars state "I am who I am." In the *Tanakh*, the term "Father"—אָב—or a reference to "Father" through the use of the term "Son"—בֵּן—are used only twenty-one times in its relationship to YHWH. We can conclude that the Jewish naming of God as "Father" in the *Tanakh* is minimal.

We have no knowledge at all of the original meaning of YHWH, and there is no detailed history of the "theology" of YHWH nor is there any history of the "philosophy" of YHWH. To say that the term means either essence or existence is deceptive. John McKenzie writes:

> The usage of the name Yahweh in the Bible shows no evidence in the OT of any etymology, and there is no evidence in the OT of a theology being built around the meaning of the name.[2]

Even if we, today, might come to know the original meaning of the name YHWH, the Jewish writers of the OT had no understanding of its meaning. In the OT, many authors avoided the name YHWH out of respect for God and they used several other names for God. Helmer Ringgren, in his book *Israelite Religion*, states the following:

> Yahweh is simply the proper name of the God of Israel; the Old Testament is not in the least concerned what it may have once meant as a Hebrew word. The Septuagint simply translates it with *kurios* "Lord," because at the time of translation motives of reference prevented people from pronouncing the name of God; they replaced it instead with ădônāy, "the Lord (lit. 'my lord')."[3]

Ringgren devotes an entire chapter on the naming of God as Yahweh and he does so by a historical description of the interrelationship of Yahwism and Paganism.[4] Today, the understanding of the word *Yahweh* is still diverse and it is still divisive. Contemporary interreligious pluralism remains in an infant stage of development, but it may develop more strongly in the twenty-first century CE.[5] If interreligious pluralism becomes stronger, the question of one God for all of these religions will slowly become a major issue.

PART TWO: THE FATHERHOOD OF GOD AND THE DIVINIZATION OF JESUS

A secondary contemporary issue is the divinization of Jesus. Biblically and theologically, this theme is closely allied to the preexistence of Jesus. My own focus is on the Christian naming of God both as "Father" and

---

2. McKenzie, "Aspects of Old Testament Thought," 1286.
3. Ringgren, *Israelite Religion*, 67–68.
4. Ringgren, *Israelite Religion*, 7–20.
5. On the internet, there are many articles which refer to the meaning of God in the Jewish, Christian, and Islamic religions. Some of these articles deny that one and the same God can be found in all three religions, while other authors claim that there is one and the same God in Judaism, Christianity, and Islam. This theme seems to be widely discussed by contemporary religious scholars. In the last chapter of this volume, I will focus on the infinity of God, which historically has not been a central theological focus of the three religions.

as "Son." As mentioned above, these two words differ from language to language: Padre, Père, Πατήρ, etc., and Hijo, Fil, υἱός, etc., but the meaning of father and son is common to all members of human life.

Human life as we know it began sometime between 200,000 and 50,000 years ago.[6] Some contemporary scientists refer to *Homo sapiens* as the "almost" human being, and then they refer to *Homo sapiens sapiens* for our own human ancestors. Whichever name you choose to use, contemporary human beings derive from these particular human beings, *Homo sapiens* or *Homo sapiens sapiens*. How these earliest human beings lived is not well-known, but in the past hundred years, scientists have gathered enough data to give us some understanding of the way in which they did live. As scientists develop more and more data on early human life, one begins to see that our ancestors were also developing human culture into more intricate ways of living.

From the beginning of *Homo sapiens sapiens*, human beings remained divided sexually, as they are today, into men and women. From a physical standpoint, their sexual life was also similar to the way it is today. Men became fathers and women became mothers. Their children were both sons and daughters. No doubt, there were many different words for father, mother, daughter, and son, but the physical aspects of both sexual life and child-birthing were basically the same as they are today. Consequently, the actual names of "father and mother, daughter and son" are simply English names. In the reality of languages which early humans had developed, the meaning of such English words as fatherhood, motherhood, daughter-hood and son-hood is basically the same, even though the words themselves are different.

These familial words could have been found in every language if there were written documents from 150,000 or 50,000 or even 3,500 years ago. However, human writing did not appear until ca. 3500 BCE. In the many centuries prior to this date, some sort of pre-writing familial words must have been used millions and millions of times.[7] The number

---

6. The dating of the origins of human life varies. My choice of 50,000 years ago is simply one of the stronger variants presented by today's scientists.

7. The word "nature" has many definitions and descriptions, e.g., one can refer to a Chinese nature, to an Islamic nature, etc. In the above paragraphs, I am using the term nature in a limited way, namely that in Christian theology, scholars focus on the "two natures" in Jesus Christ, namely a human nature and a divine nature. The divine nature is totally different from a human nature, and therefore the terms father and son have totally different meanings between a human father-son and a divine Father-Son. This differentiation complicates the very meaning of God the Father and God the Son. It

of human beings who lived prior to writing is debated by today's scientists, and these datings are not unified.

In Jewish literature, the reference to God as "Father" is basically poetic, descriptive, and metaphorical way. It is not a name which defines the "essence" or "nature" of Yahweh. When Jesus spoke of God as "Father," his listeners understood that the term "Father" was simply a descriptive word for YHWH. Since Jesus spoke in Aramaic, he used the Aramaic term for "father," namely "Abba"—אַבָּא.

From the time of Jesus down to today, Jewish Christians as well as non-Jewish Christians began to call God "Father." Most of these first-century CE Christian leaders and scholars called God "Father" in a descriptive way, but with the Gospel of John, and also with the writings of non-Jewish second-century CE Christians, such as Clement of Rome, Ignatius of Antioch, and the author of the letter describing Polycarp's martyrdom, there is a beginning of the "divinization" of Jesus. However, it is only a beginning. In the latter half of the second century CE, Justin, a major author and theologian, seems to have been a subordinationist; that is, there is only one God, and Jesus is subordinate to God the Father in an essential way. This move from descriptive to essential was caused by the divinization of Jesus, and the name they gave for the divinized Jesus was the "Son of God." In chapter 4 of this volume, I present in great detail the beginning of the historical process for the "divinization of Jesus." It was not until the second century CE that Christian leaders and scholars began to claim that Jesus was divine. Throughout the second century, the divinization of Jesus as "Son of God" had Christian promoters and Christian opponents. At the end of the second century, there were also Christian leaders and scholars who began to divinize the Holy Spirit. From the second century to the eighth century, the Christian belief in the divine Sonship of Jesus was both accepted and denied. Many Christian theologians today simply express the decisions of the earliest councils of the church which present Jesus as the "Son of God."

The first official statement on the divinization of Jesus took place at the first ecumenical council at Nicea in 325 CE. However, from 325 CE to the end of a church council at Friauli Venezia Giulia in 796 CE, the theology of the Trinity remained a dividing issue within the Christian

---

also raises the question: in the twenty-first century the meaning of "human nature" has been physically, scientifically, poetically, and philosophically analyzed. Today's understanding of nature, in my view, is totally opposed to its divinization. "Divine nature" is a phrase which has no contemporary meaning.

community. In some areas, Christian leaders and scholars were stating that Jesus was an "adoptive Son of God." The separation of the Western and Eastern Churches led to a long-standing and at times a bitter resentment between the leaders and members of both Christian communities. Members on both sides began to consider each other as members of an illegitimate church. This ecclesiastical division became a theological division as well. Trinitarian theology was included in this division, and the forms of Trinitarian theology were differently expressed by Western and Eastern Christians.

Nowhere in the Old Testament or in the New Testament is there any direct mention of a Trinitarian God. Trinitarian theology had a very slow beginning from the second century CE onward.[8] The divinization of Jesus changed the very meaning of God, and calling God "Father" was also changed. When this change took place, the term "Father" in many Christian communities ceased to be a poetic, descriptive, and metaphorical term for Yahweh. The very nature of God became a "Father-Son-Nature." Eventually, many Christians accepted a "Father-Son-Holy Spirit Nature." Officially, God's nature was "one divine nature" with "three divine persons." Officially, this began to take place in the Council of Nicea in 325 CE and it was to some extent clarified at the second ecumenical council held in Constantinople in 381 CE. However, there were many Christian groups in the early centuries which rejected a theology which divinized both Jesus and the Holy Spirit.

In the Scriptures, the terms father and son have absolutely two different meanings. The first meaning centers on human beings; the second meaning centers on a divine Father God who has a Divine Son who is also God. One can rightfully ask if there are not some better terms which might be used instead of God the Father and God the Son.

PART THREE: THE INFINITE GOD; A NAME WHICH TRANSCENDS ALL OTHER NAMES FOR GOD

Another word which describes God is infinite. In both the Old Testament and the New Testament, the words infinite and infinity are not used at all. However, in *The New Strong's Exhaustive Concordance of the Bible*, the authors state that there are three Old Testament citations which include the word "infinite," namely: Job 22:5; Psalm 147:5; and Nahum 3:9. In the

---

8. This development of Trinitarian theology is explained in detail from chs. 4–6.

New Jerusalem Bible, the English translations of the three Old Testament passages are as follows, together with Hebrew text:[9]

> Job 22:5: "Is not thy wickedness great? Are not thine iniquities without end?"
>
> הלא רעתך רבה ואין־קץ לצונתיך
>
> Psalm 147:5: "Our Lord is great, all powerful, his wisdom *beyond all telling*."
>
> דול אדונינו ורב־כח לתבונתו און מספר
>
> Nahum 3:9: "In Ethiopia and Egypt lay her strength and it was *boundless*."
>
> פוש עצמה ומצרים ואין קצה פוט ולובים היו בצזרתך

I have found several different English translations of these three citations but there is only one English translation of the Old Testament in which the authors used the term "infinite."[10] All other biblical texts used words and phrases such as unlimited, beyond all telling, and without boundaries, but they do not use the term infinite to translate various Hebrew or Greek words.

The meaning of the word infinity when applied to God is totally different from the meaning of the word infinity when used in such phrases as "potential infinity," "mathematical infinity," "spatial infinity" (there are two issues in spatial infinity: infinite divisibility of space and infinite extension of space),[11] "cosmological infinity," and "philosophical infinity."

---

9. The English translations of these three passages are taken from the New American Bible. In the New Catholic Study Bible, the three translations are: Job, "Because you have sinned so much"; Psalm 147, "His wisdom cannot be measured"; and Nahum, "There was no limit to her power." In the New Jerusalem Bible, the three translations are: Job, "More likely for your unlimited sins"; Psalm 147, "Our Lord is great, all powerful, his wisdom beyond all telling"; Nahum, "In Ethiopia and Egypt lay her strength, and it was boundless." The Hebrew word קץ means "no ending" and the Hebrew word מספר means "without measure" or "boundless." It is translated into German as "Ohne Mass"—"without measure" (Kraus, *Psalmen*, 956). The word infinity is not used at all in the Old Testament, but phrases such as "so much," "cannot be measured," "no limit," "unlimited," "beyond all telling," and "boundless."

10. The one Bible is the Gideon International Bible (1981 ed.): "Is not thy wickedness great? And thine iniquities infinite?" Job 22:5 (p. 592); also Ps 147:5 (p. 684), "His understanding is infinite." In Nah 3:9, we read, "Ethiopia and Egypt were her strength, and it was infinite."

11. See Rovelli, *Some Considerations on Infinity*. Rovelli centers on the hypersurface of a hypersphere in which space is both finite and unbounded.

Three Greek words, ἀόριστόν, which means indefinite; ἄπειρον, which means inexperienced; and ἀδιαίρετον, which means indivisible, at times have other meanings. Two of them—ἀόριστόν and ἄπειρον—are used in the New Testament, and their meaning is child or baby.[12] In my final chapter, I will explain that my meaning of infinity when applied to God is totally different from the meaning of infinity when used in mathematics, science, and philosophy.

In 2011, Wolfgang Achtner, a theological professor at Justus Liebig Universität in Giessen, Germany, wrote a detailed article on infinity, entitled "Infinity as a Transformative Concept in Science and Theology." In his essay, Achtner writes:

> Identifying infinity as an important aspect of God is nearly abandoned in contemporary theology. If it still exists, it is only used more or less in a metaphorical way. . . . The concept of infinity has migrated from a property of God to a factor in religious anthropology. . . . Any robust theology of creation has to come up with an exploration of God's infinite creative possibilities.[13]

Achtner mentions that Anaximander (610–546 BC) was the first philosopher to consider infinity. Achtner then presents, in a brief way, the explanation of infinity in Aristotle and Plotinus.[14] He then moves to St. Gregory of Nyssa, who was one of the earliest Christian scholars to use the term "infinite" in a frequent way.[15] Achtner states: "However, it was not until Gregory of Nyssa that Christian theologians started to think about God in terms of infinity in a theologically elaborated way as actual infinity."[16] Achtner continues his historical study of infinity by focusing on Dionysius the Areopagite, Thomas Aquinas, John Duns Scotus, and Nicholas of Cusa.[17]

---

12. One finds that the English translations of ἄπειρον include "child" and "baby." In the New American Bible, Heb 5:13, one reads: "being still a baby." In the New Catholic Study Bible, Heb 5:13, one reads: "Anyone who still has to drink milk is a child." In the New Oxford Annotated Bible, Heb 5:13, one reads: "For everyone who lives on milk is unskilled in the word of righteousness for he is a child." See also Arndt and Gingrich, *Greek-English Lexicon of the New Testament*, 83.

13. Achtner, "Infinity as a Transformative Concept," 47.

14. Achtner, "Infinity as a Transformative Concept," 20–23.

15. Achtner, "Infinity as a Transformative Concept," 27–31.

16. Achtner, "Infinity as a Transformative Concept," 28.

17. Achtner, "Infinity as a Transformative Concept," 31–38.

Questions Surrounding the Theology of the Triune God

There are, however, two major figures who lived in the last years of the second century to the beginning of the third century CE, namely Justin (d. 165 CE) and Clement of Alexandria (ca. 150–215 CE). For these two authors, God is far beyond the finite world, and human beings have no adequate words to describe the nature or essence of God. Neither of these two scholars, however, used the term "infinite."

Justin, in his *Second Apology*, states that God has no origin, ἄρρητος, and therefore God has existed forever. He writes:

> But to the Father of all, who is unbegotten, there is no name given.

> νομα δὲ τῷ πάντων Πατρὶ θετὸν, ἀγεννήτῳ ὄντι, οὐχ ἔστιν. Ὧι γὰρ ἂν καὶ ὀνόματι προσαγορεύηται, πρεσβύτερον ἔχει τὸν θέμενον τὸ ὄνομα.[18]

> But these words, Father, and God, and Creator, and Master, are not names, but appellations derived from his good deeds and functions.[19]

> Τὸ δὲ Πατὴρ, καὶ Θεὸς, καὶ Κτίστης, καὶ Κύριος, καὶ Δεσπότης, οὐχ ὀνόματά ἐστιν, ἀλλ' ἐκ τῶν εὐποιϊῶν καὶ τῶν ἔργων προσρήσεις.[20]

> But His Son who alone is properly called Son, the Word, who was begotten before all things, and Who was with Him, and was begotten, when in the beginning through Him He created and ordered all things, is called Christ, as he was anointed; and by Him God set all things in order, and this name itself contains an unknown signification; as also the title God is not a name, but the notion which is implanted in the matter of man, of a thing which can hardly be explained.[21]

---

18. Justin Martyr, "Second Apologia," vol. 6, n. 6, 453.

19. Quasten, *Patrology*, 208.

20. Justin Martyr, "Second Apologia," vol. 6, n. 6, 453.

21. For the English text, see Justin, *Works of Justin Martyr*, n. 6, p. 62. For the Greek text, see Justin Martyr, "Second Apologia," vol. 6, n. 6, p. 453. In Justin's *First Apology*, he calls the Father "the most true God." English ed., "Two Apologies" in *Works of Justin Martyr*, n. 6, p. 3. See also the "Son of the very God, and holding Him to be in the second place, and the Spirit of Prophecy in the third [place]." See also English ed., *Works of Justin Martyr*, n. 13, p. 9, in *Dialogue with Trypho*. In this essay, one reads: "By Another, namely, by Him Who always remains above the Heavens, Who has never been seen by any man, and Who of Himself holds converse with none; Whom we term the Creator of all things and the Father." English ed., *Works of Justin Martyr*, n. 56, p. 138.

For Justin, God is totally transcendent, and because of God's transcendence God cannot be named. Justin in his philosophical way of thinking and writing states that God is not substantially present in creation, rather it is the Logos—Λόγος σπερματικός—who brings about creation and the Logos is the only way through which a human mind and heart can come to believe in God. For Justin, it is the Logos who bridges the infinite gap between the "Father God" and creation. For Justin, the Logos is neither "Trinitarian" nor "Binatarian." Prior to creation, the Logos was simply a power in the depths of God. The Logos emerges from the Father in order to create the world. Some patrologists have concluded that Justin is at least tainted with subordinationism. They may be correct. However, the focus in this present volume is on the infinity of God and because of divine infinity, no one religion today has a complete meaning of an infinite God.

Clement of Alexandria wrote in a very clear way that God was infinite. Moreover, he enumerates several names for God, but for Clement God is beyond all human names in a way that is similar to Justin's statement above. The following citations from Clement indicate his view that God is infinite and that God is nameless.

In the second century CE, these two major Christian leaders tell us that God is unnameable. All human names for God signify something about the nature of God, but the nature of God is beyond any and all efforts of human intelligence. Today, we might also say that God is infinite, and therefore no human mind has a complete understanding of God's divine nature. We have only glimpses of God's being. Through these glimpses of God, we can conclude that there is a God, and that God is infinite.

Medieval theologians like Thomas Aquinas and Bonaventure stated in an affirmative way that God was infinite. For Thomas and Bonaventure—as well as other medieval theologians—divine infinity was not presented as the major aspect of God's being. Rather, both of these scholars presented infinity as simply an "attribute" of God.[22]

In *De Primo Principio*, John Duns Scotus writes: "Nona Conclusio: Te esse infinitum et incomprehensibilem a finito" (Ninth Conclusion: You are infinite and incomprehensible for a finite mind). The key

---

22. See my volume *Infinity of God and a Finite World*, ch. 5, "The Theology of the Existence and Infinity of God in the Writings of Bonaventure," 83–121; also ch. 6, "The Theology of the Existence and Infinity of God in the Writings of Thomas Aquinas," 123–68.

words in Scotus's presentation are: God is "infinite" and therefore God is "incomprehensible."[23] Scotus wrote this volume just prior to his death, and his naming of God as infinite and incomprehensible is his final description of God.

In chapter 7 of this volume, I am suggesting—and only suggesting—that for all religions there might be just one God, namely the Infinite God. All other names for God focus on something finite, for example, God is all-powerful, God is all-knowing, and God is all-merciful. Secondary names for God are extremely important, but these secondary divine names reveal, only to some degree, one or the other major aspect of the Infinite God.

There are two major issues which contemporary Christian theologians have begun to consider in an in-depth way, namely:

1. The validity of the term "Father" for God, and the validity of the term "Son of God" for Jesus when used as a major aspect of God. Do the terms "Father" and "Son" have any essential meaning for divinity? From a human standpoint, God is essentially neither a "Father" nor a "Son." Nor do these two words have some exclusive meaning when they refer to divinity. They are human words which define a human father and a human son.

2. The meaning of the term "infinite" when used as a major aspect of God. In many theological textbooks, the term infinite is considered only as an "attribute" of God. Infinity is in no way an attribute, even a divine attribute. If, in religious thinking, God is called infinite, the meaning of infinite is not the same as mathematical infinity, philosophical infinity, metaphysical infinity, physical infinity, etc. Divine infinity has no affiliation with any and all other infinities. We believe in the infinity of God; we do not rationally understand the infinity of God.

---

23. *Infinity of God*, ch. 7, "The Theology of the Existence and Infinity of God in the Writings of John Duns Scotus," 169–218.

SUMMARY: THE NAMING OF GOD AS "FATHER" AND GOD AS INFINITE

God Is Named Father

In the Old Testament, the name "Father" when applied to God is poetic, descriptive, and metaphorical. In the "Song of Moses" (Deut 32:4–6) we read: "A trustworthy God who does no wrong. He is the Honest, the Upright One! . . . Is this not your Father who gave you being?"(הֲלוֹא־הוּא אָבִיךָ קָּנֶךָ). In the twenty-first century CE, religious Jews still sing the beautiful Jewish hymn *Abinu Malkeinu* (מלכנו אבינו).

In today's Christian communities, a major prayer is the "Our Father." In the first century CE, Luke includes the Lord's Prayer in his Gospel (11:2–4), and in a longer format Matthew also includes the Our Father (Matt 6:9–13). In both Gospels, naming God "Father" is not a reference to God in a substantive way. Rather, the naming of God as "Father" is poetic, descriptive, and metaphorical. Catherine Mowry Lacugna states the following:

> [In the New Testament] God is beyond all names. . . . Fatherhood is clearly an analogous or metaphorical term and cannot be applied literally to God's being. God is as much like as unlike human fathers.[24]

In the second century CE, a few Christians began the divinization of Jesus and in doing so Jesus was called "the Son of God." When this began to take place, the phrase "the nature of God" was radically changed for our human thinking. This is the second issue. We now have only one divine nature but two individualized persons: God the Father and God the Son. At the end of the second century CE, the Holy Spirit was considered as the third and equal person of the Trinity.

In the second-century Christian world, a major change took place. The terms nature and person were no longer poetic, descriptive, and metaphorical. These three terms—Father, Son, and Holy Spirit—were used to describe the Trinitarian God. The *Catechism of the Catholic Church* explains this use of terms.

> The Church uses (I) the term "substance" (rendered also at times by "essence" or "nature") to designate the divine being in its unity, (II) the term "person" or "hypostasis" to designate the

---

24. Lacugna, "Fatherhood of God," 520.

Father, Son and Holy Spirit in the real distinction among them, and (III) the term "relation" to signify the fact that their distinction lies in the relationship of each to the others.²⁵

This statement is understandable if one has been taught Greek philosophy, which both the Christian church and the Greco-Roman society were using at that early period of time. The terms—essence, nature, person, hypostasis, and relation as used in the above citation—are all based on Greek philosophy. The philosophies of scholars in the twentieth century, such as Martin Heidegger, Edmund Husserl, Albert Camus, and Jean-Paul Sartre, no longer use the terminology of Plato and Aristotle as their primary referent. The ecclesiastical leaders of the Catholic Church have been mostly traditionalists, that is, retaining the theological understanding of Catholic faith as presented basically by Thomistic theologians.

In various English Bibles, the above four words are translated in different way: οὐσία, φύσια, ὑπόστασις, and συγγένεια. In today's English Christian literature regarding Jesus, the above Greek words are rather common not only in theology but also in philosophy. However, they are not universally accepted as the only philosophical terms which can describe all reality. Asian languages have quite different names for substance, essence, person, and relationship. The Euro-Americans do not think philosophically in a "yin and yang manner," but the Chinese have understood the universe in and through the philosophical terms yin and yang for centuries.²⁶ The same could be said for many other major languages.

Today's scientists also have a totally different way of naming the basic aspects of our world. Often, "philosophical terms" are not used by contemporary scientists. Rather, they use "scientific terms." Nonetheless, the tendency of contemporary Western theologians, philosophers, and scientists is to use Western words, all of which are limited in their meaning. In 1936, Charles A. Moore and Wing-tsit Chan, both professors at the University of Hawaii, began the project of writing a source book on Asian philosophy. Two source books developed, one on Indian philosophy and the other on Chinese philosophy. Both Indian philosophy and Chinese philosophy are totally different from today's Western philosophy. None of these philosophies have the final philosophical word, and in the Western

---

25. Catholic Church, *Catechism of the Catholic Church*, n. 252, p. 66.

26. See Chan, *Source Book of Chinese Philosophy*, 244: "The Yin Yang doctrine is very simple but its influence has been extensive. No aspect of Chinese civilization—metaphysics, medicine, government, or art—has escaped its imprint."

university world, many professors and religious scholars focus only on the philosophies of the West.

God Is Infinite

In her writings, Lacugna has also presented a serious question: "Why has the doctrine of the Trinity, often claimed to be the center of Christian faith, been neglected, evaded, or even derided in what Rahner has called an 'anti-trinitarian timidity'?"

However, there has been at least a beginning re-theologizing the Trinity. She states:

> Today Trinitarian theology is being recovered. . . . In the past few years virtually every theological journey and many others oriented to pastoral, liturgical, and spiritual questions have begun to include significant scholarly articles on issues related to the Trinity.[27]

Aristotle Papanikolaou has written an article on the Trinitarian theologies of Sergius Bulgakov, Vladimir Lossky, and John Zizioulas. These three scholars have presented mutually incompatible trajectories in Orthodox theology today.[28] Nonetheless, these theologians have become a major part of today's renewal of Trinitarian theology.

One might comment that from Karl Barth down to the end of the twentieth century, a major theological reconsideration of the Trinity has begun to take place. From the beginning of the twenty-first century to today, Christian scholars in a worldwide way have presented excellent books and articles on the Trinity which differ from the standard theologies of the Trinity. One of the major differences focuses on the infinity of God.

The *Catechism of the Catholic Church* employs only the Western format of theology with its early Greek philosophical language. However, one might ask: Can the theology of the Roman Catholic Church be presented only in a medieval and post-Reformation Western philosophical and theological format? The *Catechism* mentions "infinity" only in a brief way. In n. 270, one reads: "Finally by his infinite mercy, for he displays his power at its height by freely forgiving sins." In n. 256, one reads: "The infinite co-naturality of three infinites." In the final chapter, I will focus in

---

27. Lacugna, "Trinitarian Mystery of God," 152.
28. See Papanikolaou, "Sophia, Apophasis, and Communion," 243–58.

a lengthy way on the infinity of God. In the chapters which follow, I begin with a summary of several contemporary theologians who have presented a rethinking of the Trinitarian theology of a Triune God (ch. 2). This is followed by several chapters in which I present in a detailed way the religious history in which the Jewish religion and subsequently the Christian religion referred to God as "Father" (chs. 3–6). Finally, in chapter 7, I offer a naming of God which includes all religions, namely the one and only Infinite God.

2

Contemporary Theologians and Their Tentative Theologies of God

INTRODUCTORY OBSERVATIONS

Prior to the first century CE, a Trinitarian God was totally unknown. From the end of the first century down to the present, the issue of a Trinitarian God has been stated and restated. In the Christian presentations of God, there can be no separation of the One God and the Triune God. Richard McBrien expresses this interconnection as follows:

> To distinguish the "one God" from the "Triune God," even for purposes of theological analysis is to distort radically the distinctive understanding of God. For the Christian, there is only one God, and that one God is triune.[1]

McBrien's statement has been expressed over and over again in Christian literature, namely that there is only one God and the one God is triune. For Christians, God has been triune from the second century down to today.

In the twentieth and twenty-first centuries CE, major theologians—Protestant, Catholic, and Orthodox—have written a wide range of books and articles on the Trinity. These presentations are not simply a repeat of the standard theologies of the Trinity. Rather, they offer new theological

1. McBrien, *Catholicism*, 276.

insights into a Trinitarian God.² Peter Phan, in the preface of his recent volume *The Cambridge Companion to the Trinity*, presents these new views of the Trinity in a positive way:

> One of the pleasant surprises in contemporary theology is the widespread revival of the doctrine of the Trinity. Long shunted to the wings [of theological writings], the Trinity is now occupying center stage.³

In a later chapter in the same volume, entitled "Systematic Issues in Trinitarian Theology," Phan offers his own reconsideration in a detailed way. He writes: "One of the much-debated issues in Trinitarian theology today concerns the relationship between the economic Trinity and the immanent Trinity, with three interrelated questions."⁴ Phan's three questions are as follows.

Phan's First Question

> Is it possible and necessary to speak of the immanent, or transcendent, or ontological Trinity, that is, the eternal relations among Father, Son, and Spirit at all? Are not reflections on the economic Trinity, that is, on what God has revealed Godself to be namely, Father, Son, and Spirit and their distinct activities in history, already sufficient? Is the God *in se* (in God's self) nothing more than the God *pro nobis* (for us)?⁵

One might respond to Phan's question by saying that we are able to speak about the economic Trinity, since the economic Trinity is God's presence and activity within our finite and human world. However, since the immanent Trinity is within the inner life of God, we have little to no knowledge of God's internal nature, and thus we need to be careful whenever we refer to the immanent Trinity. Karl Rahner presented a brief statement,

---

2. A listing of the number of contemporary books and articles on the Trinity is beyond the limits of this volume. Peter Phan, in a volume which he edited, *The Cambridge Companion to the Trinity*, lists twenty-one major contemporary authors who have written on the Trinity. Each of the authors who have presented a chapter for his book also offers at the conclusion of his/her essay a listing of books on aspects of the Trinity cited by the author. See also Hunt, *Trinity: Nexus of Christian Faith*. She has a nine-page bibliography of books and articles on the Trinity, written from 1960–2005.

3. Phan, *Cambridge Companion to the Trinity*, xiii.

4. Phan, *Cambridge Companion to the Trinity*, 16.

5. Phan, *Cambridge Companion to the Trinity*, 16.

which has been cited as "Rahner's Rule": namely, "The 'economic' Trinity is the 'immanent' Trinity and the 'immanent' Trinity is the 'economic' Trinity."[6] Rahner offers a lengthy explanation of his "rule" in volume 6 of the German edition of his *Schriften zur Theologie*.[7] Rahner was not the first theologian to unite the immanent and economic theologies of the Triune God. Karl Barth, without using the two words of immanent and economic, states his theological position as follows:

> That He [Jesus] is both at one and the same time. He is the promise and the command, the Gospel and the Law, the address of God to man and the claim of God upon man. That He is both as the Word of God spoken in His work, as the Word of God which has become work, is something which belongs to Himself as the eternal Son of God for himself and prior to us.[8]

We have faith, hope, and love in God the Father, Son, and Holy Spirit, but there is something more, for there is God whom we encounter and from whom we have our being. This God we cannot apprehend or exhaust.[9]

Jürgen Moltmann, in his volume *The Trinity and the Kingdom*, is somewhat skeptical of Rahner's position on the unity of the economic and immanent Trinity. In his section on Rahner, he refers to his axiom: "The economic Trinity is the immanent Trinity and vice versa." Moltmann states that Rahner's union of "God with us" and "We with God" is modalism. He concludes his section on Rahner with these words: "Is there really any 'greater danger' than this modalism'?"[10]

Who and what God is remains unknowable; this unknowable God, however, has revealed aspects of his nature to us. In other words, when one speaks of God, one is speaking only of a "revealed" God, not the "total" God. The problematic issue of this juncture or conjuncture of God's infinite nature on the one hand and God's revealed nature on the other hand is not easily acceptable. Rahner's rule may be correct, but it is not totally clear, since the infinite nature of God surpasses the finite nature of

---

6. See Rahner, *Theological Investigations*, 1:144–48. On p. 148, Rahner refers to the immanent and to the economic Trinity. In *Theological Investigations*, 2:176–79, Rahner explains that "Homo videt faciem, Deus autem cor."

7. However, in vol. 4, Rahner focuses in depth on the economic-immanent trinity. The German text states Rahner's own position at great length: see *Schriften zur Theologie*, IV (Einsiedeln, Switzerland: Benziger, 1962), 125–33.

8. See Barth, *Doctrine of Reconciliation*, 53.

9. Barth, *Doctrine of Reconciliation*, 4.

10. Moltmann, *Trinität und Reich Gottes*, 148.

human beings. Consequently, our knowledge of an infinite God remains unknowable to any and every finite mind.

Phan's Second Question

> Is the so-called psychological model that uses the human mind (Augustine's *mens* or *memoria*), with its twofold operation of knowing and loving (*intelligentia* and *amor*) as an analogy of the immanent Trinity still valid and useful? . . . Does it not inevitably lead to modalism and does it not produce ahistorical, spiritually sterile speculations, unmoored from God's activities in history?[11]

Michel René Barnes, in his study on the issue of Augustinian theology, refers to Augustine's interest in the common operations of the Trinity. He writes: "Augustine's use of the noetic triad—the 'psychological analogy'—represents an attempt by Augustine to understand the unity of the Trinity as articulated in the doctrine of common operations. . . . Similarly, the operations which pertain not only to all three persons but also those assigned to one person are done inseparably or in common. We cannot know what it means for three to act inseparably and in common with the other two."[12] Barnes is simply reminding us that Augustine's *De Trinitate* is not an exposition on the doctrine of the Trinity *per se*; it is a study of the problematic human way of knowing God rather than what is the meaning of Trinity.[13]

Barnes then states that in the writings of Augustine, there are three foundational features that remain constant: (1) the doctrine of the perfect immaterial nature of divine existence, (2) the doctrine of the common operations of the Trinity, and (3) the doctrine that theological language is meant to purify our thoughts about God as a necessary precondition to thinking about God.[14] Barnes remarks that "the question arises as to why topoi fundamental to Latin Trinitarian theology for two hundred years are not fundamental in any explicit way in *On the Trinity* (by Augustine)."[15] Barnes states that Augustine's focus is on Trinitarian hermeneutics or

---

11. Phan, *Cambridge Companion to the Trinity*, 1.

12. Barnes, "Latin Trinitarian Theology," 80. Augustine was born in 354 CE and he died in 430 CE.

13. Barnes, "Latin Trinitarian Theology," 79–81.

14. Barnes, "Latin Trinitarian Theology," 79–81.

15. Barnes, "Latin Trinitarian Theology," 78.

epistemology, namely does the human mind have the ability to know God in a Trinitarian way? His focus is on the human mind, rather than on the Trinitarian nature of God.

Augustine also established a basic approach to our theology of God, namely God is totally different from all created beings. What is it that causes this divide? For Augustine, all created realities have something materialistic about them. God alone is totally immaterial. For Augustine, a true theology of God and of a Trinitarian God must exhibit an absolute aspect of the separation God on the one hand, and human nature on the other hand.

Phan's Third Question

> How are the economic Trinity and the economic Trinity related to each other? Is the immanent Trinity eternal, existing independently of its creative, redemptive and sanctifying work in the world, or is it in the process of being constituted as Father, Son, and Spirit by their activities in history? If the former position is held, and hence the immanent Trinity is totally unaffected by the flow of history into which the Logos has really and truly entered and taken upon himself in Jesus of Nazareth, then the historicity of God's self-revelation, which is Christianity's distinctive teaching, is not taken in all of its radical consequences.[16]

According to Barnes, Augustine would not have answered this question with a technical explanation since "a flesh-bound habit of thought cannot grasp that the persons of the Trinity are equal." For Augustine, the true answer to this third question is not found in intellectual discourse but in "the discipline of faith, which trains our mind and forms our heart, and thus enables us to think properly about God the Trinity as all equal."[17]

These three questions are very important for contemporary theological discussions on the Trinity and they need to be answered by the best Trinitarian theologians. However, I want to suggest that there is yet another question which today needs to be studied. This issue has to do with the naming of the Trinitarian God as "Father" and as "Son." At the divine level, what can the term "Father" possibly mean? In the history of Judaism, God has been called "Father" for centuries. Its first canonical

---

16. Phan, *Cambridge Companion to the Trinity*, 17.
17. Barnes, "Latin Trinitarian Theology," 81. The quote is from the opening sentence of chapter 8 of Augustine's *De Trinitate*.

appearance can be found in Exodus and in Deuteronomy. In the history of Christianity, the preaching of Jesus himself probably included the naming of God as "Father." In the majority of New Testament writings, God is called "Father" again and again, and Jesus is referred to as the "Son of God" over and over again.

THE MAJOR CHANGES IN CHRISTIAN TRINITARIAN THEOLOGY WHICH TOOK PLACE IN THE TWENTIETH CENTURY

Before we consider the above historical issues, let us explore today's resurgence of Trinitarian theology. Anne Hunt, in her volume *Trinity: Nexus of the Mysteries of Christian Faith*, presents a careful and detailed overview of Trinitarian theology from 1900 to 2002.[18] She lists author after author who have, during this space of time, written on the Trinity in a new theological framework.[19] Her volume is strongly Roman Catholic, but she does mention at some length the Trinitarian theologies of Jürgen Moltmann, John Zizioulas, Christoph Schwöbel, and Wolfhart Pannenberg.

In 2011, Peter Phan edited his book on the Trinity, *The Cambridge Companion to the Trinity*, in which almost one-half of the text is dedicated to contemporary theologians—Catholic and non-Catholic—who have written on the Trinity.[20] Some of the authors in this volume even discuss the Trinity in dialogue with other religions: such as Confucianism and Taoism, Hinduism, Buddhism, Judaism, and Islam. In a very strong way, the current theology of the Trinity has become a major issue both ecumenically and interreligiously. One can clearly conclude that the long-standing Christian theology on the Trinity has been radically re-questioned and revised in the twentieth and twenty-first centuries.

The major twentieth-century changes in Trinitarian theology can be found in the works of Karl Barth (1886–1968), Karl Rahner (1904–1984), Wolfhart Pannenberg (1928–2014), and Jürgen Moltmann (1926–2014). These four scholars, each in his own way, centered on the unification of the immanent Trinity and the economic Trinity. The immanent Trinity had focused only on the eternal Trinity, whereas the economic Trinity

---

18. Hunt, *Trinity*.
19. Hunt, *Trinity*; see her lengthy bibliography, 235–42.
20. Phan, *Cambridge Companion to the Trinity*, 173–411.

had interfaced with creation. For the above theologians, the immanent Trinity is the same as the economic Trinity, and the economic Trinity is the same as the immanent Trinity. However, the contemporary changes in Trinitarian theology move far beyond the issue of the immanent/economic distinction.

It was the Trinitarian writings of these four theologians that encouraged several other Christian theologians to re-study Trinitarian theology.[21] Let us consider in some detail the revised theologies of Trinity as presented by the four major theologians.

Karl Barth

Karl Barth, from his early writings on the Trinity to his later and more mature Trinitarian writings, stressed the unity of the immanent Trinity and the economic Trinity. In a special way, he focuses on the Father-Son description; he writes:

> As applied to Jesus Christ we can legitimately call the term "Son of God" a true but inadequate and an inadequate but true insight and statement. . . . The true and living God is the one whose Godhead consists in this history, who in these three modes of being the One God, the Eternal, the Holy, the Merciful, the one who loves in freedom and is free in his love.[22]

Barth does not deny the Trinitarian doctrine, but he clearly describes the Trinity in a way that is not usual.

> By Father, Son and Spirit, we do not mean what is commonly suggested by the word "person." This designation was accepted—not without opposition—on linguistic propositions which no longer obtain today. . . . The one name of the one God is the threefold name of Father, Son and Holy Spirit. The one "personality" of God, the one active and speaking divine Ego, is Father, Son and Holy Spirit.[23]

Barth goes on to explain this viewpoint. He states that we have one God in self-repetition and this repetition is a threefold mode of being. God

---

21. In the bibliography at the end of this volume I have listed almost all the major theologians who have contributed to the contemporary renewal of Trinitarian theology.

22. Barth, *Doctrine of Reconciliation*, 203ff.

23. Barth, *Doctrine of Reconciliation*, 204–5.

exists as the mutual interconnection and relationship of three differing modes of one and the same Supreme Being. Modality and relationship are key aspects of Barth's theology of Trinity.

In her volume *Trinity: Nexus of the Mysteries of Christian Faith*, Anne Hunt explains the role of Barth in today's renewal of Trinitarian theology:

> Karl Barth, one of the great Protestant theologians of the twentieth century whose work marks a watershed in German Protestant Trinitarian theology, placed the mystery of the Trinity at the head of his revelation-centered Christian theology, recognizing its decisive and controlling role in regard to the whole theological enterprise.[24]

This citation might appear as an academic and pompous statement, but the main issue is simply this: Barth begins with the reconciliation of our sinfulness in and through the life, death, and resurrection of Jesus. One does not start with the Trinity itself. Rather, Barth begins his understanding of God with the reconciliation which Jesus attained for all men and women. The focus on the Triune God along with reconciliation is explained in some detail by Peter Goodwin Heltzel and Christian T. Collins Winn in their chapter on Barth in *The Cambridge Companion to the Trinity*.[25] The conclusion of their essay states:

> Barth's Trinitarian doctrine deployed in the doctrine of reconciliation is Trinitarian theology at its best. It not only provides a new horizon for uniting creation, reconciliation, and eschatology for Christian theology, but it also presses for the proclamation of a prophetic social ethic in an age of "lordless powers."[26]

Barth certainly led Western theology into a reconsideration of almost every aspect of the Christian faith and Christian theology. Both Heltzel and Winn, at the end of their chapter, state:

> Recent discussions of the Trinity and election in Barth's theology have placed new attention on God's triune activity in the space-time manifold of history. This "turn to history" has helped us see with new eyes the way in which Barth "historicized" the doctrine of God. However, much of the recent scholarship has focused on the ways in which election affects the divine nature.

---

24. Hunt, *Trinity*, 4.
25. Heltzel and Winn, "Karl Barth," in Phan, *Cambridge Companion*, 173–91.
26. Heltzel and Winn, "Karl Barth," 186.

> In this chapter, we have sought to dislocate the debate on Trinity and election, and relocate it in a discussion of Trinity, history and ethics.[27]

Barth's Trinitarian doctrine, they add, which is deployed in the doctrine of reconciliation, is Trinitarian reflection at its best.

Karl Rahner

In many ways, Barth's position began the current renewal of Trinitarian theology, but Karl Rahner must be cited as a scholar whose writings also began the renewal of today's Trinitarian theology. Rahner expressed a major approach of the twentieth-century renewal of Trinitarian doctrine by writing: "The economic Trinity is the immanent Trinity and the immanent Trinity is the economic Trinity."[28] This phrase unites the two usual foci of Trinitarian teaching: the immanent aspect and the economic aspect. Both Augustine and Thomas Aquinas presented lengthy explanations of the one God and only then did they move to a Trinitarian God.[29]

Rahner's union of the immanent and the economic trinities is basically accomplished in his presentation of God as both "Father" and as "Son." Only on the basis of this interrelationship does he turn to the Holy Spirit. However, in Rahner's approach the Fatherhood of God is fundamentally manifested in two modalities. Peter Phan expresses this triadic view of Rahner as follows:

> Rahner argues that, given the fact of God's self-communication in two modes, which we experience a posteriori in history and is made known to us through revelation, it is possible and necessary to "deduce" from the economic Trinity to the immanent Trinity for otherwise God's self-communication would not be a *self*-communication.[30]

---

27. Heltzel and Winn, "Karl Barth," 185.

28. See Rahner, "Remarks on the Dogmatic Treatise 'De Trinitate,'" in *Theological Investigations*, 4:87.

29. This format, namely a lengthy presentation on the existence of the one God followed by the existence of a Trinitarian God, was the standard approach of Catholic neo-scholastic theological textbooks which were used in almost all Catholic seminaries from Vatican I to Vatican II.

30. Phan, "Mystery of Grace and Salvation: Karl Rahner's Theology of the Trinity," in *Cambridge Companion to the Trinity*, 205.

Rahner delivered a lecture entitled "*Theos in the New Testament*" to a small theological study circle in Vienna and was intended merely to prepare the way for further discussion.[31] In his essay, Rahner does not take into account the various "dates" at which each of the various parts of the New Testament were written. Paul is the first author, and his seven genuine letters were written from 50 to 58 CE.[32] Paul describes Jesus as "Pre-existent Son," "Christos," and "Kyrios." One can ask: did Paul believe that Jesus was God? Joseph Fitzmeier carefully analyzes each of these titles as used in the letters of Paul.[33] He states: "Only in Romans 9:5, does Paul possibly call Jesus Christ Θεός, 'God,' and that is a highly controverted text."[34]

Chronologically, the use of terms, such as those mentioned above, have a historical diversity in the New Testament. In the Gospel of John, the authors might use the same written terms as used by Paul, but, given the development of the Jesus community from 50 CE (Paul) to 90–100 CE ("John"), the understanding of Jesus, the Logos, had deepened.

Rahner, in the above lecture and in most of his writings, does not take into account the historical changes in the understanding of Jesus and of the Trinity in the different "books" of the New Testament. Paul is chronologically the first author in the New Testament. Paul's explanation of Jesus is different from the explanation of Jesus which is presented by the authors of the Gospel of "John." The Johannine Gospel almost presents a divine Trinity, but the Johannine Gospel is not a story about Jesus, but it is a story about what God has done in Jesus. What I miss in Rahner's writings on the Trinity in the New Testament is the "historical" development of a theology of God. The understanding of God as found in the writings of Paul and in the Gospel of Mark is the Jewish God Yahweh. There is no reference to a Trinitarian God in the writings of Paul and Mark. In Luke, who is not Jewish, we have little to no idea what his meaning of God, Θεός, might be. In the Gospel of Matthew, the term "God"

---

31. Rahner, "Theos in the New Testament," English trans. in *Theological Investigations*, 1:79–48.

32. See Fitzmyer, "Pauline Theology," in *NJBC*, 1384. There are seven uncontested letters of Paul: 1 Thessalonians, 50–51 CE; Galatians, 54 CE; Philippians (3 distinct letters), the first and second, 54–57 CE, and third 58 CE; 1 Corinthians, 54 CE; 2 Corinthians, 55 CE; Romans, 57–58 CE; Philemon, 56–57 CE.

33. See Fitzmyer, "Pauline Theology," 1393–94.

34. Fitzmyer, "Pauline Theology," 1395.

refers to YHWH. In the Gospel of John, there is an "almost Trinitarian theology."[35]

Jürgen Moltmann

Jürgen Moltmann bases his Trinitarian theology in line with Barth and Rahner, but his view of the Trinitarian unity is one which is a continuing unity down to the present and beyond. Moltmann, himself, describes his differing way as follows:

> The economic Trinity completes and perfects itself to immanent Trinity when the history and experience of salvation are completed and perfected. When everything is "in God" and "God is in all," then the economic Trinity is raised into and is transcended in the immanent Trinity.[36]

Perhaps, the most significant Trinitarian issue in Moltmann's Trinitarian theology is his position on a "suffering God." In his major publication, *The Trinity and the Kingdom*, he presents in a careful way a Trinitarian theology of a God who can suffer. An entire chapter is focused on "The Passion of God." In these pages, he describes the meaning of the pathos, the sorrow, the tragedy, and the suffering of God. For Moltmann, God's suffering is based on God's freedom and love.[37] In the final chapter of his book, Moltmann recapitulates his position in a very careful way:

> If we see the Almighty in Trinitarian terms, he is not the archetype of the mighty ones of this world. He is the Father of the Christ who was crucified and raised for us. As the Father of Jesus Christ, he is almighty because he exposes himself to the experience of suffering, pain, helplessness and death. But what he *is* is not almighty power; what he *is* is love. It is his passionate, passible love that is almighty, nothing else.[38]

Veli-Matti Kärkkäinen, in his essay "The Trinitarian Doctrines of Jürgen Moltmann and Wolfhart Pannenberg in the Context of Contemporary Discussion," states that "these two German theologians both echo and have shaped nearly all the key themes of the document of the Trinity in

---

35. I will discuss these various understandings of God in chapter 3.

36. Moltmann, *Trinität und Reich Gottes*; English translation by Margaret Kohl, *Trinity and the Kingdom of God*, 161.

37. Moltmann, *Trinity and the Kingdom of God*, pt. 2, "The Passion of God," 21–60.

38. Moltmann, *Trinity and the Kingdom of God*, pt. 2, "The Passion of God," 197.

contemporary theology."³⁹ Moltmann spent about twenty years to produce his highly respected book *Trinität und Reich Gottes*.⁴⁰ In his preface, he notes that today the best theology takes place in "Ecumenical Fellowship." For Moltmann, this includes the Western Christian churches and the Eastern Christian churches, but it moves beyond the Christian domain, for he also includes the theology of God as presented in many ways by the Jewish communities.

> But if the Son proceeded from the Father alone, then this has to be conceived of as both a begetting and as a birth. And this means a radical transformation of the Father image; a father who both begets and bears his son is not merely a father in the male sense. He is a motherly father too. He is no longer defined in unisexual, patriarchal terms but—if we allow for the metaphor of language—bisexually and transsexually. He has to be understood as the motherly Father of the only Son he has brought forth, and at the same time as the fatherly Mother of his only begotten Son.⁴¹

Moltmann cites a passage which is found in the documents of the Council of Toledo in 675 CE.

> Nec enim de nihilo, neque de aliqua alia substantia, sed de Patris utero, id est, de substantia eius idem Filius genitus vel natus esse credendus est.⁴²

Margaret Kohl's English translation of the passage from the Council of Toledo reads as follows:

> It must be held that the Son was created neither out of nothingness nor yet out of any substance but that he was begotten or born out of the Father's womb, that is, out of his very essence.⁴³

Moltmann adds another startling sentence, by which he wants to clarify his own understanding of the conciliar statement. He writes: "Whatever may be said about God's gynaecology according to this explanation, the

---

39. Kärkkäinen, "Trinitarian Doctrines," 223.
40. See Kärkkäinen, "Trinitarian Doctrines," 224.
41. Moltmann, *Trinity and the Kingdom of God*, 164.
42. Denzinger, *Enchridion Symbolorum*, n. 526, p. 176. The Council of Toledo in 675 took place under Prince Wamba, a military man.
43. See Kohl's English translation of Moltmann's citation of the Council of Toledo in 675 CE in Moltmann, *Trinity and the Kingdom of God*, 165.

point of these bi-sexual statements about the trinitarian Father is the radical rejection of monotheism, which is always patriarchal."[44]

Both the statement of Moltmann which is cited above and the statement from the Council of Toledo clearly reinterpret what the words "father" and "mother" had meant since the beginning of human nature. The statements describe God neither as a father nor a son in the ordinary sense of a human father and a human son. Given today's understanding of sexuality, the terms human fatherhood and gynecology do not help us in our explanation of the Trinity. We might continue to refer to God as Father, but only in a poetic, descriptive, and metaphorical way, and we might continue calling Jesus the Son of God, but only in a descriptive way. "Son of God" is also poetic, descriptive, and metaphorical. At present, most Anglican, Orthodox, Protestant, and Roman Catholics refer to Jesus' divinity when they say: "Jesus, the Son of God."

Wolfhart Pannenberg

In order to understand the Trinitarian theology of Wolfhart Pannenberg, we need to repeat the citation of Kärkkäinen in which he unites the theologies of Moltmann and Pannenberg:

> These two German theologians both echo and have shaped nearly all the key themes of the document of the Trinity in contemporary theology.[45]

There are, however, differences between these two theologians. In the writings of Pannenberg, there seems to be a rejection of the immanent-economic distinction. He stresses the economic Trinity in an overriding way. Second, the union of Father and Son, in the writings of Pannenberg, does not appear to be a "moral union" which involves an ontological relationship nor does it involve an eternal generation of the Son.[46] Christoph Schwöbel writes:

> How can the three persons of the Trinity be understood as presenting one divine essence without reducing them to moments or aspects of the one essential Godhead and without positing

---

44. Moltmann, *Trinity and the Kingdom of God*, 165.
45. Kärkkäinen, "Trinitarian Doctrines," 223.
46. See the lengthy analysis of Pannenberg's understanding of the Trinity in Kärkkäinen, "Trinitarian Doctrines," 229–38.

the divine essence as a fourth subject lurking behind the persons of Father, Son, and Spirit?[47]

Perhaps, one of the most important aspects of Pannenberg's theology of the Trinity is his position of the three Persons in one God. The three divine Persons are not differentiated by their origin, namely the Son originates from the Father, while the Holy Spirit has its origin from the Father and the Logos (Western theology) or from the Father alone (Eastern theology). The three persons are differentiated according to Pannenberg by the "relations of mutual dependence and self-distinction, characterized by mutuality and reciprocity, whereby each of the divine persons receives his divinity through the other two divine persons."[48]

On the foundation of the Trinitarian theology proposed by the four theologians mentioned above, many other well-known contemporary scholars have also contributed to today's Trinitarian renewal, such as Anne Hunt, Catherine Mowry LaCugna, Ted Peters, Claude Welch, Elizabeth Johnson, Leonardo Boff, Aristotle Papanikolaou, Sergius Bulgakov, Vladimir Lossky, John Zizioulas, and many others.[49] Today, the long-standing theologies of the Trinity are being questioned by several well-regarded theologians. This twentieth-century questioning of the classical positions of Trinitarian theology has therefore begun to change the long-standing theologies of the Trinity mentioned above. At the beginning of the twenty-first century, the questioning of the classical positions on the Trinity remains not only a major challenge but also a major development of intercultural possibilities.

THE MAJOR CHANGES IN CHRISTIAN TRINITARIAN THEOLOGY WHICH ARE TAKING PLACE IN THE TWENTY-FIRST CENTURY

On the basis of the major Trinitarian changes in the writings of Barth, Rahner, Moltmann, and Pannenberg, several Christian theologians have turned to a wider rethinking of Trinitarian theology. Phan begins his volume with a strong and insightful statement:

> While all these observations are correct, it does not mean that a full-fledged doctrine of the Trinity is already developed in the

---

47. Schwöbel, "Wolfhart Pannenberg," 192.
48. See Hunt, *Trinity*, 229.
49. See Phan, *Cambridge Companion to the Trinity*, chs. 14–20.

> New Testament. As the various chapters of this book show, the road that leads from New Testament embryonic affirmations on the Trinity to contemporary Trinitarian theologies is a long, meandering, and tortuous one, at times disappearing and reappearing in the thicket of Christian doctrines.[50]

In other words, there have been numerous theologies of the Trinity, from the second century down to the present. No single theology of the Trinity has ever unified the Christian world. In 2017, various Christian communities have accepted one or the other new form of a Trinitarian theology. A brief analysis of each of these current writers indicates that today new theologies on the Trinity are at least beginning to be part of Christian thought.

Heup Young Kim

Heup Young Kim, in his essay "The Tao in Confucianism and Taoism," states his focus as follows:

> I will discuss how the Trinity can be understood in the religio-cultural matrix of East Asia which is heavily influenced by Confucianism and Taoism. My goal is not to replace Western interpretations of the Trinity with this Eastern approach, which may at first appear strange to some. Rather, my hope is that an East Asian interpretation of the Trinity will enrich the contemporary theology of Trinity and situate it in the global context.[51]

Kim's Trinitarian goal reaches far beyond the positions of Barth, Rahner, Pannenberg, and Moltmann. He is continuing, as his notes reveal, the work of Julia Ching, Tu Wei-Ming, Wing-tsit Chan, Jung Young Lee, and Cheng Chung-ying, all of whom have written publications on this subject.[52] There are a few Chinese Trinitarian references in Wing-tsit Chan's volume *A Source Book in Chinese Philosophy*. For instance, he cites a passage from the writings of *Hsün Tzu* in which there is a cosmic triad:

---

50. See Phan, "Development of the Doctrine of the Trinity," in *Cambridge Companion to the Trinity*, 3–4.

51. Kim, "Tao in Confucianism and Taoism," 294.

52. See Chan, *Source Book in Chinese Philosophy*; also Yu-lan, *History of Chinese Philosophy*; Lee, *Trinity in Asian Perspective*; Kim, *Christ and the Tao*; Küng and Ching, *Christianity and Chinese Religions*; Ming, *New Horizons in Eastern Humanism*.

Contemporary Theologians and Their Tentative Theologies of God 31

> Although the Way of Heaven is deep, the perfect man does not deliberate over it. Although it is great, he does not devote any effort to it. ... This is what is meant by not competing with Heaven. Heaven has its seasons, earth has its wealth, and man has his government. This is how they are able to form a triad.[53]

In the *Ch'un-ch'iu fan-lu*, written by Tung Chung-Shu (ca. 179–ca. 104 BCE), we read: "From this we can see that man is distinct from other creatures and forms a trinity with Heaven and Earth."[54] There are other areas in Chinese literature which indicate a trinity such as the "yin" and the "yang." In the yin-yang, one often sees only "the yin" or "the yang," but in order to form a triad it is a necessary to add a third issue, namely "and." In the box below, the third part of the triad is the "and" which unites the yin to the yang and the yang to the yin:

"Yin"–"Yang" form only a duality
but "Yin and Yang" form a triad

Heup Young Kim suggests that there is a Confucian Trinity which includes heaven, earth, and human life. Kim writes:

> The universe is visualized as a cosmic triune family, a human being as a cosmic person, and a member of the cosmic Trinity. From this vantage point, a Confucian-Christian idea of the Trinity has been suggested.[55]

Kim describes this "Trinity" by using the insights of Cheng Chung-ying.[56] Kim suggests that one might see God the Son as "the ideal human being." One might also see God the Father as "the creative spirit in heaven." And one might also see God the Holy Spirit as "the agent of the world" since the Spirit will, at the end of world, testify that humans can and have reached an ideal status and that the creative spirit has finally helped the

---

53. See Chan, *Source Book in Chinese Philosophy*, 117, in which he cites the above passage on nature from Hsün Tzu, who was the most eminent scholar of his time. Hsün Tzu flourished for six decades 298 to 238 BCE. He has a special attraction for contemporary Chinese.

54. On pp. 273–88, Chan provides an English translation of certain chapters of Tung's essays, *Ch'un-ch'iu fun-lu* (*Luxuriant Gems of the Spring and Autumn Annals*). On p. 281, one finds Tung's use of the term "trinity" for the interrelationship of Heaven, Earth, and Human Life.

55. Kim, "Tao in Confucianism and Taoism," 298.

56. Cheng, "Trinity of Cosmology, Ecology, and Ethics," 213–15.

world come to its ultimate perfection.⁵⁷ Given the vast number of Asians in the world today, Kim's essay helps Christians see the presence of God in the many religions throughout the world.

Francis X. Clooney

The essay of Francis Clooney, who has spent many years in India, is entitled "Trinity and Hinduism."⁵⁸ Perhaps, the most important Indian document for a possible union of the Indian religions to world religions is the *Trimurti*, the "Three Forms." The *Trimurti* focuses on the three deities, Brahma, Vishnu, and Shiva. The name *Trimurti* means "the three seeds from which Hinduism has developed." Although there are many sects of Hinduism in India, only a few have accepted the *Trimurti* but most Hindu sects have not accepted it. Currently, the interplay of Trinity and *Trimurti* is minimal. There is, perhaps, openness to Hindu deities and accordingly there is openness to new ways of thinking and living. India has been a strongly religious country, and its religious framework is highly diverse. Christianity is only one of the many religions of India.

Today, there are a number of academic scholars, almost all from India, who are focused on the multi-religions of the Indian people such as Michael Amaladoss, Abraham Kadalyil, Virginia Fabella, Raimon Panikkar, Felix Wilfred, and Aloysius Pieris. The Federation of Asian Bishops Conferences began in 1970 and these leaders of the Asian Catholic world have also led the way for a rethinking of Christian religion in almost all the Asian countries. For many years, Francis Clooney has been part of this episcopal and ecclesial movement. To date, the Catholic Church itself has been Asianized in several major ways.

Michael H. Díaz

Michael H. Díaz explains the theology of the Trinity from a multicultural stance: namely, "The life-giving reality of God from black, Latin American, and US Hispanic theological perspectives."⁵⁹ A Trinitarian God was a part of the emergence of black theologies of liberation in the late 1960s,

---

57. Cheng, "Trinity of Cosmology, Ecology, and Ethics," 298. Kim refers to Cheng Chung-yin's article "Trinity of Cosmology, Ecology, and Ethics," 213–15.

58. Cheng, "Trinity of Cosmology, Ecology, and Ethics," 309–24.

59. Cheng, "Trinity of Cosmology, Ecology, and Ethics," 259–73.

and—in an independent way—in Latin American theologies of liberation around the same time, as well as the independent emergence of US Hispanic theologies of liberation in the early 1970s. James Cone, Gustavo Gutiérrez, and Virgilio Elizondo "provided distinct building-blocks in black, Latin American and U.S. Hispanic Trinitarian reflections."[60] Díaz expresses in a clear way the needed relationship between Trinitarian theology and three cultures. He writes:

> God is not only Greek or Latin, but he must be black, red, Asian, Latin American, and U.S. Hispanic, to point to a few possibilities that name the human and divine encounter. The import of liberation theologies, however, is that the poor and marginalized are the primary addressees of God's abundant life. In this sense, a theology of God that does not attend to issues of human liberation, a Trinitarian theology unable to challenge oppressive human experiences that cause death, does not reveal the life-giving mystery of God.[61]

In all of the above authors, it is the theology of the Trinity in a different culture which is the keynote. This also took place in the early centuries CE when the Trinitarian theology was explained in Greek, Latin, Syriac, Aramaic, Coptic, and Arabic. Languages are not just words, they also include ways of understanding. Moreover, over centuries languages themselves change their meanings or the insights. Biblical scholars today have put themselves back into the ways in which Hebrew writings and Greek writings were used for a given book in either the *Tanakh* or the New Testament. Often, the meanings of some words or phrases in these scriptural works are more clearly expressed by a linguistic scholar who is aware of their temporalized meanings.

Patricia Fox

Patricia A. Fox explains the Trinity from the perspective of women theologians from differing cultures in her essay "Feminist Theologies and the Trinity."[62] Fox notes that the issue of the inferiority of women in the Christian religion has lasted for two thousand years. Today she asks

---

60. Cheng, "Trinity of Cosmology, Ecology, and Ethics," 259.
61. Cheng, "Trinity of Cosmology, Ecology, and Ethics," 268–69.
62. Cheng, "Trinity of Cosmology, Ecology, and Ethics," 274–90.

that women's voices on seven positive issues be taken into account by the Christian community.

1. Pay attention to women's voices and experiences.

2. Include, as much as possible, female imaging of God's presence in our life.

3. Value women's dissonance and dissatisfactions when they criticize ecclesial issues.

4. Develop a Trinitarian theology which includes ecofeminism.

5. Reread Christian patristic and scholastic resources in the light of today's feminine wisdom.

6. Bring Trinitarian theology more deeply in the church's spiritual and the liturgical dimensions.

7. Broaden Trinitarian theology to include Eastern, Western, Northern, and Southern cultures.

James Fredericks

In his essay on Buddhism, James Fredericks explains the ways in which Pure Land Buddhism has offered a major tradition of some twenty-five centuries and which today challenges the standard Christian theologies of Trinity. His essay is very intriguing, since it moves entirely away from the Greek-Latin theology of the triune God. If the incarnation of Jesus had taken place in India among the Mahayana Buddhists who were beginning to move throughout Eastern Asia, many major religious issues which Jesus preached would have been heard by non-Semitic ears and thereby translated into a different philosophy. Francis Moloney, in his essay "Johannine Theology," wrote the following: "[The Gospel of] John is the story of Jesus of Nazareth. . . . Yet, despite appearances, [the Gospel of] John is not a story about Jesus but a story about what God had done in Jesus."[63] The same God was at work at the same time in the Mahayana movement.

---

63. Moloney, "Johannine Theology," 1418.

David B. Burrell

David Burrell explains the "Trinity in Judaism and Islam."[64] Perhaps his essay raises more questions than answers. His many attempts to explain a union between Christian teachings and Jewish or Islamic teachings are based primarily on the Christian side. The Qur'an and the path to Chalcedon are by no means similar, even though he mentions their similarity several times.

CONCLUDING OBSERVATIONS

1. The contemporary multicultural and multireligious questioning of the "standard teaching" on the Trinity is not the first occasion in Christian history when there were divergent Trinitarian theologies. However, the above multicultural authors offer their views of Trinitarian theology in the light of differing cultures and differing religions. This interplay of a Trinitarian God with the "Gods" of many other cultures and religions involves a rearrangement, at least to some degree, of the current linguistic presentation of the many Trinitarian theologies in Christian communities.

2. From the second century CE to the end of the eighth century CE, the theological meaning of Trinity was the main focus of Christian theologians.[65] In these centuries, there were several different theological views of the Trinity. Today, the theological views of the Trinity are once again differing. For instance, there are Western approaches and there are Eastern approaches. In the above listing of contemporary theologians we have seen new approaches based on the diversity of cultures.

---

64. Moloney, "Johannine Theology," 344–62.

65. The *Letter of Clement to the Corinthians* is generally dated ca. 96 CE. There is one statement in which we read in English, n. 46: "Do we not have one God, and one Christ, and one Spirit." The Greek text reads: "Ἡ οὐχὶ ἕνα Θεὸν ἔχομεν καὶ ἕνα Χριστὸν καὶ ἓν Πνεῦμα τῆς χάριτος." Only God is referred to as "one God." The others are referred to as "one Christ" and "one Spirit of love." A second similar passage is found in n. 58. MacCulloch devotes an entire chapter (MacCulloch, *Christianity*, ch. 7, "Defying Chalcedon: Asia and Africa," 451–622), to carefully but honestly explaining the many divisions of the Christian churches as regards the divinization of Jesus. Many of these Christian churches remain divided today. The historical details which MacCulloch presents help Roman Christians today to see that their Trinitarian theology has many competitors. Over and over again, the divisive issue is the divinity of Jesus.

3. We are indebted to Barth, Rahner, Pannenberg, and Moltmann for their major presentations on the Trinity. Each of these theologians has to some degree changed the Trinitarian theologies which were developed after the Council of Trent. We are equally indebted to the contemporary theologians who have raised major questions as regards the current Trinitarian theologies in a world that is multicultural, multireligious, and intersexual.

4. In chapter 1, I have simply indicated that there are several contemporary movements which are presenting new theological views on the Trinity. The majority of these views are the work of outstanding Anglican, Orthodox, Protestant, and Roman Catholic theologians. In the twentieth and twenty-first centuries there has also been a strong appearance of major reconsiderations vis-à-vis the meaning of God in the major world religions. In other words, the leaders and scholars of these different religions have at least raised the question whether each religion has its own "theology of God," or should each religion claim that God is infinite? This latter approach would indicate that each world religion has only a partial understanding of an infinite God.

Currently, some major diverse scholars have presented essays on God which are open to a single infinite God who has revealed itself in differing ways. Today's technical histories of world religions indicate to some degree that there is an infinite God who surpasses each and every human description of a denominational God. The current theology of religious pluralism represents a new way for doing theology. One might call this new way of theologizing a "dialogical interreligious theology."[66]

---

66. See for instance Jacques Dupuis's recent book *Christianity and the Religions*, an English translation by Phillip Berryman of Dupuis's *Il cristianesimo e le religioni*. In the forty-one footnotes in chapter 3, there is a listing of the many books on interreligious dialogue from 1980–1999. I have also listed many books on contemporary interreligious dialogue in the bibliography at the end of this volume.

3

The Presentation of the Term Father—אָב—in the *Tanakh* and in Early Rabbinical Texts

THERE ARE MANY THEOLOGICAL and historical issues which unite the Hebrew religion and the Christian religion. One of these connecting issues is the term "Father" as a name for God. One finds the naming of God as Father in the following instances:

- In the *Tanakh*, the term "Father," אָב, was used as a name for God, but it was used infrequently. More often the issue of God's fatherhood was indirect, such as Exodus 4:22: "Israel is my son" (יִשְׂרָאֵל בכרי בני). It was used only as a poetic, descriptive, and metaphorical term.

- In the *intertestamental period*, from 300 BCE to about 300 CE, the term "Father" was used as a name for God by many Jewish writers, but again as a poetic term for YHWH.

- In the actual *lifetime of Jesus* in the first century CE, we can only affirm that Jesus used the term "Father" for God, since there are no texts for Jesus' own statements. In the Pauline Letters (written from ca. 50–ca. 58 CE), and in the three Synoptic Gospels, the term "Father" was used as a name for God but only as a poetic term for YHWH. Paul and the authors of two Gospels, Mark and Matthew, were Jewish, and Luke was a Gentile who had become a Jewish convert.

In all of the above texts, the two terms, either אָב or Πατήρ, were references to the Jewish God, YHWH. In these writings, there are also many other Hebrew names for Yahweh, such as El—אל; Elohim—אלהים; Adonai—אדני; etc. There is also a frequent use of the term אָב as a name for YHWH in Jewish noncanonical writers from 300 BCE to 300 CE—excluding the Jewish New Testament authors. In Jewish liturgy there has been a long-standing use of the term "Father" and we see this today in the beautiful hymn, *Abinu Malkenu*—טלכנו אבינו—which is a major part of contemporary Hebrew liturgies.

Samuel Rayan, a professor at the Vidyaijyoti Institute in Delhi, used the title "Naming the Unnamable" in an essay he wrote in 1985.[1] From the earliest historical names for God down to today's cultural and sectarian names for God, Rayan states that men and women are really "naming the nameless." Rayan writes:

> Any given name names and fails to name. It reveals and leaves a great deal undisclosed, and we know it. It situates reality and points at the same time to the element of reality that escapes all attempts to grasp it and enclose it in a set of syllables. . . . The more precious the reality, the greater number of names we invent.[2]

In the Hebrew text, one can find many sources which offer names for God. Most of these names are cultural names, while some of them are sectarian names.[3] The focus of my book is basically on two specific names for God: the first specific name for God is "Father." The second specific name for God is "The Infinite God."

THE NAMING OF GOD AS FATHER

In Judaism and Christianity, God has been called "Father" for centuries. However, today, we have a scientifically detailed understanding of what the term father means. This includes a physical, psychological, historical, personal, and emotional meaning. Today, we can trace the origins of a

---

1. Rayan, "Naming the Unnamable," 8.
2. Rayan, "Naming the Unnamable," 5.
3. See for instance Wikipedia.com, s.v. "Names for God."

human "father" back to *Homo sapiens sapiens*. Contemporary scientists have stated that *Homo sapiens sapiens* first appeared in history from ca. 200,000 years ago down to ca. 50,000 years ago. In these initial years, human beings had, in their variety of languages, names for which we today in English express as "father and mother," "son and daughter," "husband and wife." In all languages, these are terms which focus exclusively on human fathers, etc. In this volume I am suggesting that the name "father" when used for God in any and every language is only a poetic, descriptive, and metaphorical title. The words "Father" and "Son" in Christian usage do not refer to the "essence" of God. Within Christianity, and also within other religions, the one name which refers only to God is "infinite."

THE NAMING OF GOD AS INFINITE

Nowhere in the *Tanakh* or in the Christian Bible can one find the term infinite. Rudy Rucker, an emeritus professor in mathematics and computer science at San Jose State University, is the author of the introduction to a recent book, *Infinity: New Research Frontiers*.[4] In his essay he refers to a variety of infinities: mathematical infinities, physical infinities, metaphysical infinities, psychological infinities, and artistic infinities. He also mentions "theological infinities." In the following pages I will present God as infinite but only as a religious and theological infinity. Christians and other religious groups may call God "infinite," but if they do so it is a matter of faith not a matter of mathematical infinities, physical infinities, metaphysical infinities, etc.[5]

In the Christian world, from the second century CE down to the present century, an explanation of God's infinity has had a strange history. In the writings of the second century CE by the Fathers of the Church, the word infinite is used sparingly. Gregory of Nyssa (ca. 335 CE–ca. 394 CE), however, is the one scholar who used the term infinite in an abundant way, particularly in his writings against the Arian bishop of Cyzicus, Eunomius, who died in 394 CE. Eunomius's approach was philosophical and therefore Gregory of Nyssa had to express his opposition in a philosophical way. Gregory's philosophical rebuttal included the following: "He [Gregory] used the common ground of the Greek metaphysics and

---

4. Rucker, "Introduction," 2.

5. I have presented religious infinity in the final chapter of this volume and I will maintain that divine infinity is a matter of belief not a matter of human thought.

its properties, on which Eunomius also agreed. By a logical inference, Gregory showed that the two metaphysical properties of God in the Greek tradition—simplicity and inalterability (ἀναλλοίωτος)—necessarily entail God's infinity."[6] The Son was adopted from the beginning and therefore he had a different nature than God the Father.

The material in chapter 3 is divided into two parts.

PART ONE: IN THE *TANAKH*, THE USE OF THE TERM "FATHER"—אָב—FOR YHWH

In the *Tanakh*, the term "Father"—אָב—refers at times to YHWH, which is the main term for God throughout the *Tanakh*. In the Hebrew tradition, the most sacred name for God was and still is YHWH—יהוה. In the Masoretic text it appears about 6,828 times. The word literally means "One is" or "He is," or as many Hebrew scholars state "I am who I am."[7] The word itself implies that YHWH always "is." It also implies that we creatures do not really know the exact name for God, since YHWH is an open-ended name.

In *The Religion of Israel*, Yehezkel Kaufmann focuses on the role of YHWH among the early years of Jewish history.[8] In chapter 3 of "Israelite Religion," Kaufmann states the following:

> In him, then, the biblical religious idea, visible in the earliest strata permeating even the "magical" legends, is of the supernal God, above every cosmic law, fate, and compulsion, unborn, unbeginning, knowing no desire, independent of matter and its forces.... An unfettered divine [being who is] transcending all being—this is the mark of biblical religion and what sets it apart from all the religions of the earth.[9]

Perhaps this description of God with all its openness and transcendence is the reason why the untranslatable title of YHWH has no definition. In the *Tanakh*, YHWH appears more times than any other name for God.

6. Achtner, "Infinity as a Transformative Concept," 29.

7. See BiblicalHebrew.org. See also McKenzie, "Aspects of Old Testament Thought," 1286–87. McKenzie refers in particular to W. F. Albright and F. M. Cross. See also Ringgren, *Israelite Religion*. In ch. 2, Ringgren focuses totally on the Israelites' understanding of God.

8. See Kaufmann, *History of Israelite Religion*, 8 vols. An English abridgement of this work was published by Moshe Greenberg, entitled *Religion of Israel*.

9. Kaufmann, *Religion of Israel*, 121.

Elohim is second and Adonai is third. In Genesis 4:26, God is called YHWH for the first time: "Then began men to call upon the name of the Lord"—בשם יהוה.

The Twenty-One Citations in the *Tanakh* in Which God Is Named אָב Directly or Indirectly

In the *Tanakh*, God is indirectly called "Father" in the book of Exodus (4:22–23): "Thus saith the Lord" (יהוה). However, it is very probable that some Jewish people called God "Father" prior to this occasion. The pentateuchal text of the book of Exodus "is a five-section compilation of diverse traditions of varying ages edited by the Priestly redactor (P) in the 6th cent. BC."[10] The origin of the Jewish naming of God, "Father," is not all that clear. Ringgren, in the introduction to *Israelite Religion*, presents a brief history of the compilation of the texts used in the Pentateuch.[11]

We have little written evidence to confirm the earliest oral or written use of the term "Father" for God by a Jewish author, and the dating of a "canonically final edition" is also unclear. However, it seems that in Palestinian Judaism, there was finally an official or canonical acceptance of certain biblical books in the first century CE.[12] Prior to the first century CE, however, Jewish leaders had unofficially completed their acceptance of the official books in the *Tanakh*, and in doing so many writings, such as Sira, Daniel, Wisdom, which were available, were rejected by a Jewish council. Thus, the origin of Exodus preceded the Jewish council's decision that Exodus was divinely inspired. But in the many years and decades and even centuries prior to the end of Babylonian exile, the book of Exodus was in the making.[13]

One might conclude that in the official writings of the Hebrew Scriptures the major names for God—prior to Moses—were El and

---

10. See Clifford, "Exodus," 44.

11. Ringgren, *Israelite Religion*, 4–8. Ringgren also gives an account of the naming of God at the time of the Patriarchs (ch. 1) and the naming of God at the beginning of Israel's religion (ch. 2). See also Alt, *Essays on Old Testament History and Religion*. See also Kauffmann, *Religion of Israel*, ch. 3, "Israelite Religion," 60–121. In these volumes, the Israelite position on the fatherhood of God, YHWH, did not necessarily begin with Moses.

12. See Brown, "Canonicity," 1037–40.

13. In the writings of Kaufmann, beginning the history of Jewish life and Jewish religion are carefully expressed in part 2 of his volume *Religion of Israel*, esp. 153–261.

Elohim, and from the time of Moses onward the essential name for God was YHWH.[14] In early Judaism, there were many other names for God, and lists of these names can be found online under the search "Jewish Names for God." However, in almost all of these computerized lists, no mention is made of the name "Father."

In 1934, Joseph Bonsirven published a major work, *Le Judaïsme au Temps de Jésus-Christ*. His section on *"Dieu-Père"* begins as follows:

> Dans l'A.T. Dieu est appelé souvent Père. Ordinairement le titre signifie une relation spéciale entre Dieu et son peuple d'Israël; les Israélites sont les fils de Dieu, parce qu'il a creé et qu'il conserve leur nation, parce qu'il leur reserve ses bienfaits; ils sont ses fils, non pas en tant qu'individus, mais en tant que membres de la nation.[15]

In a footnote for this paragraph on *Dieu-Père*, Bonsirven cites only two passages from Sirach and one from Wisdom to confirm his statement that YHWH was called "Father" frequently (*souvent*) in the Old Testament. In the Jewish world, neither Sirach nor Wisdom is considered canonical writings. For the Hebrew Scriptures, however, Bonsirven rightly adds that the term *Père*, in these citations, is only metaphorical.[16]

John McKenzie, in his essay "Aspects of Old Testament Thought," explains the basic meaning of "Father" as used for God in the Old Testament. He writes:

> The analogy of *father-son* may appear to be primarily a natural relationship; but when it is seen in the context of other analogies and the character of parent-child relationship is examined, it becomes evident that even here it is the freely associated community of persons that is meant. Yahweh is never called the physical progenitor of Israel; he "begets" Israel by forming a people for himself. The attitudes that appear in the father-son analogy are the personal attitudes of love, devotion, and obedience, and not

---

14. For a detailed examination of the texts and versions of the Hebrew Scripture see "Texts and Versions," in Brown et al., *NJBC*, 1083–12. For my listing of the term Father—אב—for God in the OT, I have used Strong, *New Exhaustive Concordance of the Bible*, and Gesenius, *Hebrew and English Lexicon of the Old Testament*. See also Arndt and Gingrich, *Greek-English Lexicon of the New Testament*.

15. See Bonsirven, *Le Judaism Palestinien*, 138–39.

16. Bonsirven, *Le Judaism Palestinien*, 138–39; see also Schlatter, *Wie sprach Josephus von Gott*.

the relations of carnal kinship. The sonship of Israel is adoptive, not natural.[17]

The conclusion of McKenzie's paragraph may need further clarification. The theological understanding of God as the Father of Israel is based neither on a natural fatherhood nor on an adoptive fatherhood insofar as we understand adoption. A human father is totally different from God as Father. The use of the term "Father" for YHWH in the *Tanakh* is used by at least fourteen different Jewish authors, none of whom knew each other. Thus, there may be different nuances vis-à-vis the meaning of God as "Father."

The following citations from the Hebrew Scriptures indicate in a clear way that the Hebrew leaders, prior to the intertestamental period, distanced themselves from naming God "Father." Even in the few citations of God as "Father," there are differing views of God as "Father." Some citations seem to refer to a description (not definition) of the nature of God as "Father." Most citations refer to God as "Father" in a more poetic way. A few citations refer to God as "Father" with negative overtones. There are differing thrusts in the citations of God as "Father." Consequently, I have placed a symbol—✻—for each of the citations of the name "Father" for God in the following way.

1. Citations which strongly focus on the fatherly nature of God are marked by a single symbol ✻. The authors of these citations do not say that God's very nature is that of a father. They simply say that God could easily be described as a "Father." For instance, in the book of Exodus, the very first citation of "Father" for God, states that God is the "Father of Israel." The author is simply describing but not defining God.

2. Citations which focus more poetically on the fatherly nature of God are marked with two symbols ✻ ✻.

3. Citations which appear to have some hesitant and even negative overtones regarding the fatherly nature of God are marked with three symbols ✻ ✻ ✻.

---

17. McKenzie, "Aspects of Old Testament Thought," 1297n75. This citation is important for the thesis of this book. When we say that in the Trinity, there is a "God the Father" and a "God the Son," we can ask whether this relationship is simply analogous and adoptive, but the term is not used in a natural or physical way. On the other hand, is the Father-Son relationship an essential aspect of God? See chapter 5 for this problematic naming of God.

None of these citations are focused on the essential nature of God. For the Jewish people, YHWH is the name which comes closest to the nature of God, but the name YHWH is not translatable since it is a name which at best points to the Hidden God, but does not name God in a defining way. YHWH, in certain parts of Jewish history, was and is the only God. All other gods are non-gods.[18]

In the Tanakh, Yahweh Is Called Father Directly—אָב—or Indirectly in a Phrase such as—"He is my Son"—בֵּן

There are twenty-one citations in the *Tanakh* in which Yahweh is either called "Father" in a direct way or Yahweh is referred to as "Father" in an indirect way The indirect reference takes place when the Lord states that "Israel is my son."

Exodus 4:22–23: God is the Father of Israel—✲

> You will then say to Pharaoh: "This is what Yahweh says: Israel is my first-born son, my first born (בכיב שראל בני). I told you: Let my son go and worship me; but since you refuse to let him go, well then I will put your first born-son to death."

In the first three chapters of Exodus, the author has already mentioned God several times prior to the above citation.[19] In ch. 4:22–23, YHWH indirectly tells Pharaoh twice that he is the "Father" of Israel, for he says that Israel is his firstborn son. In this sentence, God indirectly claims to be a father (אָב) of the Israelites, and not simply the Father of one person,

---

18. See Kaufmann, *Religion of Israel*, 127-31. Kaufmann stresses that the land of the Israelites is sacred and that in this land the Jewish people must worship YHWH. On p. 130, he writes: "In alien lands, one cannot worship YHWH." On p. 134, he writes: "The imposition of a new religion upon an entire people always involves the assistance of and promotion by the temporal power. This is the lesson of the spread of Mazdaism, Christianity, and Islam." On p. 128, he writes: "Thus while YHWH governs and manifests his activity everywhere—in Sodom, Shinar, Egypt, Nineveh, and Tarshish—the area of his sanctity is restricted to the boundaries of the land of Israel." Kaufmann's explanations of the one God raise many religious questions. His stance of YHWH as the only true God needs some rethinking.

19. The author (or authors) of these three chapters refers to God as Elohim אלהים—see ch. 1, 26 times; in ch. 2, 13 times, one of them v. 4b uses for the first time Yahweh Elohim, יהוה אלהים; and in ch. 3, 12 times. In ch. 4, God is called YHWH for the second time.

such as Moses.[20] Brevard Childs, in his book on Exodus, states: "That Israel is Yahweh's first-born son is a metaphor which expresses the unique relationship between God and his people."[21]

Father-Son is most often used as a human relationship between an older male and a younger male, who has his origin through the sexual union of a particular man and a particular woman. In the text from Exodus as well as other books of the Old Testament, the wording, Father-Son, is used in an analogous way, which describes a personal attitude of love, devotion, and obedience. The sonship of Israel is adoptive not natural and in the above citation it is not the adoption of one person. God is the father of all Israelites, and therefore the use of the term "Father" refers in a general way to the Jewish population.

The book of Exodus was put together by a redactor in the sixth century BCE. Consequently the material which was compiled in the sixth century came from pre-sixth-century material, which remains unknown.[22] Moses lived sometime between 1300 and 1050 BCE.[23] Therefore, one cannot say that the words of Moses given above are his exact words. In the course of Jewish history up to the writing of Exodus, the phraseology of Moses speaking to Pharaoh developed sometime in the intervening years and thus it is the main author of Exodus who gives us a picture of Moses speaking to Pharaoh. The phrase Father of Israel cannot be judged as the exact wording of Moses himself.

Deuteronomy 14:1: You are the children of the Lord, your God—

> And the Lord spoke to Moses, saying: Speak unto the children of the Lord your God (אתם ליהוה אלהיכם). You shall not gash yourselves nor shave the hair above your foreheads for the dead. For you are a people sacred to the Lord, your God, who has chosen you from all the nations on the face of the earth to be a people peculiarly his own.[24]

---

20. The Hebrew text is taken from Hertz, *Pentateuch and Haftorahs*, and in a footnote for v. 22 one reads: "The other nations, too, are God's children." See p. 221.

21. Childs, *Book of Exodus*, 202.

22. See Speiser, *Genesis*, 15–16, for the use of Yahweh in the *Tanakh*.

23. The date of Moses' birth varies; some scholars argue that his life began in 1520 BCE, others suggest 1393/1392 BCE; still others suggest 2368 BCE; others suggest the dates stated in this paragraph, namely sometime between 1300 and 1050 BCE.

24. For the Hebrew text, see Hertz, *Pentateuch and Haftorahs*, 808.

In this citation, the term "father" is not used. Yahweh is telling his people that they have been chosen as a special group. They are the children of God, and children are usually close to their own fathers. Once again, this passage just as the one above does not focus on a "natural father" of a "natural child." God's fatherhood is a poetic, descriptive, and metaphorical fatherhood of the Jewish people. God's children need not copy the customs of the gentiles.

The dating of Deuteronomy is very tenuous. Since the book gathers together many legal situations, one would expect that some "laws" were a compilation of many regulations of various times prior to its compilation. This passage, however, agrees with many other citations of YHWH as the Father of Israel. It is the fatherly nature of God which is emphasized.

Deuteronomy 32:5–6: God is the Father who created Israel—✳✳

> Yet basely, [as Moses says] has he been treated by his degenerate children (בניו), a perverse and crooked race! Is the Lord to be thus repaid by you, O stupid and foolish people? Is he not your father (אביך) who created you? Has he not made you and established you?[25]

Chapter 32 in Deuteronomy presents the "Song of Moses," and in it God is called "Father." Again it is the "Father of Israel" not the Father of a single individual. In the three citations from the Pentateuch which are just cited, God is called Father. God's fatherhood is not, however, described in any full way. In all three citations, God is not the Father of an individual. The citations simply imply that God has a fatherly nature and his children are the children of Israel.[26]

2 Samuel 7:8, 14: God is the Father of David—✳✳

> Now then, speak thus to my servant David: "The Lord or Host has this to say: . . . I will be a father to him (David) and he shall be a son to me" (אני אהיה־לו לאב והוא יהיה־לי לב).[27]

---

25. English text, New American Bible, 329. For the Hebrew text, see Rosenbaum and Silbermann, *Hamisha humshe torah*, 159.

26. See Blenkinsopp, "Deuteronomy," 108. Blenkinsopp states along with many others that "The Song of Moses" is an addition to the final pages of Deuteronomy. Moses is probably not the author of the "Song of Moses."

27. English text from the New American Bible, 474; Hebrew text in Goldman,

In the above citation from the Second Book of Samuel, YHWH is presented as the "Father of David." In Exodus and Deuteronomy, God was the Father of Israel; in the above passage from 2 Samuel, God is the father of only one person, David. However, the use of the future tense indicates that the father-son relationship refers to a time in David's life when he will be close to YHWH: "I will be . . ." Again, the relationship describes the fatherly nature of God, not simply to a large community but to an individual, and this description is poetic, descriptive, and metaphorical.

1 Chronicles 17:4, 11–13: *God is the Father of only one of David's sons*—✳✳

> The word of God came to Nathan: "Go and tell my servant David. Thus says the Lord . . . I will raise up your offspring after you who will be one of your own sons, and I will his kingdom. He it is who shall build me a house, and I will establish his throne forever. I will be a father (לאב) to him, and he will be a son (לבן) to me."[28]

In this passage, the author clearly states that a son of David will build the temple. David had wanted to build the temple, but Yahweh had different plans. The son of David will build the temple and will also be a king of Israel. Yahweh *will be a father to this son of David*, namely of Solomon. In this passage, YHWH is called the Father (לאב) of Solomon not the father of David. In the Jewish tradition, Solomon was honored as a "son" of God; this is an honorary title not a physical title.

1 Chronicles 29:10: *God is the eternal Father of Israel*—✳✳

> Then David blessed the Lord in the presence of the whole assembly, praying in these words: "Blessed may you be, O Lord, God (יהוה) of Israel, our Father (אבינו) from eternity to eternity."[29]

In this passage, David refers to YHWH as the Father of the Jewish people. Once again we move from God as the Father of an individual, namely

---

Samuel, 226–27.

28. English text, New American Bible, 617. For the Hebrew text, see Slotki, *Chronicles*, 99.

29. English text, the New American Bible, 632. For the Hebrew text, see Slotki, *Chronicles*, 156.

Solomon, to God as the Father of the Israelites. Clearly this use of Father for God is poetic. David is describing God's relationship to Israel from its beginning to its ending in a metaphorical way. In the Jewish Scripture, the close interrelationship of YHWH to the Jewish people is clearly stated. No other group of human beings can claim YHWH as Father.

Job 1:6: Sons of God—✳✳

> One day when the sons of God (Elohim, בני האלהים) came to present themselves before the Lord, Satan also came among them.

In this verse, the author of Job is presenting God (*Elohim*) in an anthropomorphic way. God is described as an Oriental monarch. He is seated on his throne, and his servants are presenting their reports. Roland Murphy states that these servants were called the "Sons of Elohim," and were ministers of Yahweh. Among them is the Adversary, "the Satan," not to be treated as a proper name, but "as the prosecutor who spies on men's wrongdoings and reports it to his master."[30] "He is not yet the 'devil' of later Jewish and Christian theology; to identify him as such distorts the understanding of the book [of Job]."[31] In this passage, the phrase "Sons of God" centers on a reduced group of YHWH's ministers. In this context, even "Satan" is a minister of YHWH.

Psalm 2:7: You are my son—✳

> The Lord (יהוה) said to me, "You are my son (בנ אתה) this day I have begotten you. Ask of me and I will give you the nations for an inheritance and the ends of the earth for your possession."

In the Hebrew text, God is not referred to as "Lord." Rather, God is referred to as Yahweh: אתה יהוה אמר אלי בני. The text seems to indicate that "this day" is a day when YHWH adopted (begotten) the "Messiah" who now is given universal reign: In the text of this psalm, there is no indication that the chosen one was a "natural" son of God. Rather, a human person is adopted to be a son of YHWH and also one who will be the ruler of nations. In verse 11, we read: "Serve the Lord with fear and

---

30. Murphy, "Job," in Brown et al., *NJBC*, 470.
31. Murphy, "Job," in Brown et al., *NJBC*, 470.

rejoice before him; with trembling pay homage to him." The Hebrew words are "kiss the son" not "pay homage to him." In Hebrew the word "kiss" is נשק. In the *New Jerome Biblical Commentary*, "Psalms," one reads that this is an awkward phrase and many proposals have been offered.[32]

Psalm 68:6: God is the father of orphans—✳✳

> The father of orphans (אבי יתומים) defender of widows, such is God in his holy dwelling. God (אלהים) gives the lonely a home to live in, leads prisoners out into prosperity, but rebels must live in the bare wastelands.

Psalm 68 is probably the most obscure and confusing of all the psalms. Scholars like William Albright see about thirty verses which begin their first line of strophe copied from a range of Hebrew hymns.[33] Hans-Joachim Kraus, in his first volume of *Psalmen*, also takes into account the large diversity of this "hymn." He writes:

> Es gibt im Psalter wohl kaum ein Lied, das in seiner Textverderbnis und Zusammenhanglosigkeit den Interpreten vor so grosse Aufgaben stellt wie—geäußert worden sind, weit auseinander.[34]

> Bei der Frage nach Gattung des Ps. 68 wird man von den dominierenden Elementen der Formsprache ausgehen müssen. Die Form des Hymnus ist in 4–7, 20ff., 25–28, 35ff., klar zu erkennen. Daneben stehen ganz anderen Elemente.[35]

The few passages of the psalm itself cited above by Kraus are seen as part of the original form of the psalm.[36] However, most of the psalm verses come from a variety of sources and the passages are often a listing of many verses from different sources. Kraus, in a lengthy passage, cites the various passages from a variety of non-interconnected sources.[37] Nonetheless, the description of YHWH as Father of the poor and needy is, in

---

32. See Kselman and Barré, "Psalms," 527.
33. Albright, "Catalogue of Early Hebrew Lyric Poems."
34. Kraus, *Psalmen*, 468.
35. Kraus, *Psalmen*, 469. Kraus dedicates fourteen pages to his analysis of Psalm 68, and a major part of it focuses on the mystifying conglomeration of the verses.
36. Kraus, *Psalmen*, 468.
37. Kraus, *Psalmen*, 469. Kraus lists in sixteen lines twenty-two different themes, each taken from a different source.

itself, a powerful description of a loving God, and this passage seems to be original to the psalm.

Psalm 89:27: God is the Father of David—✳✳

> He [David] shall say of me, "You are my Father (אבי), my God, (אלי), the Rock of my salvation."³⁸

This psalm was written by a very educated Jewish person and in many editions of the Psalms a title is presented for such a poem, namely a *maskil*. The name *maskil* is not in the original text. The use of the term *maskil* stems from the time of the Haskelah movement, a European Jewish enlightenment from 1770–1789, which was an effort to reeducate Eastern European Jews in the Hebrew Scripture. This psalm was, perhaps, written by Ethan the Ezrahite at the time of the division into two kingdoms, Israel and Judah (922 BCE). In other words, many European Jews—and perhaps others—considered this psalm as a very special hymn written by a very special Jewish poet and consequently the poem came to be called a *maskil*. Notice here that it is an individual, David, who refers to YHWH as "my Father." However, at the very beginning of the psalm, vv. 3–4, the author mentions that YHWH made a covenant with David. It is only after this covenant that David says: "You are my Father."

Psalm 103:13: YHWH is a compassionate father—✳✳

> As a father (אב) has compassion on his children (בנים), so the Lord has compassion on those who fear him.³⁹

In this verse of Psalm 103, God is described as similar to a father who has compassion (רחם) on his children. It is evident that YHWH is not essentially a "Father." Rather, he is "like a good human father who in a tender way loves his children."

---

38. English trans. in the New Jerusalem Bible, 906.

39. English trans. in the New Jerusalem Bible, 1013. Hebrew text, see *Hebrew Bible: Hagiographa*, 4:1055.

Isaiah 1:2, 3: YHWH is a disowned father—✳✳✳

> Hear, O heavens, and listen, O earth, for the Lord (יהוה) speaks: Sons (בנים) have I raised and reared, but they have disowned me. An ox knows its owner, and an ass, its master's manger; but Israel does not know, my people have not understood.[40]

The Israelites had abandoned their allegiance to YHWH, who is presented in the above verse as a Father. YHWH is speaking to the Israelites, but he does not state directly that he is a Father. God says in a metaphorical way: "Sons have I raised and reared, but they have disowned me." Israel is more stupid and stubborn than an ox or an ass, two animals which in Old Testament Judaism are not considered special animals. Worse than these two animals, the above statement is a clear description of God as a Father, but the passage is very brief. Joseph Jensen in his commentary on Proto-Isaiah uses strong language on this passage. He writes that Yahweh had taken care of his Israelite children, but their parents seriously failed to instruct their children. Both young and older Israelites became seriously disobedient and rebellious against the words of Yahweh who describes them as worse than their oxen or jackasses. Yahweh is telling the Israelites that their elders and their children are worse than the two animals mentioned above.

Isaiah 63:16: YHWH is Israel's father—✳✳

> O Lord, hold not back for you are our Father (אבינו). Were Abraham not to know us, nor Israel to acknowledge us, You, Lord are our Father (אבינו), our redeemer you are named forever.[41]

Trito-Isaiah 64:7: God is our father—✳✳

These two passages from Trito-Isaiah are almost identical, and therefore the following paragraphs refer to both of them. Carroll Stuhlmueller notes that the author is twice "defending his status as an authentic

---

40. For the English text see: New American Bible, 1263. For the Hebrew text, see Slotki, *Isaiah*, 1–2.

41. For the English text see the New American Bible, 1349. For the Hebrew text, see Solti, *Isaiah*, 309–10.

Israelite and a true child of God."[42] The main theme of the two psalms is the following: "Human life is moving from sorrow to a new heaven and a new earth." The author, by using the term "Father," is saying to God that he is God's child and in some way deserves to be a member of this *new heaven and new earth*.[43]

Jeremiah 3:4–5: Israel's first rejection and YHWH's loving and forgiving nature—✳✳✳

> Even now on, do you not cry out to me "My Father (אבי)? My beloved ever since I was young! Will he keep up his anger forever? Will he maintain his wrath to the end?" This is what you say; but still go on sinning, being so obstinate.[44]

Israel's first rejection takes place through its disregard of YHWH and its many relationships with other lovers. Such a woman ignores her husband and spends time with other men. Such infidelity often ends in divorce, and Israel's infidelity ends in a divorce from YHWH. "In the days of King Josiah, Yahweh said to me: 'Have you seen what disloyal Israel has done? How she has made her way up to every high hill and to every green tree and played the whore there? I thought, After doing all this she would come back to me, but she did not come back.'" The Lord referred to her traitor sister, Judah, who was equally adulterous. The text then stops. Jeremiah moves to the conditions for forgiveness and the return of Israel.

YHWH had given a message to Jeremiah, telling him to repeat his words to Israel. The section begins with YHWH's earnest desire to forgive Israel. "Then the Lord said to me: 'Rebel Israel is inwardly more just than traitorous Judah. Go and proclaim these words towards the north [to Israel] and say: Return, rebel Israel, says the Lord, I will not remain angry with you for I am merciful'" (3:11–12). Then, YHWH says to Israel: "You would call me, 'My Father' I thought and never cease following Me" (3:19). In this section it is the Israelites, not individuals, who should ask YHWH if they can call God "Father."[45]

---

42. Stuhlmueller, "Deutero-Isaiah and Trito Isaiah," in Brown et al., *NJBC*, 347.

43. Stuhlmueller, "Deutero-Isaiah and Trito Isaiah," in Brown et al., *NJBC*, 347.

44. English trans., New American Bible, 1367. For the Hebrew text, see Bright, *Jeremiah*, 3:4–5, p. 19.

45. The context seems to indicate a universality in God's Fatherhood.

Jeremiah 3:19: YHWH loves Israel and pleads for her to return—✶✶

> I had thought: How I should treat you as sons (בנים) and give you a pleasant land, a heritage most beautiful among the nations! You would call me "My Father" (אבי) I thought, and never cease following me. But you like a woman betraying her lover, House of Israel, you have betrayed me, Yahweh says.

Jeremiah 31:8–9: Israel rejects YHWH again and eventually asks God for forgiveness, just as the father of Israel had once before forgiven Israel—

> The Lord (יהוה) has of the north. . . . With them, the blind and the lame, women with children delivered his people. . . . Behold I will bring them back from the land, women in labor—all together a mighty throng will return here! In tears will they return, in prayer I shall lead the. . . . For I am a father (לאב) to Israel, and Ephraim is my first-born (בכרי).[46]

In Jeremiah 31:8–9, the Israelites are finally returning from exile and YHWH is renewing his fatherly love. The tribe of Ephraim is the Father's firstborn not because it is superior to Judah, but because YHWH wills to renew his fatherly love for Ephraim once again. God loves freely. The tribes of Israel can do nothing for YHWH. God freely responds to tribal actions, since forgiveness is a gratuitous gift from YHWH. In this text, the focus is not on an individual person; YHWH is the "father" of Israel in a wide sense, and in a privileged sense Ephraim is YHWH's firstborn. McKenzie clarifies the Hebrew meaning of God's relation to Israel:

> The OT uses a number of analogies to designate the relationship of God to Israel. The analogy of father-son may appear to be primarily a natural relationship; but when it is seen in the context of other analogies and the character of the parent-child relationship is examined, it becomes evident that even here it is the freely associated community of persons that is meant. Yahweh is never called the physical progenitor of Israel; he "begets" Israel by forming a people for himself. The attitudes that appear in the father-son analogy are the personal attributes of love,

---

46. The English text is taken from the New Jerusalem Bible, ch. 31, p. 1346. For the Hebrew text, see Bright, *Jeremiah*, ch. 31:7, 8.

> devotion, and obedience, and not the relations of carnal kinship. The sonship of Israel is adoptive, not natural.⁴⁷

If McKenzie is correct in his position that YHWH is the "father of Israel" in an adoptive way, one could ask: is this also true among the Jewish people of the first century CE as well as all further centuries down to today.

Jeremiah 31:19: Is Ephraim not my favored son?—✸✸

> Is Ephraim not my favorite son (הבן יקיר לי אפרים) I still remember him with favor; my heart stirs for him. I must show him mercy, says the Lord.⁴⁸

Once again, in the same chapter, it is not a single person that is a child of God, but an entire tribe. The Ephraimites were located northeast of Jerusalem in a mountainous area, and the tribe had a long history. In Genesis 48:12–20 we read that Joseph blessed Ephraim with his right hand and Manasseh with his left hand. In the text above, the Ephraimites are singled out as the "child in whom YHWH delights." This "child" is an entire tribe and is called "my favorite son."

Hosea 11:1-11: YHWH loved his son—✸✸

> When Israel was a child, I loved him, and out of Egypt, I called my son (לבני). But the more I called them, the farther they went away from me; they offered sacrifice to Baal and burnt incense to idols. (Hosea 11:1–2)⁴⁹

Hosea 11:1-11 has been called "one of the high points of the OT revelation of God's nature." The text itself is at times corrupt, but "YHWH's fatherly love and Israel's ungrateful response are punished which calls forth God's love to produce Israel's redemption." Rabbi Lehrman describes this passage as follows: "God's relationship to His people is described tenderly under the image of a father's love for his child."⁵⁰ However, in 11:8–11 YHWH says: "How could I give you up, O Ephraim, or deliver you up,

---

47. See McKenzie, "Aspects of Old Testament Thought," 1297.
48. For the Hebrew text, see Freedman, *Jeremiah*, 208.
49. For the Hebrew text, see "Hosea," in Cohen, *Twelve Prophets*, 41–42.
50. Lehrman, "Hosea," in Cohen, *Twelve Prophets*, 41–42.

O Israel? . . . Out of Egypt they shall come trembling like sparrows, from the land of Assyria like doves and I will resettle them in their homes, says the Lord." Hosea presents us with a heavenly Father who is abounding in love.

Malachi 1:2, 6: YHWH loves Israel—✴✴

> I have loved you, says Yahweh. But you ask "How have you shown your love to us?" Was not Esau Jacob's brother? declares Yahweh; even so I loved Jacob but I hated Esau. . . . The son honors his father, the slave stands in awe of his master. If I am indeed a father (אני ואם־אב) where is the honor due to me?[51]

The book of Malachi begins with the Lord speaking to Israel through Malachi, a name which means "my messenger." In the opening lines (v. 1), the author focuses on the love of God for Israel, but a few lines later (v. 6), he reminds Israel that he freely loves Israel over Judah, just as he had freely loved Jacob over Esau. Therefore, the Lord asks Israel, which had called God "Father," "Where is the honor due to me, your Father?" Eli Cashdan clarifies this Jacob-Esau issue: "The Edomites (the descendants of Esau) were in Josephus' description 'a tumultuous nation,' while Israel was a people with a deeper religious instinct and realization of the will of God and therefore worthy of his love."[52]

Malachi 2:10: Leaders of post-exilic Israel have dishonored God, their father—✴✴

> Have we not all the one Father (אב)? Has not the one God created us? Why then do we break faith with each other, violating the covenant of our fathers?[53]

The Israelites are presented as one family ("Have we not all the one Father—YHWH?"). The Israelites are the children of the one God. This is different than the situation of other people, for they all have their differing fathers or Gods. The unity of Israel under the fatherhood of YHWH is an honor that they should never demean. The focus of the argument

---

51. Malachi, English text, New Jerusalem Bible, 1544. For the Hebrew text, see Cohen, *Twelve Prophets*, 338–39.

52. Eli Cashdan, "Malachy," in Cohen *Twelve Prophets*, 337.

53. For the Hebrew text, see "Hosea," in Cohen, *Twelve Prophets*, 345.

in these verses is that the Israelites should maintain their respect for YHWH. Those who do so will be God's "most prize possession," for they are like the son who serves his father. For those who do not love and serve God, YHWH says that "all the proud and all the evil doers will be the stubble, for the Lord will set them ablaze." Likewise, this passage indicates that the Israelites should only marry Israelites. Malachi is the final book of the canonical Hebrew Scripture, and today most scholars would place its date of composition at ca. 430 BCE.

Conclusions for Part One

The above twenty-one citations in which the authors refer to YHWH as Father or that YHWH has sons are not earth-shaking.[54] The twenty-one citations are not all from one source. Fourteen different books of the Jewish Scriptures are cited, but that does not mean that there were fourteen authors. Almost all of these books have been reedited several times and consequently different authors might have inserted "Father" in their re-editing. Nonetheless, we can make the following conclusions.

1. In the *Tanakh*, there are only twenty-one times in which God is called "Father" either directly or indirectly. The citations speak of God as Father in a positive and respectful way with the exception of Isaiah. In the entire *Tanakh*, there are no passages which state that one should not call YHWH "Father."

2. Diarmaid MacCulloch, in his volume *Christianity: The First Three Thousand Years*, devotes an entire chapter to the names for the Hebrew God. In footnote 14, page 54, MacCullough explains both the meaning and the history of the name YHWH, יהוה.[55] There are only a few books in the Old Testament in which the authors use the term "Father," אָב. The authors also use the term YHWH to name God, and do so far more than any other divine name.

At times today, it is puzzling why many contemporary Jewish authors, who are analyzing the *Tanakh*, do not refer to the Jewish usage of God as "Father." For instance, Yehezkel Kaufmann, in his volume *The Religion*

---

54. Maertens, in his volume *Bible Themes: A Source Book*, suggests a few others, such as Prov 3:12; Ps 67:6; etc., but too often the reference is unclear.

55. See the entire second chapter (47–73) of MacCulloch, *Christianity*, and esp. 1022n14.

of Israel, does not mention Yahweh as Father at all. The same can be said of Albrecht Alt's volume *Kleine Schriften zur Geschichte des Volkes Israel*. In his book, there is no mention of God as Father.[56] Joachim Jeremias, in his volume *New Testament Theology*, states a questionable position: "Nowhere, however, in the Old Testament do we find God addressed as Father."[57] Often the passages speak of the fatherhood of God in an indirect way such as Exodus 4:22–23: "Israel is my son, my first-born." However, there are passages in which YHWH calls himself "Father" such as 1 Chronicles 17:13: "I shall be his father and he will be my son."[58]

PART TWO: THE USE OF THE TERM "FATHER" FOR YHWH IN THE "INTERTESTAMENTAL PERIOD"

The classification of the "intertestamental period" differs from scholar to scholar. Martin McNamara, in his volume *Intertestamental Literature*, has an opening statement on the terms apocrypha, pseudepigrapha, and deuterocanonical writings composed during the intertestamental period.[59] He writes:

> Writings composed during the intertestamental period are often referred to as the Apocrypha, Pseudepigrapha, or by Roman Catholic writers as Deuterocanonical. The terminology has originated in denominational settings and can at times be confusing.[60]

McNamara clearly states that Jewish scholars, Protestant scholars, and Roman Catholic scholars differ in their application of the above names. In the introduction, McNamara explains the difficulties in naming the Jewish and Jewish Christian writings from 200 BCE to 300 CE. "Pseudepigrapha" is also a possible name for "Intertestamental Literature."

There are other competent authors who also have used various names for pseudepigrapha, such as R. H. Charles, James H. Charlesworth,

---

56. Alt, *Kleine Schriften zur Geschichte des Volkes Israel*. English translation by R.A. Wilson in Alt, *Essays on Old Testament*.

57. Jeremias, *New Testament Theology*, 63.

58. See also Ps 68:5; Jer 3:19; Mal 1:6.

59. In the second stage, I am excluding the Jewish New Testament writers who frequently use the term Father for God. These Jewish authors will be presented in the "Third Stage."

60. McNamara, *Intertestamental Literature*, 17.

Alexander Pahnoyotav, James Damila, Richard Bauckham, and Willis Barnstone.[61]

In my title for this section of the chapter, I am using the term "Transitional Period" since there is no agreed-upon title for this material. Under this heading, I bring together the major writings of Jewish authors from ca. 300 BCE to ca. 300 CE, in which one finds the term "Father" in reference to God.

In this, the term "Father" is found in the apocryphal, pseudepigraphal, and deuterocanonical Hebrew literature. It would be far too much to review every Judaic use of the term "Father" for God from 300 BCE to 300 CE. Consequently, I have selected the following Jewish writings as an adequate exemplification of the Jewish leaders and scholars whose works were written in the above-mentioned time line. During this period, there is a proliferation of naming God "Father" in Jewish writings. This proliferation, as far as I can tell, helped in a major way to provide a base for the use of the term "Father" by Christian Jews in the first century CE, such as Jesus, Paul, Mark, Matthew, etc.

Since the term "Father" for God was used only twenty-one times in the Hebrew Scripture, I was expecting that, in the first century CE, Jesus' generous use of the term Father for God would have met with some notable opposition. However, in the New Testament writings, reference to God as Father occurs again and again and again, and there is generally no serious complaint from his Jewish audience. There are, however, two instances when the Jewish leaders condemned Jesus for calling God "Father." In stage 3, I will focus on these two passages in detail.

The Jewish use of the term "Father" for YHWH appears frequently in the Jewish literature of the intertestamental period. From 300 BCE to 300 CE there are many Jewish texts in which YHWH is called Father. The following citations are only a few instances that the authors refer to God as "Father."

Wisdom 2:16: A Misuse of the Term "Father" for God

> He [the wicked Jew] judges us debased; he holds aloof from our paths as from things impure. He calls blest the destiny of the just and boasts that God is his Father. Let us see whether his words

---

61. See Charles, *Apocrypha and Pseudepigrapha*; Charlesworth, *Pseudepigrapha of the Old Testament*; Pahnoyotav et al., *Old Testament Pseudepigrapha*. In Barnstone, *Other Bible*, see the introduction, xvii–xxiii, for a definition of Pseudepigrapha.

be true; let us find out what will happen to him. For if the just one be the son of God, he [God] will defend him and deliver him from the hands of his foes.

Addison G. Wright states: "If we assign to it [the book of Wisdom] a date in the last half of the 1st cent. BC, we shall not be far from wrong. Wisdom is the last of the OT books."[62] From the book of Wisdom 1:16—2:24, the author presents a speech which the wicked Jews in Alexandria might have given. In this section, the wicked Jews maintain that there is no life after death. "No one is known to have come back from the nether world" (2:1). The wicked Jews mock those Jews who claim that God is their Father. The wicked Jews are atheistic, completely this-worldly, and therefore hedonistic. The "wicked Jews" deride the "religious Jews" who boast that YHWH is their "Father." The opposite, of course, is that the good Jews who live a life that honors YHWH will receive God's love.

Wisdom 14:3: Some Israelites Call YHWH "Father"

> But your providence, O Father, guides it [namely, a sea voyage by Jewish people] for you have furnished even in the sea a road and through the waves a steady path.

This is a remarkable passage. Addison Wright indicates that the author clearly states that God is the guide of every ship, not just the ship of Noah. God makes navigation safe. A road is usually on solid ground, but God can make a road through the ocean waters. The author is not focused on a Creator God, but on a Father God, who cares for his children even if they are on a boat. God the Father is a caring Father-God, and he looks after his many sons and daughters.[63] There is another passage in Wisdom in which God is called Father, but textually it is negative about God the Father. Wisdom 2:10 reads: "It was the wicked . . . who said among themselves . . . that the just man . . . boasts that God is his Father." This passage is a mockery of God.[64]

---

62. Wright, "Wisdom," in Brown et al., *NJBC*, 510. Wright is following the Catholic numeration of the biblical books. In the *Tanakh*, the book of Wisdom is not included; in the Christian Bibles the book of Wisdom is included in the Old Testament.

63. Wright, "Wisdom," in Brown et al., *NJBC*, 512.

64. Wisdom 1:16 and 2:13.

Ecclesiasticus/Sirach 23:1–2

> Lord, Father and Master of my life [Κύριε, πάτερ καὶ δέσποτα ζωῆς μου] permit me not to fall by them! Who will apply the lash to my thoughts, and to my mind the rod of discipline, that my failings may not be spared, nor the sins of my heart overlooked?

Ecclesiasticus/Sirach 23:4

> Lord, Father and God of my life [Κύριε, πάτερ καὶ ζωῆς μου] abandon me not into their control. A brazen look allows me not; ward off passion from my heart.[65]

In these two citations, which are almost joined together, the author of Ben Sira uses the Hebrew term for "Father" only two times. Alexander Di Lella in his essay on "Sirach," concludes that it was Ben Sira himself who probably wrote his book in Hebrew about 180 BCE.[66] In many Christian Bibles, the translation of the book of "Sirach" is referred to as "Ecclesiasticus." However, the book of Sirach has nothing to do with the Christian churches. Rather, it provides us with a major insight into the Jewish faith at the end of the second century BCE and the first twenty-five years of the first century BCE.

Ben Sira was a native of Jerusalem who had devoted his entire adult life to the study of Hebrew Law, Hebrew Prophets, and other major Jewish religious writings. Di Lella states that his purpose in writing "Sirach" was "to demonstrate that the Jewish way of life was superior to the Hellenistic culture and its blandishments and that true wisdom was to be found in Jerusalem, and not in Athens. Hence, the good Jew should not give in to the temptation to follow the Greek way of life."[67]

The Hebrew text of Ben Sira was probably based on his notes as a professor, and thus the text is a conglomeration of many of his professional lectures. He died around 175 BCE. The Greek translation of this

---

65. English text of *Sirach* in the New American Bible, p. 1207. For the Greek text of *Sirach* see Knabenbauer, *Commentarius in Ecclesiasticum*. This volume contains both a Greek and a Hebrew text as well as a Latin text. The Greek and Latin texts for the citation are in the main section of the book; the Hebrew text is in an appendix at the end of the volume, I–LXXXIII.

66. Di Lella, "Sirach," in Brown et al., *NJBC*, 496.

67. Di Lella, "Sirach," in Brown et al., *NJBC*, 496. See also Di Lella, *Wisdom of Ben Sira*, 16.

The Presentation of the Term Father in the *Tanakh* 61

volume was made by Ben Sira's grandson who lived in Alexandria. The Greek translation was published around 117 BCE. One could say that in its Hebrew text and even more so in its Greek text it became very popular in the Jewish world.[68]

In the English translation, part 2 of the introduction is entitled "Ben Sira and His Times." The author begins with a lengthy comment by Ben Sira's grandson, who described his grandfather in some detail.[69] Evidently his father was a well-known and a well-honored Jewish professor in Judea. With the Greek translation, his fame increased in a strong way.

Joseph Knabenbauer, in his volume *Commentarius in Ecclesiasticum*, states that the nephew of Ben Sirach added an appendix to his uncle's work. He entitled it as chapter 51: "Oratio Iesu filii Sirach distichis viginti (hebr)."[70] In ch. 10 one reads: "'Ἐπικαλεσάμεν Κύριον πατέρα Κυρίου μου" (I have invoked the Lord, the Father of my Lord). Today, scholars do not accept chapter 51 as part of the original text written by Ben Sira in Hebrew, nor does one find chapter 51 in the Greek translation written by Ben Sira's grandson. R. A. F. Mackenzie, in his commentary *Sirach*, states this negative conclusion as follows:

> The piece [ch. 51] is an appendix to the book. However, it may have been Ben Sira's work. More doubtful in origin is the collective thanksgiving, similar in style to Ps. 136, which the Hebrew manuscripts insert between vv. 12 and 13 (see NAB note). It does not appear in the Greek translation, so was probably not part of Ben Sira's original text.[71]

One can conclude the following: both Ben Sira in 180 BCE and his grandson in 117 BCE were unafraid to use the term "Father" for YHWH

---

68. See Di Lella's preface in the Anchor Bible Series, *Wisdom of Ben Sira*, which was translated into English by Patrick Skehan and Alexander Di Lella. However, one should read the preface, in which Di Lella relates the circumstances of the death of Patrick Skehan, and how much of the volume was authored by Skehan and how much was authored by Di Lella.

69. Di Lella, *Wisdom of Ben Sira*, 8–16.

70. Knabenbauer, *Commentarius in Ecclesiasticum*, 466–73. Nikel, in his volume *Das Buch Jesus Sirach*, offers a lengthy discussion on calling God "Father." Nikel states that at the time of Ben Sira's grandson, YHWH was often referred to as "Father." He also cites many Mideastern nonbiblical texts which refer to God as "Father." Jeremias argues that no one but Jesus had addressed God as "Father." However, in the citations above, there seem to be instances in the Greek text in which God is addressed as "Father."

71. MacKenzie, *Sirach*, 194.

(23:1–4). Calling God "Father" was a name for God which was acceptable to the Jews in the second century BCE. The author of chapter 51 also referred to God as "Father," and his usage was also an acceptable Jewish name for God, even though we do not know when and by whom chapter 51 was added to the book of Sirach.

2 Esdras 7:28

The second book of Esdras is a composite work, written in Hebrew or Aramaic between 100–300 CE, but these texts are no longer available. Today, we have a Syriac and a Latin text of this volume. Section 1, chs. 1–2, are clearly Christian texts, written probably in the second century. Section 2, chs. 3–14, are Hebrew or Aramaic texts written by a Jewish author and focus on Jewish themes. Section 3 is a Christian conclusion, written perhaps in the third century. The following passage is from the Jewish author who refers to the Messiah as "my son." We find this in 2 Esdras 7:28:

> For my Son the Messiah shall be revealed with those who are with him, and those who remain shall rejoice four hundred years. And after these years my son the Messiah shall die, and all who draw human breath.[72]

Testament of the Twelve Patriarchs

Martin McNamara states that this volume "is a collection of twelve independent *Testaments*, one for each of Jacob's twelve sons."[73] Each of the twelve Patriarchs centers his personal *Testament* on a few aspects, good or bad, of his own life. The *Testament of Levi* is the longest of these patriarchal *Testaments*. In the *Testament of Levi*, there is one reference to God as Father (18:6–7), namely:

> The heavens shall be opened, and from the temple of glory sanctification shall come upon him [namely, the "New Priest" 18:2] with the Father's voice as from Abraham to Isaac, and the glory

---

72. See McNamara, *Intertestamental Literature*, 75. See also Myers, *I and II Esdras*, 208. On p. 253, Myers states in his notes: "Christian tampering [of the text] can be detected from the insertion of 'Jesus' in vs. 28 and 'sons' in vss. 28–29)."

73. McNamara, *Intertestamental Literature*, 99.

of the Most High shall be uttered over him, and the spirit of understanding and sanctification shall rest upon him.[74]

The twelve *Testaments* are extant in Greek, Armenian, and Slavonic. There are two Greek manuscripts, but recently scholars have found sections of an Aramaic version of the *Testament of Levi* in the Qumran documents. Some scholars claim that the *Testament of Levi* was written in the first century CE, since the wording, in a few places, is similar to passages in the New Testament. Other scholars maintain that the *Testament of Levi* was written around 130–120 BCE.

Contemporary scholars are also divided over the issue of the original language of Levi: was it Aramaic or was it Greek? The *Testament of Levi* is the longest of the twelve *Testaments*. Parts of the document, it seems, were written in either Hebrew or Aramaic. There are Hasidic and Maccabean traces in it, but there are also Christian additions within it.

The Testament of Abraham

The *Testament of Abraham* was written either in Palestine or in Egypt. The dating of the document is unclear, moving from the first century BCE to the first century CE. There are two documents, both written in Greek. One document is half as long as the other document. In *The Testament of Abraham*, the term "Father" in reference to YHWH occurs three times:

> XVI: Coming with great fear it [Death] stood before the Invisible Father, down to Abraham, my friend, take him, and bring him to me.
> XX: And they set it [Abraham's soul] there to worship YHWH the Father. There came the undefiled voice of YHWH, the Father.[75]

In these two passages, we read that God is called "the Father," in an authoritative way but also in a loving way. Throughout *The Testament of Abraham*, God's love for Abraham is expressed again and again.

---

74. McNamara, *Intertestamental Literature*, 101. See also Russell, *Method & Message*, 337–40.

75. An English edition of the entire *Testament of Abraham* can be found at Yachanan.com. See also "The Testament of Abraham," in McNamara, *Intertestamental Literature*, 104–5.

Psuedo-Daniel

Pseudo-Daniel is an Aramaic document which was probably written in the last third of the first century BCE. Most authors claim that it is a Jewish document, and in the document the important person is called the "Son of the Most High." Catholic scholars, such as Joseph Fitzmyer, do not consider the document to be a Christian document. What Jewish person, therefore, is referred to as "Son of the Most High"? The authorship is disputed. Some scholars suggest that he is a Jewish king or a major Jewish personage.

The source of Pseudo-Daniel is basically unknown, although in the documents of Qumran, Pseudo-Daniel provides us with the text itself.[76] It would seem that in the Qumran documents we might conclude that the "Son of the Most High" refers to an important Jewish person rather than Jesus. However, the dating of the Qumran scrolls, 100 BCE to 60 CE, could allow for a reference to Jesus.

Three Maccabees

In the "Prayer of the priest, Eleazar" (Maccabees 6:2–15) we read:

> King of Great Power, Almighty God Most High, governing all creation with mercy, look upon the descendants of Abraham, O Father, upon the children of the sainted Jacob, a people of your consecrated portion who are perishing as foreigners in a foreign land.

This document was written in Alexandria by a Greek-speaking Jewish scholar. Most writers conclude that it was written in the latter half of the first century BCE. The use of the term "Father" is simply another instance in which a Jewish author refers to God as Father. There are many other passages in Jewish writings from 200 BCE to 300 CE, which refer to God as Father. For instance, in the Shemoneh 'Eshreh (שמננה צשרה) we read: "Graciously favor us, Our Father, with understanding from Thee, and discernment and insight out of thy Torah." In the *Kaddish de-Rabbanan*, there are two prayers. The first prayer reads: "May the prayers and supplications of the whole house of Israel be accepted by their Father who is

---

76. See Eisenman and Wise, *Dead Sea Scrolls Uncovered*. An English translation and the original Hebrew document are available online at www.bibliotecaleyades.net/scrolls.

in heaven." The second prayer is for teachers, disciples, and disciples of their disciples: "May they have abundant peace, loving kindness, ample sustenance and salvation from their Father in heaven."[77]

The Other Bible, ed. Willis Barnstone

Another important book of Jewish prayers and sacred writings is *The Other Bible*, edited by Willis Barnstone.[78] In this volume of 742 pages, there are many citations taken from Jewish writings which are not found in canonical texts. Many of the texts are deeply spiritual and they are a testimony to the depth of Jewish spirituality. In these texts, God is called Father again and again.

In *The Other Bible*, some texts are Jewish Pseudepigrapha, such as the *Book of the Secrets of Enoch* also called *Second Enoch*. In this book, God speaks to Enoch: "Go down to earth and tell my sons all things I have spoken to you."[79] Another Jewish Pseudepigrapha is *The Odes of Solomon*. In Ode 19, God is called "Father." In Ode 41, God is called "The Father of Truth." In Ode 42, one reads: "The dead ran toward me, crying: Son of God, pity us."[80] Another source is *The Gospel of Truth*, which is "full of Jewish mystical speculation and lacks any explicitly criticism of the Jews or Jewish Christianity," and each page of the text mentions "Father."[81] *The Gospel of the Hebrews* is a Jewish-Christian text, composed perhaps in the middle of the first century CE. This text is cited by Cyril of Alexandria. One reads:

> When Christ wished to come upon the earth to men, the good Father summoned a mighty power in Heaven, which was called Michael, and entrusted Christ to the care thereof.[82]

---

77. *Kaddish*, n. 3, McNamara, *Intertestamental Literature*, 209.

78. Barnstone, *Other Bible*.

79. Barnstone, *Other Bible*, 7. In Barnstone's book, the author cites this passage from *The Book of the Secrets of Enoch*. In the following footnotes, I refer only to the pages in Barnstone's volume. The titles of each citation are in the body of my paragraphs, not in the footnotes.

80. Barnstone, *Other Bible*, 267–85: esp. 279, 283, 285.

81. Barnstone, *Other Bible*, 287, 288, 289, 290–97.

82. Cameron, "The Gospel of the Hebrews," in Barnstone, *Other Bible*, 335. The text is taken from Cyril of Jerusalem, *Discourse on Mary Theotokos*, 12a.

The *Book of the Secrets of Enoch* is part of the Jewish Pseudepigrapha, and it spans a period from 200 BCE to 100 CE. In this book, we read: "[My spirit] ascended into heaven and I saw the holy sons of God."[83] In *The Apocalypse of Ezra*, the "Son of God" is mentioned three times.[84] These are only some of the references to God as Father in Hebrew religious literature from 200 BCE to 100 CE; one could easily add many more citations from Jewish writings during the same three hundred years.

The introduction of Barnstone's book truly helps the reader understand how many of the citations have a dual editing; Christians have read and revised Jewish documents, Gnostics have read and revised Christian texts, and Jewish texts have been read and revised into the formats of Midrash, Pseudepigrapha, and early Kabbala. In all of these writings we cannot help but appreciate the depth and breadth of human beings understanding of religious literature. All three groups are searching for the meaning of an infinite God.

A Rabbinic Anthology, ed. G. Montefiore and H. Loewe

In the volume *A Rabbinic Anthology*, the authors—Claude Goldsmith and Herbert Lowe—have provided us with a very thorough compilation, in which rabbi after rabbi is cited and in many of these texts the rabbis use the term Father in reference to YHWH.

The first chapter of this book is entitled "The Nature and Character of God and His Relations with Man." There is a paragraph, written by the authors, which brings up the question of the Trinity. The author writes:

> I have not come across any passage which seriously truly tackles the *Homo sapiens sapiens* Christian conception of the Trinity or which attempts to show that a Unity, which is simple and pure Unity, is a higher or truer conception of the Divine Nature than a Unity of a Trinity or than a Trinity in Unity. Where the Rabbis reply to the minim (heretics, sectaries, and sometimes Christians), they always represent these minim as believing in many Gods. In other words, the doctrine of the Trinity (if that is referred to) is construed to mean Tritheism, which indeed was, and perhaps still is, its vulgar corruption.[85]

83. Barnstone, *Other Bible*, 492 and 493.

84. Barnstone, *Other Bible*, 515 and 516.

85. Montefiore and Loewe, *Rabbinic Anthology*. See also the introduction by Montefiore, in which he refers to the Trinity (lii).

The introduction by Montefiore offers us many details regarding similar anthologies of rabbinic literature. This volume gathers citations from the first century to the fifth century. Many citations are anonymous but in Montefiore's view there is a unity or a compatibility of the rabbinical writings in these five centuries.

The use of the term "Father" for YHWH is found again and again in this anthology.[86] The "rabbis" who are cited are basically from the second, third, and fourth centuries CE. In an appendix, the authors list the number of rabbis cited and indicate the centuries in which they were writing. The majority of rabbis lived in the second century CE down to the fifth century CE.[87]

Montefiore has written an excursus entitled "The Use of the Adjectives, 'Jewish' and 'Christian' in England."[88] In this excursus, he focuses on passages, both Jewish and Christian, which praise Jewish religion and almost condemn the Christian religion, and vice versa. This history of inter-religion contempt has had, historically, many centuries of deep contempt for each other, and other times, when the contempt was mitigated. Even today, Jewish-Christian negative relationships are still extant, but there are also developing relationships between the two religions which have a positive goal. Montefiore's excursus is an important and honest document.

A second excursus in *A Rabbinic Anthology* was written by R. H. Snape.[89] Snape was the first editor of *A Rabbinic Anthology*, published in 1937. In this excursus, Snape, in a lengthy and detailed way, described the Jewish-Christian relationship from the Pauline writings in the New Testament down to the end of the fourth century. The Christian church started in a brief way when Paul was writing his letters. The rabbis in this anthology date from the first to the sixth century CE. During the first two centuries CE, Christian and Jewish writers were in literary contact with one another. In the third century, Christian writers for the most part had become Hellenized, and thus their antagonists were basically Greek philosophers. Snape offers us a very detailed interreligious relationship,

---

86. In the index, see "Father (God)," "Father in Heaven," and "God," 795.

87. Montefiore and Loewe, *Rabbinic Anthology*, 713–37.

88. Montefiore, "Excursus I," in Montefiore and Loewe, *Rabbinic Anthology*, 609–16.

89. See the 1937 1st ed. of *Rabbinic Theology*. In this edition, Montefiore and Loewe were the authors; R. H. Snape was the editor and he wrote a preface for the book, which is republished in the 1974 ed. of the same work, 617–39.

pro and con, for the first two centuries.⁹⁰ Snape indicates that there were times when Jewish-Christian relationships were positive but also there were many times when the relationship was negative.

Concluding Observations for Part One and Part Two

On the issue of calling God "Father," אָב, Jewish authors consistently used אָב as a poetic name for God. Thereby, they avoided at least a few times the use of YHWH which was the most sacred word for God. In the intertestamental period, Jewish authors continued to use the term "Father" in a poetic, descriptive, and metaphorical way. These Jewish writers were religiously Jewish writers who lived from the last centuries BCE down to the end of the third century CE. As far as we know, these Jewish writers called God "Father" without any major protests by their fellow Jews. In the texts from Barnstone's *The Other Bible*, the naming of God as Father is found abundantly in the writings of both Jewish and Jewish-Christian scholars. One can conclude that in the first century CE, when the New Testament was written, the term "Father" had become one of the secondary names for God in order to avoid the use of the term YHWH.

1. From 200 BCE to about 300 CE, Jewish people living in Palestine began to use either Aramaic or Hebrew as their daily languages. Outside of Judea, Greek also became a foundational language throughout the Hebrew world. The Greek term πατήρ—father—was used for God—Yahweh—in a generous way. Bruce Metzger provides us with a history of Koine Greek, which affected the entire Roman Empire.⁹¹ At the time of Jesus and throughout the first century CE, many Jews were Greek speaking, and therefore they could read the writings of Paul and the Synoptics in an understandable way. In the few years of his public life, Jesus preached to the Jews again and again, using the Aramaic term Father for God. Even though the Jewish listeners did not become disciples of Jesus, they still understood what Jesus meant when he called God "Father." They, too, in the first half of the first century CE, spoke of God as "Father." Jesus was not arrested for his use of the term "Father" for YHWH; rather he was arrested by the Jewish leadership for his claim to be the Messiah.

---

90. Snape, *Rabbinic Theology*, 623.
91. See Metzger, "Language of the New Testament," 7:43–46.

The Presentation of the Term Father in the *Tanakh*   69

2. In the closing decades of the first century CE, the Jewish community experienced the destruction of their temple by the Romans. Little by little, the Romans took over the entire area of Palestine. Many Jewish men and women and Jewish-Christian men and women were killed or incarcerated. Another revolt took place in 132–135 CE. In this second scourge, Rome took over the entire Jewish structure and Jews could no longer even visit the Jerusalem area. As a result of these two destructive anti-Jewish wars, data regarding Jewish communities at that time is minimal. We can, however, state that these Jewish people continued to call YHWH "Father."

3. At the end of the first century CE, non-Jewish Christians began to move into gentile areas and in a short time non-Jews became the leaders of most Christian communities. It was in this period of time—90 CE onward—that the Gospel of John was written.[92] His Gospel is Hellenized in a strong way and the authors have centered on the divinization of Jesus and on the love of one another. The author or authors used the Greek term Πατήρ as a name for God.

4. Greek-speaking non-Jewish leaders and scholars became the influential members in almost all Christian communities. This dominance of non-Jewish Christians lasted down to today. Christian leaders, though divided among their constituents, are "gentiles" not "Jews." Nonetheless, over many centuries, the interconnection of Jewish religion and Christian religion has been a part of both religions. In both of these religions there are some Jewish elements and some Christian elements.

5. In the second century, the Christian communities slowly but surely began to face the issue of the divinization of Jesus. In the Christian world, there were and still are several different approaches to this issue. From the Reformation onward, the overriding issue in Catholic theology was ecclesiology, not the Trinity. However, in the latter half of the twentieth century and the beginning of the twenty-first century, Trinitarian theology, not ecclesiology, has become a major focus of many contemporary Christian writers. Ecumenism has seriously questioned the meaning and the theology of a Trinitarian

---

92. Raymond Brown gives us a detailed explanation of the contents in John's Gospel. See his *Introduction to the New Testament*, ch. 11, 333–82. Brown expresses his views on several key issues from 362–75.

God, since interreligious ecumenism does not demand that all people believe that God is Trinitarian.[93]

6. The contemporary God-problem has its roots in the early centuries of the Christian world. For Christians, there is only one God and that God is Trinitarian. Nonetheless, during the lifetime of Jesus, as also during the lifetime of Paul, Mark, Luke and Matthew, the God about whom they preached was not a Trinitarian God. Rather, it was the Jewish God—"Israel is my son" (ישראל בכרי בני).[94] It is only with the members of the Johannine community at the end of the first century and the beginning of the second century, and with Clement of Rome (ca. 96 CE) and Ignatius of Antioch (d. 107 CE) that we have a "beginning of a Trinitarian God." In time, the Trinitarian God became the only acceptable Christian God. Today, ecumenical gatherings need to reconsider the meaning of a universal God. Today's presentations of an infinite God move a human "theology" of God far beyond a God that human men and women claim to understand at least in a small way. Today, we do not know that God is infinite; rather, we believe that God is infinite.

---

93. Toward the end of the seventh century CE, there was an ecumenical council at Nicea in which the issue that Jesus was only an adopted Son of God was denounced. This almost brought an end to the denial of Jesus' divinity in the early Western church, but the issue of Christ's divinity became a problem once again due to the writings of Peter Abelard. In 1140 CE, Abelard was condemned by the Council of Sens.

94. Luke was a gentile who became a member of the Jewish religion prior to his friendship with Paul.

4

The Use of the Term Father for YHWH in the Writings of Paul, Mark, Luke, and Matthew

IN THE FIRST-CENTURY WRITINGS of Paul, Mark, Luke, and Matthew, God is frequently called "Father." Their references to God as "Father" are in keeping with the frequent use of "Father" for God in the intertestamental period. Since the writings of Paul and the three Synoptic Gospels were written several years after Jesus died, we cannot claim that in these writings we have the "exact words" of Jesus. However, one can rightfully argue that on many occasions Jesus himself used the term Father for God, either in Aramaic or in Hebrew.

Chapter 4 is a cataloguing of all the major passages in which Paul and the three authors of the Synoptic Gospels have used the term "Father" for God. In the writings of these authors, there are no passages in which a Trinitarian God is expressed. There are, however, a few times in these writings when Jesus is referred to as the Son of God.[1] However, the naming of "God the Father" when united to the naming of "God the Son" only expresses that Jesus is called the "divine Son of God." In other words,

---

1. The divinity of Jesus as stated in the Letter to the Hebrews has been and still is a matter of dispute. Did the author clearly state that Jesus was God? See Bourke, "The Epistle to the Hebrews," in Brown et al., *NJBC*, 920–22.

there are no clear indications that in these four writings Jesus himself is the divine "Son of God."[2]

In his analysis of the first letter of Paul, which was written to the Thessalonians, Raymond Collins writes, "Paul addressed his 'thanks' to God, i.e., the monotheistic God of the Jewish tradition; his reason is the fruitful reception of the gospel by Thessalonian Christians."[3] In other words, Paul is speaking to a Jewish audience and the reference to God is to Yahweh, the main Jewish God. In an essay by Joseph Fitzmyer, "Pauline Theology," we read again that for Paul, God was Yahweh. Fitzmyer writes:

> The Father who revealed his Son to Paul was the same God that Paul the Pharisee had always served. He [YHWH] was the creator, the lord of history, the God who continually saved his people Israel, and who proved to be the lord of the covenant despite Israel's infidelities.[4]

THE USE OF THE TERM "FATHER" FOR GOD AND THE TERM "SON OF GOD" FOR JESUS IN THE PAULINE LETTERS

We begin with the Pauline letters since they are chronologically the earliest writings in the New Testament. Between 50 and 59 CE, Paul wrote five letters and in all of them Paul uses the term "Father" (Πατήρ) for God. Daniel Patte describes Paul as follows:

> Paul was a Jew of the tribe of Benjamin, a Pharisee raised in Tarsus with a solid Hellenistic and Jewish education, who zealously persecuted the church. Paul was converted [to the Jesus community] c. 33/34.[5]

In his five letters, Paul refers to God as "Father" twenty-six times and in these references God is YHWH, not the Trinity. These passages include Paul's direct use of "Father" for God, as well as an indirect use whenever

---

2. See Bredin, *Rediscovering Jesus*, ch. 11, 229–59. In this chapter Bredin in a thorough way refers to many names of Jesus. At the end of his chapter he states that in John 20:28, Jesus is called "God" at least once. In my volume, the Gospel of John appears in ch. 5 which centers on 1000 CE.

3. Collins, "The First Letter to the Thessalonians," in Brown et al., *NJBC*, 772.

4. Fitzmyer, "Pauline Theology," 138.

5. "Paul the Apostle," in Patte, *Cambridge Dictionary of Christianity*, 932–34.

he states that Jesus is God's own son. Because of his training in Jewish writing, Paul already knew that God loved him. He even mentions that as far as Jewish religious traditions were concerned, he was blameless. "As for uprightness embodied in the Law, I was faultless" (Phil 3:6). In his letters, Paul refers to God as Father, but he does not fully explain his use of the term father for YHWH. In the New Testament, his letters are not gospels. Nor are they what we call today "theological essays." Raymond Brown acknowledges that Paul is a unique author. He writes: "In the whole library of Christianity, it is hard to match his impassioned eloquence. . . . That eloquence has been a key factor in the ongoing appreciation in places and times that he would never have envisioned."[6] As regards Paul's understanding of who Jesus is, Joseph Fitzmyer states that "only in Romans 9:5 does Paul possibly call Jesus Christ *theos*, 'God' but this is a highly disputed text."[7]

Thessalonians—Dated ca. 50 CE

This is a genuine letter of Paul which has come down to us. It was written by Paul who at that time was in Corinth. Raymond Collins writes: "Most probably the letter was written AD 50, but some scholars prefer to date it in AD 51."[8] Paul's first language was Greek and Hebrew was his second language. There are four passages in this letter in which Paul refers to God as "Father."

- 1 Thess 1:1: Paul, Sylvanus, and Timothy, to the church in Thessalonica which is in God the Father and the Lord Jesus Christ. Grace to you and peace.

- 1 Thess 1:2: We always thank God for all of you, mentioning you in our prayers, continually. We remember before God and Father how active is the faith, how unsparing the love, how persevering the hope, which you have found in our Lord Jesus Christ, who lives in the presence of our God and Father.

- 1 Thess 3:11–13: Now may God himself, our Father, and our Lord Jesus direct our way to you, and may the Lord make you increase and abound in love for one another and for all, just as we have love

---

6. See Brown, *Introduction to the New Testament*, 451–52.
7. Fitzmyer, "Pauline Theology," 1395.
8. Collins, "First Letter to the Thessalonians," in Brown et al., *NJBC*, 773.

for you, so as to strengthen your hearts, to be blameless in holiness before our Lord comes with all his holy ones, amen.

1 Corinthians—Dated ca. 54 CE

In this letter, Paul refers to God as "Father" five times. Jerome Murphy-O'Connor, in his commentary on *One Corinthians*, refers to the first nine verses of the letter as an introduction, a greeting, and a thanksgiving. In these nine verses, Paul twice refers to God as "Father."[9]

In chapter 8, Paul realizes that in Corinth there are many people whom Paul refers to as those who believe in many so-called gods. However, "for us," Paul writes, there is only one God. Murphy-O'Connor suggests that the description of God the Father and Jesus as his Son may have been taken from a baptismal liturgy, but this has only a few sources. He also states that 15:20–28 is a thesis.[10] By the use of the term thesis, he seems to be saying that in these words we find the meaning of human life. Christ has been raised from the dead and the followers of Christ will also be raised from the dead. Moreover, the risen Jesus had appeared to many of his followers. Last of all, Paul says, Jesus appeared to Paul himself. Paul may have been the least of the apostles, but he toiled harder than all of them. Paul says that he had already preached this message to the Corinthians, and toward the very end of his letter he writes: "Therefore, whether it be I or they, so we preached and so you believed" (1 Cor 15:11). With all of the above citations in mind, carefully read the following passages from Paul's letter to the Corinthians.

- 1 Cor 1:3: Grace to you and peace from God our Father and the Lord Jesus Christ.
- 1 Cor 1:9: You can rely on God, who has called you to be partners with his Son, Jesus Christ Our Lord.
- 1 Cor 8:5–6: Indeed, even though there are so-called gods in heaven and on earth (there are, to be sure, many "gods" and many "lords"), yet for us there is one God, the Father, from whom all things are and

---

9. Murphy-O'Connor, "First Letter to the Corinthians," in Brown et al., *NJBC*, 800.

10. Murphy-O'Connor, "First Letter to the Corinthians," in Brown et al., *NJBC*, 812. The word "thesis" does not seem to describe the style of Paul's letters. There are only a few philosophical sentences in Paul's own writings.

The Use of the Term Father in Paul, Mark, Luke and Matthew 75

for whom we exist, and one Lord Jesus Christ, through whom all things are, and through whom we exist.

- 1 Cor 15:22–23: For just as in Adam all die, so too in Christ shall all be brought to life, but each one in proper order: Christ the first fruits; then, at his coming, those who belong to Christ; then comes the end, when he hands over the kingdom to his God and Father.
- 1 Cor 15:28: When everything is subjected to him, then the Son himself will be subjected to the one who subjected everything to him, so that God may be all in all. (The phrase "the Son himself" implies that God is his Father.)

2 Corinthians—Dated ca. 55 CE

Biblical scholars today say that this second letter is really a conflation of Paul's subsequent letters to the Corinthians. Therefore, it is not a unified composition. Letter A is contained in chs. 1–9. Letter B is contained in chs. 10–13. Letter A is written in a measured tone and a careful language.

- 2 Cor 1:1–3: Paul, an apostle of Christ Jesus by the will of God, and Timothy our Brother, to the church of God that is in Corinth, with all the holy ones throughout Achaia: grace to you and peace from God our Father and the Lord Jesus Christ. Blessed be the God and Father of our Lord Jesus Christ, the Father of compassion and the God of all encouragement.
- 2 Cor 1:18–19: As God is faithful, our word to you is not "yes" and "no." For the Son of God, Jesus Christ, who was proclaimed to you by us, that is, Silvanus and Timothy and me, was not "yes" and "no," but "yes" has been in him (God is the Father of Jesus).
- 2 Cor 11:30–31: If I must boast, I will boast about things that show how weak I am. The God and Father of the Lord Jesus Christ—blessed be his name forever—knows that I am not lying.

Galatians—Dated ca. 54/55 or 57 CE

The province of Galatia was in an area which today is in the middle section of Turkey. At the time of Paul, there was a northern section of Galatia and a lower section of Galatia. Paul had probably been in both areas, but in the northern area were the real Galatians of the Indo-Aryans who were related to the Celtic and the Gallic populations.

The Letter to the Galatians is unique. Brown writes: "In some ways this [letter] has been considered the most Pauline of the Pauline writings, the one in which anger has caused Paul to say what he really thinks."[11] Paul had been with the Galatians for a lengthy period of time due to illness. After Paul had left the northern Galatians, some Jewish preachers came into the Galatian city and preached a Jewish-oriented Christian spirituality. They mentioned that Abraham was their Father even though the Galatians were not Jewish. The Jewish preachers also told the Indo-Aryans that they had to be circumcised. When Paul wrote to these Galatians, his anger burst out here and there, since they had rejected Paul's form of Christian life. Paul's main focus in this letter is on God the Father who blessed both the followers of Abraham and who has also blessed the gentiles, especially those from the northern part of Galatia. Paul writes:

> Consider the experience of Abraham; as the scripture says: "He believed God, and because of his faith God accepted him as righteous." You should realize, then, that the real descendants of Abraham are the people who have faith. The scriptures predicted that God would put the Gentiles right with himself through faith. And so the scripture announced the Good News to Abraham: "Through you God will bless all mankind." Abraham believed and was blessed; so all who believe are blessed as he—Abraham—was. (Gal 3:6–9)

It is on this basis that Paul writes to the Galatians. In the letter, Paul strongly insists that they not only dedicate themselves to Abraham, but even more so they should live by the standards given God the Father through his son, Jesus Christ. In his Letter to the Galatians, he mentions God the Father and his Son Jesus four times.

- Gal 1:1: Paul, an apostle not from human beings nor through a human being, but from Jesus Christ and God the Father who raised him from the dead.
- Gal 1:3–5: Grace to you and peace from God our Father and the Lord Jesus Christ, who gave himself for our sins, that he might rescue us from the present evil age in accord with the will of our God and Father, to whom be glory forever and ever. Amen.

---

11. "Letter to the Galatians," in Brown, *Introduction to the New Testament*, 467.

- Gal 1:15–16: But when [God], who from my mother's womb had set me apart and called me, through his grace, was pleased to reveal his Son to me, so that I might proclaim him to the Gentiles. (The fatherhood of God is indirectly stated by calling Jesus "his Son.")

- Gal 2:20: Yet I live, no longer I, but Christ lives in me; insofar as I now live in the flesh, I live by faith in the Son of God, who has loved me and given himself up for me. (Once again Jesus is referred to as Son of God and thus the fatherhood of God is indirectly stated.)

- Gal 4:4–6: But when the fullness of time had come, God sent his Son, born of a woman, born under the law, to ransom those under the law, so a that we might receive adoption as sons. As proof that you are sons, God has sent the Spirit of his Son into our hearts, crying out "Abba, Father."

Philippians—Dated 54–58 CE

The Letter to the Philippians is unique. Scholars are divided on its structure since it is not too well unified.[12] There is a poem in this letter which Paul might not have written, and Pauline scholars have changed, added to, and left out verses of the poem. Paul did not write this poem but he may have changed a few passages here and there. Raymond Brown devotes three pages to the poems which New Testament authors have included in their writings. He notes that in Paul's Letter to the Philippians this poem contains the most memorable lines ever penned by the apostle. In many Bibles, this poem has been translated in a variety of texts.

New Catholic Study Bible:	He always had the nature of God, but he did not think that by force he should try to become equal with God.
New Jerusalem Bible:	Who being in the form of God, did not count equality with God something to be grasped.

12. Pauline scholars have proposed that the Letter to the Philippians is a compilation of three different letters which Paul sent to the Jesus community at Philippi. Letter A (4:10–20) was written ca. 54 to 57 CE. Letter B (1:1–3; 4:4–7, 21–23) was written ca. 54 to 57 CE. Letter C (3:1b–4 and 3:8–9 and 57–58) was written a few months after Letter B. See Byrne, "The Letter to the Philippians," in Brown et al., *NJBC*, 792.

New American Bible:	Who, though he was in the form of God, did not regard equality with God something to be grasped.
Greek text reads as follows:	ἁρπαγμὸν ἡγήσατο τὸ εἶναι ἴσα Θεῷ ὃς ἐν μορφῇ Θεοῦ ὑπάρχων οὐχ

Is the author of the poem or the rearranger of the poem stating that Jesus is divine? Most biblical scholars would say "no."[13]

There are three citations in the Letter to the Philippians which contain the term "Father," but Jesus is not called "Son" of the Father.

- Phil 1:2: Grace to you and peace from God our Father and the Lord Jesus Christ.
- Phil 2:11: And that every tongue should acknowledge Jesus Christ as Lord, to the glory of God the Father.
- Phil 4:20: To our God and Father, glory for ever and ever. Amen.

Philemon—Dated ca. 56–57 CE

- Phlm 1–3: To Philemon, our beloved and our coworker. . . . Grace to you and peace from God our Father and the Lord Jesus Christ.

This is a very personal letter about a slave whom Paul calls "my son." He is asking that Philemon remove his slavery status and refer to him as a close relative of Paul the apostle. In this letter, we have a glimpse, but only a glimpse, of Paul's relationship to another human being just as Jesus loved in a very tender way some of his own followers.

Romans—Dated ca. 57–58 CE

Paul wrote this letter either in Corinth or Cenchreae in the winter of 57–58. His ministry in the Eastern Mediterranean area was ended, and so Paul turned his attention to the Western Mediterranean area. He was looking forward to his first visit to Rome. This letter "is an essay-letter presenting his [Paul's] missionary reflections on the historical possibility

---

13. Brendan Byrne in his commentary on Paul's Letter to the Philippians states the following: "What is said here of Christ is that he enjoyed a Godlike way of being. . . . The Greek wording indicates, again, likeness to God rather than strict equality." See Byrne, "Letter to the Philippians," in Brown et al., *NJBC*, 794n19.

The Use of the Term Father in Paul, Mark, Luke and Matthew

of salvation, rooted in God's uprightness and love, now offered to all human beings through faith in Christ Jesus."[14]

- Rom 1:1–7: Paul, a slave of Christ Jesus, called to be an apostle, and set apart for the gospel of God which he promised previously through his prophets in the holy scriptures, the gospel about his Son of God, who descended from David according to the flesh, but established as Son of God in power according to the spirit of holiness through the resurrection from the dead, Jesus Christ our Lord. ... And to all the beloved of God in Rome [who are] called to be holy. Grace to you and peace from God our Father and the Lord Jesus Christ.

Concluding Observations regarding the Letters of Paul

The letters of Paul are extremely important for Christian scholars, since they are the first written documents we have concerning Jesus. Paul himself was a very religious Jew, even though his primary language was Greek and even though he is writing for Jewish Christians or for non-Jewish Christians. In a major way, Paul can be described as a Christian missionary to the gentiles. Nonetheless, he was in contact with the Jewish Christians in Jerusalem and in many of the towns in which Paul has sent his letters. For Paul, the message of Jesus was not confined to Judaism. Almost all of his letters have a two-pronged purpose: first of all, Paul again and again is trying to resolve problems dividing his addressees. Second, in his letters he is urging them to intensify their Christian life. Paul was still Jewish and he believed that both the message and the example of Jesus were meant for all men and women. However, Paul remained faithful to Jewish worship. Moreover, and this is highly important, Paul was not a "theologian." For many centuries up to the present, Christian scholars have written both articles and books on the "Theology of St. Paul." We see the beginnings of this "theological-philosophical" interpretation not only of Paul's writings but also the entire New Testament in the writings of such scholars as Clement of Alexandria, Tertullian, Origen, etc.[15] Fortunately, today we have major Christian scholars who reflect on the New Testament writings without wearing second-century

---

14. Fitzmyer, "Romans," in Brown et al., *NJBC*, 830.

15. See Eugene Teselle, "Philosophy and Christian Theology," in Patte, *Cambridge Dictionary of Christianity*, 958–60, for an overview of this issue.

THE USE OF THE TERM "FATHER" FOR GOD AND THE TERM "SON OF GOD" FOR JESUS IN THE GOSPEL OF MARK

In the Gospel of Mark, there is no indication of a Trinitarian God, but there is a remarkable portrayal of Jesus. The author might not have been "Mark," since the opening passage states: "The beginning of the good news of Jesus Christ." In this passage there is no mention of "Mark." At a later time, a phrase was added to this, namely: "the good news of Jesus Christ, the Son of God." In the good news itself, the focus is not on the phrase "Son of God." Rather, the focus is on the good news which a man named Jesus had preached to us.[16] The author's references to God as "Father" are all positive affirmations. This "Gospel of Mark" was written in Greek between 65 and 69 CE, and in this good news God is referred to as "Father" eight times.

At times, Mark entitles Jesus as "Son of God" and these are all positive affirmations. In no way, does the author apologize for using "Father" as a name for YHWH or the name "Son of God" for Jesus. Daniel Harrington, in his presentation of "The Gospel according to Mark," presents the coming of the Kingdom of God as central to Mark's theology. He writes: "In the Judaism of Jesus' time, the 'Kingdom of God' referred to the definitive display of God's lordship at the end of history, and its acknowledgment by all creation. . . . That kingdom is now largely hidden, though in Jesus it is inaugurated and anticipated."[17]

There are eight citations in the Gospel of Mark in which Jesus is called the "Son" of God and God is called "Father."

- Mark 1:1: The beginning of the gospel of Jesus Christ, the Son of God.[18]

---

16. See Neirynck, "Synoptic Problem," in Brown et al., *NJBC*, 587–95, esp. nn21–31.
17. See Harrington, "Gospel according to Mark," in Brown et al., *NJBC*, 597.
18. Harrington, "Gospel according to Mark," in Brown et al., *NJBC*, 599, states that the phrase *"Son of God,"* though absent from a few manuscripts, is well attested from the second century onward. It prepares for the important Marcan theme of Jesus as the Son of God, which reaches its climax in the centurion's confession (15–39).

- Mark 1:11: And a voice came from the heavens, "You are my beloved Son; with you I am well pleased."[19]

- Mark 3:11: And whenever unclean spirits saw him [Jesus] they would fall down before him and shout, "You are the Son of God." He warned them sternly not to make him known.

- Mark 5:2, 6–7: When he [Jesus] got out of the boat, at once a man from the tombs who had an unclean spirit met him. . . . Catching sight of Jesus from a distance, he ran up and prostrated himself before him, crying out in a loud voice, "What have you to do with me, Jesus, Son of the Most High God? I adjure you by God, do not torment me!"

- Mark 8:38: Whoever is ashamed of me and of my words in this faithless and sinful generation, the Son of Man will be ashamed of when he comes in his Father's glory with the holy angels.

- Mark 9:7: Then a cloud came casting a shadow over them; then from the cloud came a voice, "This is my beloved Son. Listen to him."

- Mark 14:35–36: He [Jesus] advanced a little and fell to the ground and prayed that if were possible the hour might pass by him; he said: "Abba, Father, all things are possible to you. Take this cup away from me, but not what I will but what you will."

- Mark 15:39: When the centurion who stood facing him saw how he breathed his last he said: "Truly this man was the Son of God."

Conclusions from the Gospel of Mark

All eight of Mark's references to God as Father, אב, center on the Jewish God YHWH. Jesus in these passages is not referring to the Trinity. Each of these citations expresses directly and indirectly a positive understanding of YAHWEH as Father. In Mark's Gospel there is no indication that the author needed to defend his referrals to God as Father. Naming YHWH "Father" was not new to the Jewish people. As we have seen in chapter 3, many Jewish writers prior to Mark had already used the term

---

19. Harrington, "Gospel according to Mark," in Brown et al., *NJBC*, 599. Ps 2:7 states: "The Lord said to me, 'You are my son; this day I have begotten you.'" Does Mark understand that in this passage on the baptism of Jesus God has "adopted" Jesus as his son, or is it a confirmation of the already existing relationship between God and Jesus?

"Father" for God. Consequently, Mark, felt very free to call God "Father." He also felt free to call Jesus "God's son."

Given the widespread use of the term "Father" for YHWH by the Jewish population of Palestine in the intertestamental period, there is no indication that Jesus himself was using the term "Father" and "Son" in a new or different way. The term "Father" had become a common name for YHWH from the third century BCE down to the time of Jesus. "Son" had also become a word used generally in the Hebrew world for a major leader of the Jewish world. Therefore, one cannot say that Mark's use of "Son of God" has a meaning quite different from the common Hebrew/Christian way of naming God in the first century CE. We see a similar use of the term Father in the Gospels of Matthew and Luke. Whenever Jesus uses the phrase "Son of God" it does not have a "Trinitarian" meaning; rather he is following the common Hebrew phrase for YHWH—אב—as well as the common name for the Jewish people as "sons of God." In the "Gospel of John," however, we do see a different meaning for both terms, "Father" and "Son." Franz Neirynck, in his essay the "Synoptic Problem," presents in great detail how the material in the Synoptic Gospels includes a shared material, a differentiated material, and a non-shared material.[20] Augustine had arranged the chronological order of the three Synoptic Gospels as: Matthew, then Mark, and finally Luke. Johann J. Griesbach (1745–1812 CE), a German biblical scholar, changed the chronological order to Matthew, Luke, and Mark. In 1890, J. Weiss began to include a "Q-source". Today's biblical scholars place Mark as the first-written Gospel, Luke as the second, and Matthew as the third. However, in all three Gospels there are passages which scholars refer to as "Quelle," which means that the wording used in the Gospels had a pre-gospel history, and all three evangelists in some form or another could easily have used any or all of these words which are found in the earlier manuscripts.

THE USE OF THE TERM "FATHER" FOR GOD AND THE TERM "SON OF GOD" FOR JESUS IN THE GOSPEL OF LUKE

In the past forty years, detailed commentaries on the Gospel of Luke have been written. Joseph Fitzmyer's Anchor Bible commentary, *The Gospel according to Luke*, has an introduction of 258 pages, in which Fitzmyer

---

20. Neirynck, "Synoptic Problem," in Brown et al., *NJBC*, 587–95.

presents the major positions on various aspects of the Lukan material. He also has a lengthy bibliography from pp. 259–83. In doing this he cites almost every Lukan scholar up to 1981 whose reputation is well-known.[21]

Some scholars conclude that Luke was a gentile Christian, while a few authors argue that he was a Jewish-Christian. Luke seems to have been a Syrian who lived in Antioch, the third-largest city in the Roman Empire. Luke was probably not a physician since his Greek vocabulary is simply that of well-educated citizen of Antioch. Around 80–85 CE, Luke wrote both the Gospel and Acts for well-to-do members of the Christian community in Antioch. He may have known Paul in one way or another, but Luke wrote his Gospel and Acts about twenty years after the death of Paul in ca. 62 CE. Karris states the following:

> Writing in a pluralistic Syrian Antioch in the first years of the ninth decade of the Christian era, Luke addresses a primarily Gentile audience with well-to-do members who are painfully rethinking their missionary thrusts in a hostile environment. Internal and external controversies contribute to the hostile environment. The key question of Luke's communities deals with theodicy: If God has not been faithful to the promises made to God's elect people and has allowed their holy city and temple to be destroyed, what reasons do Gentile Christians, who believe in this God, have to think that God will be faithful to promises made to them?[22]

In the writings of Luke—both in the Gospel and in Acts—we are not presented with a "reconstituted Israel." For Luke, the "synagogue was always a foreign institution." And "the future of the Gospel lies with the Gentiles."[23] Luke in a very detailed way presents his readers with a God who will safeguard the Jesus community. Luke's theology of God maintains that God will not abandon the newly-formed Jesus community. Luke refers again and again that God is a "Father-God" who will stand by and assist his children.

Let us read the passages in Luke's Gospel that mention God as Father or Jesus as the Son of God.

---

21. See Fitzmyer, *Gospel according to Luke*, 1:3–258, for text and 259–83 for bibliography. See also Marshall, *Gospel of Luke*; Johnson, *Gospel of Luke*; Karris, "Gospel according to Luke," in Brown et al., *NJBC*.

22. Karris, "Gospel according to Luke," in Brown et al., *NJBC*, 676.

23. Brown, *Introduction to the New Testament*, 270.

- Luke 1:32: Behold, you will conceive in your womb and bear a son, and you shall name him Jesus. He will be great and will be called the Son of the Most High,[24] and the Lord God will give him the throne of David his father.

- Luke 2:49: And Jesus said to them [Mary and Joseph] "Why are you looking for me? Did you not know that I must be in my Father's house?" But they did not understand what he said to them.

- Luke 3:22: And the Holy Spirit descended on him [Jesus] in bodily form like a dove. And a voice came from heaven, "You are my beloved Son, with you I am well pleased."

- Luke 4:21: And demons also came out from many [sick people] shouting, "You are the Son of God."

- Luke 8:28: When he [a man possessed by demons] saw Jesus, he cried out and fell down before him; in a loud voice he shouted, "What have you to do with me, Jesus, son of the Most High God? I beg you, do not torment me!"

- Luke 9:35: Then from the cloud came a voice that said: "This is my chosen Son; listen to him." After the voice had spoken, Jesus was found alone.

- Luke 10:21–22: [In these verses, the names "Father" or "Son" appear seven times.] At that very moment [Jesus] rejoiced in the Holy Spirit and said, "I give you praise, Father, Lord of heaven and earth, for although you have hidden these things from the wise and learned you have revealed them to the childlike, such has been your gracious will. All things have been handed over to me by my Father. No one knows who the Son is except the Father, and who the Father is except the Son and anyone to whom the Son wishes to reveal Him."

- Luke 11:1–4: Jesus was praying in a certain place, and when he had finished, one of his disciples said to him, "Lord, teach us to pray as John taught his disciples." He said to them: "When you pray, say: Our Father, hallowed be your name, your kingdom come. Give us each day our daily bread."

- Luke 11:13: If you, then, are wicked, know how to give good gifts to your children. How much more will the Father in heaven give the Holy Spirit to those who ask him?

---

24. In the Greek text, we read: οὗτος ἔσται μέγας καὶ υἱὸς ὑψίστου κληθήσεται.

The Use of the Term Father in Paul, Mark, Luke and Matthew   85

- Luke 12:32: Do not be afraid any longer, little flock, for your Father is pleased to give you the kingdom.

- Luke 22:29: It is you who have stood by me in my trials; and I confer a kingdom on you, just as my Father has conferred one on me, that you may eat and drink at my table in my kingdom; and you will sit on thrones, judging the twelve tribes of Israel.

- Luke 22:41–42: After withdrawing about a stone's throw from them and kneeling, he prayed, saying: "Father, if you are willing, take this cup away from me; still, not my will but yours be done."

- Luke 22:70–71: They all asked, "Are you then the Son of God?" He replied to them, "You say that I am." Then they said, "What further need have we for testimony? We have heard it from his own mouth."

- Luke 23:34: Then Jesus said, "Father, forgive them, for they know not what they are doing."

- Luke 23:46: Then Jesus said: "Father, into your hands I commend my spirit," and when he had said this he breathed his last.

- Luke 24:49: And behold I am sending the promise of my Father upon you; but stay in the city until you are clothed in the light.

Conclusions from the Gospel of Luke

In the Gospel of Luke, God is called "Father" or referred to as Father twenty-two times, but Luke offers no explanation as to why God should be called "Father." The author of the Gospel simply refers to God as a Father of love and forgiveness. Will the Father-God continue to safeguard his "children"? Or will the Father-God once again allow a destruction of the "newly reconstituted family"?

The above question is at the heart of Luke's Gospel and the Acts of the Apostles. Nowhere in the Gospel is there any reluctance to call God "Father" or in his references to Jesus as "the Son of God." Luke presents Jesus as a man sent by a merciful God, but also as a Holy One who has been rejected by the leaders of the Jews. Jesus is not the second person of the Trinity.

In both the Gospel and in Acts, there is a kerygmatic story, in which Luke demonstrates that God through Jesus was faithful to Israel, but "in an unexpected way [so as] to include Gentiles, the unclean, the poor, women, as well as elect people who are repentant of their initial rejection of Jesus, God's prophet and Chosen One."[25] In the Christian communities known to Luke, there were some groups who had developed stringent requirements in order to be part of their group. Some of these communities rejected the poor, but in a true community of Christians the lame, the blind, and the maimed are welcome and also those who are well-off but willing to share what they have. Luke, especially in the Acts, indicates that the message of Jesus was accepted by gentiles. This was "no accident or aberration, but part of God's plan, reaching back to creation, a plan that ultimately includes the conversion of the whole Roman world."[26]

THE USE OF THE TERM "FATHER" FOR GOD AND THE TERM "SON OF GOD" FOR JESUS IN THE GOSPEL OF MATTHEW

According to most contemporary biblical scholars, the Gospel of Matthew was written about between 80 and 90 CE. The destruction of the Jewish temple in Jerusalem had already taken place, and the Roman soldiers dominated the city. Benedict Viviano places the date of Matthew's gospel between 80 and 90 CE, but he makes the following clarification:

> Does Matthew stand inside or outside of Judaism? This question seems straight-forward but conceals an ambiguity. Supposing, as now seems likely, that Matthew's community had recently been placed outside of Judaism by the rabbis of Jamnia through a ban called the *birkat hammînîm* (ca. AD 80), it is possible that many leading members of the community felt themselves to be Jewish. . . . Thus, the Gospel represents a predominantly Jewish-Christian outlook, though open to a Gentile mission—outside the confines of Jamnian Judaism yet still defining itself over against rival Judaisms.[27]

---

25. Karris, "Gospel according to Luke," in Brown et al., *NJBC*, 676.
26. Brown, *Introduction to the New Testament*, 272.
27. Viviano, "The Gospel according to Matthew," in Brown et al., *NJBC*, 631n3. In the Anchor Bible series, the volume on *Matthew* (Garden City: Doubleday, 1971) was written by William F. Albright and C. S. Mann. In their introduction, the two authors suggest that Matthew's Gospel was written between 60 and 75 CE, but they do so readily conceding that there is no certainty to their position (clxxxiv).

In this Gospel, God is referred to as Father fifty times, either directly or indirectly through the phrase Son of God.[28] In the majority of cases, the term Father clearly refers to YHWH, but there are also indirect references to Jesus as the "Son of God." However, there are references in which Satan or Jewish leaders mock Jesus' claim that "YHWH" is truly his Father. They do so in a way that indicates that they are referring to YHWH as Father in a disbelieving and negative way. I have added an asterisk to these few passages.

Since Matthew's Gospel was not written by the apostle Matthew, contemporary biblical scholars have suggested differing authors in a general way, such as: the author was a converted rabbi or a converted scribe. Stendahl has suggested that the authorship was a group effort, but the final text was composed by a single individual in this group.

The dating of the Gospel is also a matter of discussion, but it seems that the more logical time is somewhere around 80 or 90 CE. In the citations of Paul, Mark, Luke, and Matthew, all of whom are in the first century CE, the Jewish tenor is very strong. Only at the turn of the century is there a slow change from a "Jewish-centered Christian community" to a "Greek-centered Christian community." Even though the writings of Paul, Mark, Luke, and Matthew are in Greek, the authors—like many other Jewish people of that time—were Jewish in their birth, or in their education.

William F. Albright and C. S. Mann are the authors of *The Anchor Bible: Matthew*, and in a very thorough way, these two scholars have provided us with a lengthy and detailed introduction on the Gospel of Matthew.[29] In section 7, "Kingdom: The Man and the Father," the authors point out that in Matthew there is no presentation of the concept that "Jesus is The-Man-in-his-humility; in this gospel, The Man is taken to mean a sovereignty which is true even when the Son's kingdom is understood as a temporary institution awaiting the Kingdom of the Father."[30] In a later passage in Matthew's Gospel, Jesus has been arrested and is brought

---

28. In the Acts of the Apostles there are only two citations of the word Father for God, namely 1:7 and 2:33. Both times "Father" simply means God. It is remarkable that there are no other citations of the name "Father" for God, since Luke's Gospel refers to God as Father twenty times.

29. See the lengthy introduction to Albright and Mann, *Matthew*, xix–cxcviii. This introduction provides the reader with the main issues which biblical scholars present in their writings on Matthew. The introduction also provides a historical and a theological background for those who are interested in the values of Matthew's Gospel.

30. Introduction to Albright and Mann, *Matthew*, lxxxix.

before the Jewish Sanhedrin. The high priest asked Jesus: "I charge you by the living God that you tell us whether you are the Messiah, God's Son." Jesus' answer is a puzzling one or a sort of half-answer.[31] He says: "The words are yours . . . but more than that, I tell you that from now on you will see the son of man (τὸν υἱὸν τοῦ ἀνθρώπου) seated at the right hand of the Father, and coming on the clouds of heaven" (Matt 26:64.)

Albright and Mann, throughout their volume, are very cautious. In the opening word of chapter 12, "The Messiah in Matthew," we read:

> It would be wholly out of keeping of what we have seen of the nature of a "gospel" to find in it a fully developed Christology. There is nothing in the New Testament approaching "ontology"—that which is concerned with the being, essence, or nature.[32]

Only in the second century CE are there the beginnings of a philosophical and ontological presentation of Jesus as God. One can say that from the second century on, Christian scholars and leaders began to interpret both God the Father and Jesus through Greek philosophy, and only then do we see the beginnings of a theology of Trinity. Greek words such as οὐσία, ὁμοούσιος, γεννηθῆναι, ὑποστάσις, and φύσις began to be used to define the "nature" of God, the Trinitarian persons, etc.[33]

The transition of the followers of Jesus from a Jewish-centered group to a non-Jewish-centered group is important, since the theologies of the Trinity only began to be established little by little from the second century down to the eighth century. The scholars who wrote on the divinity of Jesus and the Trinitarian God were for the most part Greek and Latin scholars, not only linguistically but also philosophically.

Let us consider all the passages in Matthew's Gospel that mention God as Father or Jesus as the Son of God. We should read these passages through Jewish eyes and not Greek philosophical eyes. And we should hear the message of Matthew's Gospel with Jewish ears and not Greek or Latin ears, much less through contemporary eyes and ears. In this listing of the term Father, the references are not all the same. The author of Matthew's Gospel uses the term "Father" and basically this means the "Father

---

31. See Viviano, "Gospel according to Matthew," in Brown et al., *NJBC*, 671.

32. See Albright and Mann, *Matthew*.

33. See also Albright and Mann, *Matthew*. From sec. 2, xxxvii, in the introduction, "Matthew in Relation to the Synoptic Gospels," down to section 12, cli, "The Messiah in Matthew," the two authors explain the meaning of "*The Man*."

of Jesus." Jesus is saying that YHWH is "My Father." Then there are other occasions when the text in Matthew reads: "Your Fathers," referring to the Fathers of the Jews. Lastly, there are several references in which Satan or Hebrew leaders or Roman soldiers in a sneering way refer the God of Jesus as "your Father."

In the following list, YHWH is referred to as Father many times. YHWH is also referred to when we read: "My Father" or "Your Father" namely the Father of the Jews. YHWH is referred to as "Father" but in a malicious way, and these citations are marked with an asterisk. Finally, God is referred to as "Father" indirectly through the words "my Son."

- Matt 3:17: And a voice came from heaven saying, "This is my beloved Son, with whom I am well pleased."
- Matt 4:3: The tempter approached and said to him, "If you are the Son of God, command that these stones become loaves of bread."*
- Matt 4:6: Then, the devil took him to the holy city, and he made him stand on the parapet of the temple, and said to him, "If you are the Son of God, throw yourself down." For it is written: "He will command his angels concerning you, and with their hands they will support you."
- Matt 6:3–4: But when you give alms, do not let your left hand know what your right hand is doing, so that your almsgiving may be secret. And your Father who sees in secret will repay you.
- Matt 6:6: But when you pray, go to your inner room, and close the door, and pray to your Father in secret. And your Father who sees in secret will repay you.
- Matt 6:7–8: In praying, do not babble like the pagans, who think that they will be heard because of their many words. Do not be like them. Your Father knows what you need before you ask him.
- Matt 6:9: This is how you are to pray: "Our Father in heaven, hallowed by your name, your will be done, on earth as in heaven."
- Matt 6:14–15: If you forgive others their transactions, your heavenly Father will forgive you. But if you do not forgive others, neither will your Father forgive your transgressions.
- Matt 6:17–18: But when you fast, anoint your head and wash your face, so that you may not appear to be fasting, except to your Father

who is hidden. And your Father who sees what is hidden will repay you.

- Matt 6:26: Look at the birds in the sky; they do not sow or reap, they gather nothing into barns, yet your heavenly Father feeds them. Are you more important than they?

- Matt 6:31–33: So do not worry and say, "What are we to eat?" or "What are we to wear?" All these things the pagans seek. Your heavenly Father knows that you need them all. But seek first the kingdom [of God] and his righteousness, and all these things will be given you besides.

- Matt 6:32–33: All these things the pagans seek. Your heavenly Father knows that you need them all. But seek first kingdom [of God] and his righteousness, and all these things will be given you besides.

- Matt 7:11: If you then, who are wicked, know how to give good gifts to your children, how much more will your heavenly Father give good things to those who ask Him?

- Matt 7:21: Not everyone who says to me, "Lord, Lord," will enter the kingdom of heaven, but only the one who does the will of my Father in heaven.

- Matt 10:20: For it will not be you who speak but the Spirit of your Father speaking through you.

- Matt 10:32–33: Everyone who acknowledges me before others I will acknowledge before my heavenly Father. But whoever denies me before others, I will deny before my heavenly Father.

- Matt 11:25–27: At that time Jesus said in reply, "I give praise to you, Father, Lord of heaven and earth, for although you have hidden these things from the wise and the learned you have revealed them to the childlike. Yes, Father, such has been your gracious will. All things have been handed over to me by my Father. No one knows the Son except the Father, and no one knows the Son and anyone to whom the Son wishes to reveal him."

- Matt 12:49–50: Jesus was still speaking to the crowds, when suddenly his mother and his brothers were standing outside and were anxious to have a word with him. But to the man who told him this, Jesus replied: "Who is my mother? Who are my brothers?" And stretching out his hand towards his disciples, he said, "Here are my mother and my brothers. Anyone who does the will of my Father in heaven is my brother, and sister, and mother."

- Matt 14:33: Those who were in the boat did him homage. "Truly you are the Son of God."
- Matt 16:13–17: Jesus put this question before his disciples, "Who do people say that the Son of Man is?" They replied: "Some say John the Baptist, some Elijah, and others say Jeremiah or one of the prophets" "But you," he said, "who do you say I am?" Simon Peter said in reply, "You are the Messiah, the Son of the living God." Jesus said to him: "Blessed are you, Simon, son of Jonah. For flesh and blood has not revealed this to you."
- Matt 16:27: For the Son of Man will come with his angels in his Father's glory, and he will then repay everyone according to his conduct.
- Matt 18:10: See that you do not despise one of these little ones, for I say to you that their angels in heaven always look upon the face of my heavenly Father.
- Matt 18:13: In just the same way, it is not the will of your heavenly Father that one of these little ones be lost.
- Matt 18:20: Again, I say to you, if two of you agree on earth about anything for which they are to pray, it shall be granted to them by my heavenly Father. For where two or three are gathered together in my name, there am I in the midst of them.
- Matt 18:34–35: Then in anger the master handed him over to the torturers. . . . So will my heavenly Father do to you, unless each of you forgives your brother from your heart.
- Matt 20:22–23: Jesus said in reply, "You do not know what you are asking. Can you drink the cup that I am going to drink?" They said to him, "We can." He replied "My cup you will indeed drink, but to sit at my right and at my left is not mine to give, but is for those for whom it has been prepared by my Father."
- Matt 23:8: As for you, do not be called Rabbi. You have but one teacher, and you are all brothers. Call no one on earth your father; you have but one Father in heaven.
- Matt 24:34–36: Amen I say to you, this generation will not pass away until all things have taken place. Heaven and earth will pass

away. But of that day and hour, no one knows, neither the angles of heaven nor the Son, but the Father alone.

- Matt 25:34: Then the king will say to those on his right, "Come, you who are blessed by my Father, inherit the kingdom prepared for you from the foundation of the world."

- Matt 26:29: I tell you from now on I shall not drink this fruit of the vine until the day when I drink new wine with you in the kingdom of my Father.

- Matt 26:39: He [Jesus] advanced a little and fell prostrate in prayer, saying, "My Father, if it is possible let this cup pass from me; yet not as I will, but as you will."

- Matt 26:42: Withdrawing a second time, he prayed again "My Father, if it is not possible that this cup pass without my drinking of it, your will be done."

- Matt 26:52–53: The Jesus said to him [Peter], "Put your sword back into its sheath, for all who take the sword will perish by the sword. Do you think that cannot call upon my Father and he will not provide me at this moment with more than twelve legions of angels? But then how would the scriptures be fulfilled which say that it must come to pass in this way?"

- Matt 26:63: Then the high priest said to him [Jesus], "I order you to tell us under oath before the living God whether you are the Messiah, the Son of God" Jesus said to him in reply, "You have said so. But I tell you: From now on you will see the Son of Man seated at the right hand of the Power and coming on the clouds of heaven."

- Matt 27:39–40: Those passing by reviled him, shaking their heads and saying, "You who would destroy the temple and rebuild it in three days, save yourself, if you are the Son of God, [and] come down from the cross."*

- Matt 27:41–43: Likewise, the chief priests with the scribes and the elders mocked him and said, "He saved others; [but] he cannot save himself. So he is the king of Israel! Let him come down from the cross now, and we will believe in him. He trusted in God; let him come down from the cross now, and we will believe in him. He trusted in God; let him deliver him now if he wants him. For he said, 'I am the Son of God.'"*

- Matt 28:18–19: Then Jesus approached and said to them: "All power in heaven and on earth has been given to me. Go, therefore, and make disciples of all nations, baptizing them in the name of the Father and of the Son, and of the Holy Spirit, teaching them to observe all that I have commanded you. And behold, I am with you always, until the end of this age."

Conclusions from the Gospel of Matthew

There is no doubt that the author of the Gospel of Matthew used the term "Father" for YHWH in an overwhelming way. He also used the indirect phrase "Son of God" for Jesus, even though the author does not mean that Jesus is the actual Son of God. The use of the term Father for YHWH in the *Tanakh* may have been minimal, but nowhere in the Hebrew Scripture is the expression "Father" for YHWH forbidden. From 300 BCE to 100 CE, the number of times that Jewish writers referred to God as Father is multiple, and there was no legislation by the Jewish leadership to curtail this naming of God.

The Jewish writers who accepted Jesus as their spiritual leader also used the term Father for YHWH, especially Paul, Mark, Luke and Matthew. One can rightly conclude that in the Jewish world, from ca. 300 BCE to the destruction of the temple in 70 CE, both Jewish writers and Jewish Christian writers used the term "Father" for YHWH not only in an overwhelming way, but also in a poetic, descriptive and metaphorical way. The three condemnatory statements made by the members of the Sanhedrin against Jesus' acceptance of the term "Son of God" implied that Jesus was using the term Father in a disgraceful way, namely Mark 14:61; Luke 22:70–71; Matt 26:63–66. The three statements are miniscule when compared to the overwhelming positive use to the term "Father" for God in the Pauline letters and the three Synoptic Gospels.

As regards the divinity of the Holy Spirit, there is a strange passage in Matthew's Gospel. In the English translation of Matthew's Gospel, one reads (Matt 1:8): "Before they [Mary and Joseph] came to live together she was found to be with child through the Holy Spirit." In the Greek text, one reads: ἐκ πνεύματος ἁγίου. There is no article—e.g., "the" or "a" or "an"—so the real translation is not the Holy Spirit but a holy spirit. In this passage, Matthew is not thinking in a Trinitarian framework.

CONCLUDING OBSERVATIONS

1. In the writings of Paul and in the writings of the authors of the three Synoptic Gospels there are abundant references to God—YHWH—as "Father" and to Jesus as "Son of God." Jesus and his first followers were almost all Jewish. Nowhere in the writings of Paul and the Synoptic authors do we find any references that they were relinquishing the Jewish name for God, YHWH—יהוה. Jesus also used the Aramaic term "Father" for God, but to cite a particular verse and claim that Jesus was calling God Father because he was actually God the Son and state that this passage was personally used by Jesus would be extremely difficult to prove. Nonetheless, we can state that Jesus used the term "Father" for the Jewish God—יהוה—during his lifetime, but he used it in a poetical, descriptive, and metaphorical way.[34]

2. In the above writings, the use of the term "Father" for YHWH—אָב and Πατήρ—had slowly become commonplace throughout the Jewish world, and the title of "Son of God" for Jesus had also become commonplace among his disciples. However, the three Synoptic texts (Mark, Matthew, Luke), which focus on the interrogation of Jesus by the Sanhedrin, ask: "Are you the Son of God?" For the high priests, this question meant: are you the son of YHWH—יהוה? In his response, Jesus claims to be the "Son of God." In Mark and in Matthew, the leaders state that Jesus is blasphemous. Blasphemy means that one has seriously said something against YHWH. Given the context of the three citations, the question does not mean that Jesus has claimed to be YHWH, but it does express a personal closeness to YHWH.

3. In the many citations from Paul, Mark, Luke, and Matthew, we have seen the beginnings of Jewish men and women who have accepted Jesus as the center of their lives. By accepting Jesus, one might ask, can they be called "Christians"? In the Acts of the Apostles, the author uses the term "Christians" for the first time in the New Testament, Acts 12:26. As regards its earliest meaning, Richard Dillon in his essay on "Acts of the Apostles" states: "Christians: the use of this

---

34. Contemporary biblical scholars date the Synoptic Gospels as follows: Mark, ca. 68–73 CE, Matthew between 80 and 90 CE, and Luke from 80 and 85 CE. Most biblical scholars today state that Jesus, along with almost all the Hebrew people spoke in Aramaic rather than Hebrew.

name by outsiders attests that at Antioch the 'Christian people' first stood out as a sect distinct from Judaism."[35] During the lifetime of Jesus his followers were probably not called "Christians."

By the end of the first century CE, Christians had to some extent moved away from the Jewish religious framework and developed new religious communities which were almost non-Jewish. These Christian communities had their own leaders and authors, as well as their saints and sinners. The main writings of these "Christian authors" eventually included the letters of Paul as well as the four Gospels, the Acts of the Apostles, and a few other letters such as the book of Revelation. These writings eventually became the New Testament, which Christians by far and large consider to be the word of God.

---

35. Dillon, "Acts of the Apostles," in Brown et al., *NJBC*, 747. See also Cavadini, "Jewish Christianity," 706. Cavadini argues that in Jewish Christianity, the interconnection of Christians with Jews was not a clear divide until 90 CE. The division was a process rather than a one-moment situation.

5

The Beginning of Trinitarian Theology (100 to 300 CE)

THE NEW TESTAMENT DOES not contain a doctrine per se of the Trinity, in the sense of an understanding that there are three distinct persons within the one divine nature. The title for this chapter does not mean, therefore, that the Trinity itself begins in the second century; rather this chapter presents the first-ever "sort-of-a-theology of the Trinity." In the first century CE, neither Paul nor the three authors of the Synoptic Gospels referred to a Trinitarian God.

In the Gospel of John, however, one finds the first "indications" of a possible theology of a Trinitarian God, and a few Christian writers in the early part of the second century present the naming of God the Father and his Son. Their focus was on the divinity of Jesus together with the divinity of God the Father. At the end of the second century, Christian writers began to include the divinization of the Holy Spirit. As a result, a "theology of the Trinitarian God" began to take place.

The theological arguments over the divinization of Jesus—and also of the Holy Spirit—remained central to both the western and eastern regions of the Roman Empire. However, Arianists and other theological writers remained anti-Trinitarian down to the beginning of the ninth century. In the ninth century, the final split of the Western and Eastern Christian churches took place. Theologians in both the Eastern and Western churches maintained differing theologies on the Trinity and in both churches there remained, in a lesser way, Christians who did not accept a Trinitarian God.[1]

PART ONE: GENERAL OVERVIEW OF TRINITARIAN THINKING IN THE FIRST AND SECOND CENTURIES

There are two phrases in the New Testament, namely ὁ υἱὸς τοῦ Θεοῦ and υἱὸς Θεοῦ, which are not crystal clear. Walter Bauer, in the English translation of his *Greek-English Lexicon of the New Testament and Other Early Christian Literature*, writes: "In Judaism this [title—Son of God] was at least not a frequently-used honorary title for the Messiah." He then remarks: "In the pagan world, on the other hand, sons of the gods in a special sense are not only known to myth and legend, but definite historical personalities are also designated as such."[2] In this same dictionary, the section on God—Θεός—contains certain passages in which the authors use the word Θεός for Jesus, but the text does so "without necessarily equating Christ with the Father."[3] One can say that in the Pauline letters and in the three Synoptic Gospels, Jesus is deeply honored, but he is not divinized in the same way that God the Father is divinized.

In his essay "The Trinity in the Greek Fathers," John Anthony McGuckin states that there is a "sparse collection of second-century [Greek] theologians."[4] However, Quasten, in his first volume of *Patrology*, does not offer a sparse collection of Christian authors; rather, he mentions a fairly large number of second-century Christian authors who wrote on the Trinity.[5]

There is an evening hymn, entitled "Φῶς ἱλαρόν," which was written in the second century and is still used in the liturgy of the Presanctified of the Greek Church. In this hymn we hear:

---

1. See Hunt, *Trinity*, 10.

2. See Bauer, *Greek-English Lexicon*, 834–35; English translation by Gingrich and Danker. In the section on ὁ υἱὸς τοῦ Θεοῦ, the author Bauer and the revisers of Bauer's volume provide a thorough explanation of Greek words and phrases used in the New Testament.

3. Bauer, *Greek-English Lexicon*, 357.

4. McGucken, "Trinity in the Greek Fathers," in Phan, *Cambridge Companion to the Trinity*, 4.

5. The first volume of Quasten's *Patrology* contains ca. 300 pages, beginning with Clement of Rome (d. ca. 101 CE) and ending with Irenaeus (d. ca. 202). It is difficult to say that the second-century scholars constituted a "sparse collection."

Serene light of the Holy Glory of the Father everlasting Jesus Christ....
We praise the Father and the Son and the Holy Spirit of God.[6]

The issue of the divinization of Jesus dominated Christian scholarship from the second century to the ninth century CE. During these eight hundred years, many major Christian theologians argued that Jesus was both human and divine, while other major Christian theologians argued that there is only one God, namely the Father, and that Jesus was not divine nor was the Holy Spirit divine.

The names for God which were chosen in the divinization process for God were "Father" and "Son." In chapter 3 and in chapter 4, I have presented a listing of the many, many times that Jewish and Jewish Christian authors referred directly to God as YHWH—יהוה—or indirectly as Father—אב, or ὁ Πατήρ. These authors referred to God indirectly when they used the phrase "Son of God." In the book of Exodus (4:22–23) for instance, we read: "Thus saith the Lord (יהוה) Israel is my son" (יִשְׂרָאֵ֥ל בְּכֹרִ֖י). In Psalm 2:7 we read: "Yahweh said to me: You are my son, today I have fathered you" (יהוה אמר אלי בני אתה אני היום ילדתיך). In both of these citations, the authors do not say in a direct way: God is "Father." Rather, the authors indirectly call God "Father" by saying: "Israel" or "you" are my Son.

The focus of this chapter is on the origins of Trinitarian theology. The focus is not simply on the naming of God as "Father" or on the naming of Jesus as "Son of God." Rather, this chapter focuses on the most important Christian theologians in the second and third centuries CE who have presented God as the divine "Father" and the divine "Son." This chapter also includes major Christian theologians in the second and third centuries CE who have presented only the divine "Father" and theologically they have denied the divinization of Jesus. In this latter group, we need to understand the fundamental reasons why they rejected the divinization of Jesus. Since the divinization of Jesus continued to be a major theme in Christian theology down to the beginning of the ninth century, we need to analyze the pro and con theologies of both positions. This bi-polar division has become part and parcel of contemporary Trinitarian theology.

---

6. Quasten, *Patrology*, 1:159.

The Main Theologians in the Second Century Who Either Presented or Rejected the Divinization of Jesus Christ

The theological divinization of Jesus began in the final two years of the first century. We find this in some degree in the Gospel of John, and in the writings of Clement of Rome, Ignatius of Antioch, Polycarp of Smyrna, and Aristides of Athens. At first, the divinization of Jesus was only mentioned but not theologized. In the second step, the divinization of Jesus, was explained theologically but only in an initial format. We find a more detailed theology of the divinization of Jesus, both pro and con, in the writings of Appolinaris of Hierapolis, Athanagoras of Athens, and Theophilus of Antioch as well as a non-divinization of Jesus in Justin and Clement of Alexandria. Let us begin chronologically with the texts on the divinization of Jesus, in which there is union of God as Father and God as Son.

The Authors of the Gospel of John

The Johannine Gospel was probably written between 90 and 110 CE, and in the Gospel text there are 120 references to God as Father and to Jesus as his Son. The Johannine community had originally been a part of a Jewish community, but this ended when John's community was expelled from the synagogue. A large portion of the community moved to Ephesus and most biblical scholars state that John's Gospel was basically written in Ephesus but attained its final version in the first decade of the second century.[7]

In the Gospel, the relationship of the Father to the Son and the Son to the Father is intense. Brown published two volumes which focused on the divinity of Jesus in John's Gospel, namely, *Jesus, God and Man*,[8] and

---

7. The Gospel of John was written at the turn of the first and second centuries and it is the product of several authors. See Perkins, "The Gospel according to John," in Brown et al., *NJBC*, 946–47. She states: "The importance of the community's history of faith in shaping the Johannine tradition makes preoccupation with a single Johannine author inappropriate today." See also Moloney, "Johannine Theology," in Brown et al., *NJBC*, 1417–19. His presentation is closer to a Trinitarian theology than a monotheistic theology. See 1418nn8–9; see also 1419–20n17. Other important sections are nn38–49. The close relationship of God the Father and his Son Jesus is stated, but there is no reference in the Gospel of a Trinitarian God.

8. See Brown, *Jesus God and Man*.

an *Introduction to New Testament Theology*.[9] His final conclusion in *Jesus, God and Man* reads:

> Unless we understand that Jesus was truly human, we cannot comprehend the depth of God's love. . . . A Jesus for whom the future was as much a mystery, a dread, and a hope as it is for us and yet, at the same time, a Jesus who would say, "Not my will but yours"—this is a Jesus who could effectively show us how to live, for this is a Jesus who would have gone through life's real trials.[10]

In Brown's *Introduction to New Testament Christology*, one needs to read the careful wording in appendix 3, "Did New Testament Christians Call Jesus God?" as well as in the wording of appendix 4, "Features in the Christology of the Gospel according to John."[11] In the first appendix, Brown analyzes every possible New Testament passage in which Jesus was *not called* God, and then every possible passage in which Jesus *could, perhaps, and even maybe was called* God. Brown's final words in this second appendix are:

> Firm adherence to the later theological and ontological developments that led to a confession of Jesus Christ as "true God of true God" must not cause believers to overvalue and undervalue the less developed NT confession.[12]

John's Gospel can be described as a "new approach" to God which thereby includes a new approach to Jesus. In this new approach to God, the author or authors go beyond the insights of Paul and the authors of the Synoptic Gospels, the Johannine authors present the life, death, and resurrection of Jesus as a mirror in which we can see a loving and caring God. As created human beings, we are limited in understanding and honoring God, and therefore the author or authors go out of their way to indicate who the God of Jesus Christ truly is. There is a deep relationship, in this Gospel, between God the Father and his "Son" Jesus and thus the Johannine Jesus becomes a mirror or a window in and through whom we are able to experience the paternal depth of God in a more contemplative way. The Johannine relationship of God the Father to Jesus as the "Son of

---

9. See Brown, *Introduction to New Testament Christology*.
10. Brown, *Jesus, God and Man*, 105.
11. Brown, *Introduction to New Testament Christology*, 171–213.
12. Brown, *Introduction to New Testament Christology*, 213.

The Beginning of Trinitarian Theology (100 to 300 CE)

God" began the opening a new window from which Christians in the second century onward eventually began to call God a "Trinitarian God."[13]

Brown states clearly that Jesus "comes from God."[14] There is, however, some preparation for Brown's position. Thomas Rausch describes his dating of the four Gospels as follows: "Mark (AD 60) presents Jesus as Son of God from the time of his baptism at the Jordan. Matthew and Luke (AD 85), both with accounts of the virginal conception, see Jesus as Son of God from the time of his conception by the Holy Spirit. The 'preexistence' christology of John's gospel (AD 90) represents the high water mark of this development."[15]

Clement of Rome

In recent times, the *Letter to the Corinthians* by Clement of Rome (d. 101) has been reevaluated by major authors.[16] In the letter itself, there is no mention of the author's name, "Clement," and scholars over the past fifty years have debated his authorship. The majority of patristic scholars today consider Clement as the author of this letter. In this letter, Clement strongly indicates that God the Father is the one and only God. He writes:

> The Creator and Master of the Universe Himself exults in his works. Thus, by his transcendent might He established the heavens, and by His incomprehensible understanding He ordered them; the earth He separated from the water now circling it, and firmly grounded it on the unshakable foundation of His own

---

13. Brown describes the process of writing this text as follows: "Some [authors] think that the sources [of the Johannine gospel, namely] (collection of 'signs'; collection of discourses; and passion narrative) were combined; others think of a process of several editions. In either case, plausibly the body of the Gospel was completed by one writer and a redactor later made additions (chap. 21; perhaps 1:1–18); but no text of the gospel has been preserved without these 'additions.'" See *Introduction to the New Testament*, ch. 11, p. 334.

14. Brown, *Introduction to the New Testament*, 333. Brown refers to many redactors who have added to the Johannine writings.

15. Thomas Rausch, "Development of Doctrine," in Komonchak et al., *New Dictionary of Theology*, 281.

16. See Quasten, *Patrology*, 1:51–53. In these pages, Quasten cites ca. forty authors who have written on Clement of Rome. I will use the English translation from Kleist, *Epistles of St. Clement of Rome and St. Ignatius of Antioch*, 45. I will also cite Goodspeed, *Apostolic Fathers*, 47–81; Lightfoot and Harmer, *Apostolic Fathers*, 28–64. McGucken, "Trinity in the Greek Fathers," in Phan, *Cambridge Companion to the Trinity*, 49–69. Above all see Holmes, *Apostolic Fathers*, 22–78.

> will.... Finally, the most excellent and greatest being, man, He formed with His sacred and faultless hands in the likeness of His own image.[17]

In this citation, God the Father is the source of all creation. Clement again and again refers to God the Father with no mention of the Son and the Holy Spirit. In his *Letter to the Corinthians*, there are two possible references to the Trinity. In the first reference, he simply states the terms; "Father-Son-Spirit." He offers no explanation of the relationship of these three names. This citation seems to have some connection to Ephesians 4:5–6, but in Paul's letter there is no clear mention of a divine Holy Spirit. Paul uses the term Spirit but he does not mean a Trinitarian Holy Spirit. He writes:

> Or, do we not have one God and one Christ and one Spirit of grace, a Spirit that was poured out upon us.[18]

> Ἢ οὐχὶ ἕνα Θεὸν ἔχομεν καὶ ἕνα Χριστὸν καὶ ἕν Πνεῦμα τῆς χάριτος τὸ ἐκχυθὲν ἐφ' ἡμᾶς.

In a later paragraph of the *Letter to the Corinthians*, Clement refers to the three names for a second time, but once again he simply mentions Father, Son, and Holy Spirit without any further description.

> For, as truly as God lives, as truly as the Lord Jesus Christ and the Holy Spirit live—so truly will he [a Christian] ... be enrolled and be in good standing among the number of those who are on the way to salvation through Jesus Christ.[19]

> Ζῇ ὁ Θεὸς καὶ Ζῇ ὁ Κύριος Ἰησοῦς Χριστὸς καὶ τὸ Πνεῦμα τὸ Ἅγιον ... οὗτος ἐντεταγμένος καὶ ἐλλόγιμος ἔσται εἰς τὸν ἀριθμὸν τῶν σωζομένων διὰ Ἰησοῦ Χριστοῦ.

In these two citations, only the Father is ὁ θεός; the relationship of Jesus and the Holy Spirit to the Father—ὁ θεός—remains unexpressed. Clement, in two other citations from his letter to the Corinthians refers to the

---

17. Clement, *Epistle to the Corinthians*, n. 33. English trans. Kleist, *Epistles*, 29. For the original Greek text see Ἐπιστολή πρός Κορίνθιους I, in Migne, *Patrologia Graeca*, vol. 1, column 273.

18. Greek original text, Ἐπιστολή πρός Κορίνθιους I, in Minge *Patrologia Graeca*, vol. 1, column 304. For the English translation, see Kleist, *Epistles*, 38.

19. See Kleist, *Epistles*, 45n58. The Greek text is from Rouët de Journel's *Enchiridion Patristicum*, 10n28.

one and only God. There is no mention that Jesus is divine in the same way God is divine.

> Let all the nations know that Thou art the only God, that Jesus Christ is Thy Son, that we are Thy people and the sheep of Thy pasture.[20]

> To Thee, who alone art able to bestow these and even greater blessings upon us, we render thanks and praise through whom be to Thee the glory and majesty nor and for all generations and forever and ever more. Amen.[21]

Clement, in a way that is similar to certain texts in John's Gospel, seems to say that Jesus is not quite divine. Clement refers to Jesus and to the Holy Spirit, but these citations merely state that God the Father has some sort of relationship to both Jesus and the Holy Spirit, but there is no "theology of the Trinity" in his letter. Throughout the *Letter of Clement*, Jesus is frequently mentioned, and whenever Jesus is mentioned, the author explains how Jesus brings our needs, our hopes, and our lives to God the Father. For Clement, Jesus is close to God but not close enough to be "divinized."[22]

Ignatius of Antioch

Our knowledge of Ignatius of Antioch is limited. He is known primarily through the seven letters he wrote at the end of his life (ca. 35–107 CE). He seems to have been ordained as bishop of Antioch. He was in his seventies when he was arrested by the Roman government and he was taken in chains under military guard from Antioch to Rome where he was eventually martyred. In their journey from Antioch to Rome, the armed guard took two brief respites, the first at Smyrna, present-day Izmir, and the second at Troas.[23]

---

20. Kleist, *Epistles*, 46n59.
21. Kleist, *Epistles*, 47n61.
22. For a general understanding of editing the Greek Fathers, see Herbert Musurillo, "Some Textual Problems in the Editing of the Greek Fathers," *Studia Patristica* III (Berlin: Akademie Verlag, 1961), 85–96. His essay states that one needs to understand the historical time in which various patristic statements are made. We cannot read into these statements the meaning of certain words which had one interpretation in an early century and a quite different meaning in our own century.
23. Antioch is about 450 miles to Smyrna/Izmir. Troas is about 125 miles from Izmir.

In both cities, Christians brought Ignatius stationary and writing utensils. In Smyrna, Ignatius wrote three letters to Christian communities which he knew quite well: namely to the Christians in Ephesus (the capital of the Roman province in Asia); to the Christians in Magnesia (a city about 12 miles south of Ephesus); and to the Christians at Tralles (a city about 17 miles from Magnesia). A fourth letter was sent to the Christians in Rome. From Smyrna, Ignatius was taken to the city of Troas (Troy) in the northwest corner of Asia Minor. In Troas, Ignatius wrote the letters to the Christians at Philadelphia (today this Turkish city is called Alaşehir, just south of Canakkale). He also wrote a letter to the Christians at Smyrna and another letter to Polycarp the bishop of Smyrna.

Six of these letters are about the presence of God and Jesus in the lives of the Christians; only in his letter to the Romans did Ignatius claim that his arrest by the Romans was wrong. He did not strike out at his enemies. Rather, his letters consistently urged the Christian communities to maintain their love for God, for Jesus, and for the Christian church.

Mention of the Holy Spirit is also made, but with no precise description. In the Gospel of John, Jesus is almost divinized and therefore all Christians who believe in Jesus are to some degree in the presence of God the Father. Clement might have been born of Jewish parentage, for he draws heavily on passages from the Old Testament. He, too, mentions that there is a relationship of the human Jesus to God, but he does not state that Jesus is divinized. If Ignatius was a gentile and he honored a God, this God would not have been YHWH. However, we do not have any indication of his understanding of God as it appears in the two citations below. He uses the Greek term Θεός, but there is no indication as to its exact meaning. In the Greek world of the first and second centuries CE, the name Θεός had a number of different meanings.[24]

John Anthony McGuckin urges us to reflect on Ignatius as a spiritual writer in a much different way. Most commentators, he writes, want to find in his writings early traces of later Trinitarian theology. He explains his own position as follows:

> We will better appreciate the ancients if we lay aside the above flawed methodology and remember that they are singing in a different key, or—to change metaphors—that they are working under a different light. Approach their differences on their own

---

24. See Arndt and Gingrich, *Greek-English Lexicon*, 356–58, for the use and meaning of ὁ Θεός. This English lexicon is basically a translation of Walter Bauer's *Griechisch-Deutshes Wörterbuch zu den Schriften des Neuen Testaments* (Berlin 1949–1952).

The Beginning of Trinitarian Theology (100 to 300 CE)

terms (as if looking under purple light instead of daylight) and we will see a wholly different set of facts.²⁵

As you read the following citations, place yourself in the same position as that of Ignatius: he has been arrested and was under armed guard; a bloody death awaited him; he took time to write to his many friends urging them to love God. In each letter, he places the focus on the recipients not on himself for he urges them to deepen their love for God, for Jesus, and for the Christian church.

In the following paragraph, Karl Baus describes the historical situation that Ignatius was in when he was writing his letters.

> In attempting to assess the value of the *Corpus Ignatianum* as a source of information on post-apostolic theology and religion, one must not overlook the fact that the seven letters were written more or less ex-tempore by a prisoner condemned to death, under the eyes of his not very considerate gaolers. The letters are not well-weighed theological treatises composed in conditions of tranquility, but the spontaneous outpourings of a courageous leader, full of love for Christ and a longing for martyrdom.²⁶

Baus implies that Ignatius was not a major theologian. He was writing his letters without a library for references. He is speaking as a Christian man who is about to die. We cannot refer to these letters in the same way a scholar refers to a theological treatise.

1. In his *Letter to the Ephesians*, Ignatius wrote the following:

   > [You are] animated by one faith and in union with Jesus Christ, who in the flesh was of the line of David, the Son of Man and the Son of God. (n. 20)

   > Συνέρχεσθε ἐν μιᾷ πίστει καὶ ἐν Ἰησοῦ Χριστῷ τῷ κατὰ σάρκα ἐκ γένους Δαυίδ, τῷ Υἱῷ ἀνθρώπου καὶ Υἱῷ Θεοῦ.²⁷

2. In his *Letter to the Magnesians*, Ignatius wrote the following:

   > There is one God who manifested himself through Jesus Christ, His Son—who, being His Word, came forth out of the silence

---

25. McGucken, "Trinity in the Greek Fathers," in Phan, *Cambridge Companion to the Trinity*, 52.

26. Baus, *Handbook of Church History*, 1:138–39.

27. English translation by Kleist, *Epistles*, n. 20, p. 60. For the Greek text, see Migne, *Patrologia Graeca*, 5:661.

into the world and won the full approval of Him whose Ambassador He was. (n. 8)

Be zealous, therefore, to stand squarely on the decrees of the Lord and Apostles, that in all things whatsoever you may prosper, in body and in soul, in faith and in love, in the Son and the Father and the Spirit. (n. 13)

3. In his *Letter to the Trallians*, Ignatius wrote the following:

Stop your ears therefore when anyone speaks to you who stands apart from Jesus Christ...who also really rose from the dead, since His Father raised him up. (n. 9)

4. In his *Letter to the Romans*, Ignatius refers again to Jesus as God:

Ignatius, also called Theophorus, to the church that has found mercy in the transcendent Majesty of the Most High Father and of Jesus Christ, His only Son. (intro.)

5. In his *Letter to the Philadelphians*, Ignatius writes:

To the Church of God the Father and the Lord Jesus Christ which is at Philadelphia in Asia; a church which has found mercy and is irrevocably of one mind with God. (intro.)

6. In his *Letter to the Smyrnaeans*, Ignatius writes:

I extol God and Father of our Lord Jesus Christ, the God who granted you through him such wisdom. (n. 1, 1)

Δοξάζω Ἰησον Χριστὸν τὸν Θεὸν τὸν οὕτως ὑμᾶς σωφίσαντα.

7. In his *Letter to Polycarp*, Ignatius writes:

Ignatius to Polycarp, who is bishop of the Churches of Smyrna, or rather has for his bishop, God, the Father and the Lord Jesus Christ.

And therefore, I praise you for everything: I bless you [God the Father] and I glorify you through the eternal and heavenly High Priest, Jesus Christ, your beloved Son, through whom be glory to you together with Him and the Holy Spirit, both now and for the ages to come. Amen.

Δἀρχιερεύς Ἰησοῦ Χριστοῦ, ἀγαπητοῦ σου παιδός, δι'οὗ σοὶ σὺν αὐτῷ καὶ Πνεύματι Αγιων ʼ ῳη δόξα καὶ νῦν καὶ εἰς τοὺς μελλοντας αἰῶνας. Ἀμήν.

The Beginning of Trinitarian Theology (100 to 300 CE)

In the above three sources—namely the Gospel of John, Clement's *Epistle to the Corinthians*, and the *Letters of Ignatius*—there is no direct reference to the Trinity. In the history of Trinitarian theology, the mere mention that Jesus is the Son of God is the first step. In this first step, Jesus could be explained as the adopted Son of God. The second step is the development of a theology in which the divine nature of God the Father is the same nature of God the Son. By using the term "nature" for both human nature and divine nature, several Christian scholars in the second century unfortunately did not explain the difference between human nature and divine nature. They simply used the word in a descriptive way which eventually with Justin and Clement of Alexandria developed into a more definitive way. The third step is a theology on the divinity of God which includes the Holy Spirit.[28]

The Gospel of John, the Letter of Clement of Rome, and the Letters of Ignatius of Antioch offer us only the first step regarding the divinity of Jesus. In this first step, there is no clear theological presentation in the above three sources that the divine nature of Jesus is truly equal to the divine nature of God the Father. There is a mention that Jesus is the Son of God with no further theological explanation as to what this entails.

The Epistle of Barnabas

There is a letter which is attributed to Barnabas (early second-century text), but the letter is really an announcement that Barnabas had been martyred. James Kleist begins his analysis of the letter with these words:

> We do not know who the author of the Epistle of Barnabas is, or when and where he wrote, or to what specific group of Christian readers he addressed his words of warning. Nor is the meaning of some allusions to his time beyond all doubt. One thing is certain: it is only from this epistle that we learn the interesting fact that between the destruction of Jerusalem and the second catastrophe in Hadrian's time, Judaism, which had been a disturber of peace from earliest times, had raised its head so high as to become a grave danger to a certain Christian community.[29]

---

28. The meaning of the word "nature" in Christian theology has had a complicated history from the earliest theology of the meaning of nature which is essentially the same for the Father as well as the Son and the Holy Spirit.

29. Kleist, *The Didache, The Epistle of Barnabas, The Epistles and the Martyrdom of St. Polycarp, The Fragments of Papias, and the Epistle to Diognetus*, 29.

In the text of the letter, "Barnabas" makes a statement in which God the Father is mentioned as speaking with someone else, since the author uses the phrase "Let us . . ." The text reads:

> If the Lord [Jesus] submitted to suffering for our souls—He, the Lord of the universe, to whom at the foundation of the world God [the Father] had said "*Let us make man according to our image and likeness*,"—then how did it happen that he submitted to suffering at the hands of men?[30]

Kleist states that the two words "Let us" refer to the Holy Trinity.[31] Quasten, however, states that the phrase "Let us" means only "Father and Son."[32]

A few pages later, the author of Barnabas refers to the suffering of Jesus: "The Son of God, although he is Lord and Judge of the living and the dead, underwent suffering so that his affliction might give us life."[33] In the entire *Epistle of Barnabas*, the author refers to the Holy Spirit only six times, while he mentions the Father and Son again and again. The paucity of references to the Holy Spirit indicates in a strong way that the author of *Epistle of Barnabas* had no idea of a Trinitarian God. On the basis of the text of this document, one can ask: Is Jesus, as the Son of God, coequal with God and therefore divine? Or is Jesus "divine" in the sense of being close to the Father but not equal to the Father? The letter does not give a clear answer to the divinity of Jesus or to his equality with the Father.

Aristides

Aristides was an Athenian philosopher who had become a Christian. He died in 133/134 CE. He wrote an *Apology*, entitled "To Imperator Adrianus Caesar from the Athenian Philosopher Aristides." He delivered the *Apology* to the emperor Hadrian around 125 CE. In chapter 15, he writes:

> Some Christians have written a genealogy of the Lord, Jesus Christ. He is believed to be the Son of the Most High God, who

---

30. *Barnabas* (Kleist), 43. Kleist explains this at 171n47. Kleist cites the text of Genesis 1:26, which states: "Let us make man according our image and likeness." The plural "our" is a reference to the "Blessed Trinity."

31. See Kleist, *Didache . . .*, 171. In the footnote for this reference, Kleist states that "in Genesis I, 26 the plural 'we' is a reference to the Blessed Trinity" (171n47).

32. See Quasten, in *Patrology*, 1:87. Quasten states that the plural relates only to God the Father speaking to his Son.

33. *Barnabas* (Kleist), 46.

in the Holy Spirit came down from heaven for the salvation of men and women, and he assumed [human] flesh from the holy virgin without semen and without corruption.[34]

Again, we have only a brief statement of God, his Son, and the Holy Spirit.[35] Aristides does not offer us either a philosophical or a theological clarification of the Christian Triune God. It seems that one cannot say that Aristides believed in a "Trinitarian God," since he does not clearly indicate that all three are equally divine.

Marcion

In the second century CE, Marcion of Sinope (d. ca. 160) became one of the most unacceptable Christians in ecclesiastical history. Hans Jonas describes him as follows:

> Marcion "occupies a unique position in gnostic thought, as well as in the history of the Christian Church. In the latter respect, he was the most resolutely and undilutedly 'Christian' of the Gnostics, and for this very reason his was the greatest challenge to Christian orthodoxy."[36]

He came to Rome in 135 CE, but in 144 CE he was expelled from his Roman church. He founded his own church with its own bishops, priests, and deacons.[37] In the second century, he was a fairly influential person and a prominent leader against the Christian way of life. His writings indicate that the acceptance of Jesus as Son of God was impossible. The initial success of Marcion's community stirred Irenaeus, Tertullian, and

---

34. See Aristides, *Apologia*, n. 15. A Greek and a Latin text can be found in Rouët de Journel's *Enchiridion Patristicum*, 40. The above English translation is my own. See also the English translation of D. M. Kay, "The Apology of Aristides the Philosopher," available online at http://www.earlychristianwritings.com/text/aristides-kay.html.

35. For the writings of Aristides, there are an Armenian version and a Syriac version. In the Armenian version the Holy Spirit is mentioned only once and this occurs in the final chapter. In the Syriac edition, I did not find any mention of the Holy Spirit at all. To say that Aristides believed in a Trinitarian God is, in my view, not very clear. The text of Aristides which is used in Rouët de Journel's *Enchiridion Patristicum*, 40–41, mentions the Holy Spirit twice, but again in a very secondary way.

36. Jonas, *Gnostic Religion*, 137. Jonas devotes seventeen pages—a complete chapter—to Marcion. Marcion was part of a Christian community until 144 CE when he was expelled from the Christian community. Marcion then established a new "Christian Church." He died in 160 CE.

37. See Eugene TeSelle, "Marcion," in Patte, *Cambridge Dictionary of Christianity*, 759.

Origen to answer in their writings by lengthy passages against Marcion's theology. Marcion died around 160 CE.[38]

Justin

Justin was born in Samaria around 100/110 CE from pagan parents. He was a very talented individual, and as a young man he kept looking for a school that would challenge his intelligence. He became a philosopher and a prolific writer. However, only three texts have come down to us: two *Apologies* and his *Dialogue with the Jew, Trypho*. Justin offers no theology of the Trinity, but he does accept the Christian God, whom he calls "God the Father," and this God is without origin and is inexpressible (ἄρρητος).[39]

However, in a later passage he writes that the terms God, Father, Creator and Master, are not real names. They are simply appellations derived from his good deeds and functions. The appellation "God" is not a name, but an opinion implanted in the nature of men regarding a reality that can hardly be explained. I cite the following passage from Justin:

> But a proper name for the Father of all things, who is unbegotten, there is none. For whoever is called by a name, has a person older than himself who gives him the name.[40]

> Ὄνομα δὲ τῷ πάντων Πατρὶ θετόν, ἀγεννήτῳ ὄντι, οὐχ ἔστιν. Ὧι γὰρ ἂν καὶ ὀνόματι προσαγορεύηται, πρεσβύτερον ἔχει τὸν θέμενον τὸ ὄνομα.[41]

> But the terms Father, and God, and Creator, and Lord and Master, are not names, but terms of address derived from His benefits and His works.[42]

> Τὸ δὲ Πατὴρ, καὶ Θεὸς, καὶ Κτίστης, καὶ Κύριος, καὶ Δεσπότης, οὐχ ὀνόματά ἐστιν, ἀλλ' ἐκ τῶν εὐποιϊῶν καὶ τῶν ἔργων προσρήσεις.[43]

---

38. See Holmes, *Apostolic Fathers*; in the chapter on the Martyrdom of Polycarp (222–48), we read that Marcion is called by Polycarp: "Yes, I recognize you, the First-born of Satan" (citation from p. 245).

39. See Quasten, *Patrology*, 1:207. Quasten states that for Justin "God is without origin (ἄρρητος).

40. Quasten, *Patrology*, 1:207–8.

41. For the Greek text, see Migne, *Patrologia Graeca*, vol. 6, col. 453.

42. English text, n. 6, 61–62.

43. Greek text, Migne, *Patrologia Graeca*, n. 6, col. 453.

> But His Son who alone is properly called Son, the Word, who was begotten before all things, and Who was with Him, and was begotten, when in the beginning through Him He created and ordered all things, is called Christ, as he was anointed; and by Him God set all things in order, and this name itself contains an unknown signification; as also the title God is not a name, but the notion which is implanted in the matter of man, of a thing which can hardly be explained.[44]

In the above passages, Justin is stating that we do not know the true name of God. It is we who have named him God, Father, Creator, Lord, and Master, but none of these names tells us who God really is. All the above names, including the name God, are human expressions of the one who is "all in all." In other words, God's nature is totally beyond our natural intelligence.

Jesus, the Son of God, is called "the Son begotten by the Father." The name "Son of God" is also only a human expression of the "unknown holiness." In his writings, Justin calls him God, but actually we do not have any knowledge of a proper name for the one who is above all names. The names "Father God" or the "Son of the Father God," or the "Holy Spirit" are human names for the one and only "unknown holiness."

This passage of Justin on the "no name" for God has been studied at great length in Jules Lebreton's *Histoire du Dogme de la Trinité*.[45] Johannes Quasten also devotes many pages to the writings of Justin, and he states: "It seems that Justin tends toward subordinationism as far as the relation between the Logos and the Father is concerned."[46]

Justin's references to the divinity of the Holy Spirit are brief but clear: In his *First Apology*, he writes:

> Our teacher of these things is Jesus Christ . . . and he is the Son of God (Υἱὸν αὐτοῦ τοῦ ὄντως Θεοῦ μαθόντες) and holding Him

---

44. English text, n. 6, p. 62. In Justin's *First Apology*, he calls the Father "the most true God" (n. 6); he also refers to the "Son of the very God, and holding Him to be in the second place, and the Spirit of Prophecy in the third [place]" (n. 13, p. 9). In *The Dialogue with Trypho*, one reads: "By Another, namely, by Him Who always remains above the Heavens, Who has never been seen by any man, and Who of Himself holds converse with none; Whom we term the Creator of all things and the Father" (n. 56, p. 138). The Greek text is in *Patrologia Graeca*, 6, Πρὸς Τρύφωνα Ἰουδαῖον Διάλογος, nn. 596–97.

45. Jules Lebreton, *Histoire du Dogme de la Trinité*, (Paris: Gabriel Beauchesne, 1928), Tome II, Livre V, Chapitre I, "Saint Justin," 411–28.

46. Quasten, *Patrology*, 1:209.

to be in the second place (καὶ ἐν Δευτέρᾳ χώρᾳ ἔχοντες) and the Spirit of prophecy in the third [place] (Πνευμά τε προφητικὸν ἐν Τρίτῃ τάξει).[47]

Throughout the entire *First Apology*, Justin refers again and again to the Father, the Son, and the Holy Spirit. For Justin, the Trinity is the divine God and he acknowledges that this God is triune. Even though no one knows the true name of "God," we humans have used several of our finite words when we speak of an unspeakable God, and one of these terms is "The Trinitarian God." For Justin, the true name and essence of God is unknowable.

In my view, Justin's position on "God" is very helpful to our contemporary religious world. The Jews had a name for God, YHWH, but its meaning was not clear and it still is not clear. Christians have had several names for God, but there are Christians throughout the second century down to the twenty-first century, who claim that the very name of God is "God" or "Father" or "Creator" or "Trinity." From the earliest times, Christian missionaries and Christian scholars have stated that there is only one God and that God is Trinity—Father, Son, and Holy Spirit. Justin, however, makes his claim that since God is unsurpassable, we cannot know the name of God. Therefore, a "Trinitarian God" is a name for God, but it, too, does not tell us what the nature of God is.

When we consider today the many names which men and women have used to designate the "God" of all creation, we are aware that there have been and still are multiple names for the divine Creator. In many religions, the belief in a "named" reality is treasured by its adherents. In the post-Vatican II world, the number of interreligious meetings has multiplied. Many Catholics and many Christians attend these meetings. Most Christians tend to believe that the "Christian God" is the one and only true God. In these ecumenical sessions, there is no common name for God.

Justin's position on "God" challenges us today. If we cannot know the primary name for "God," can we argue that the Christian God is the only God? Justin remained very Christian and died for his faith in the Christian God. His phrasing above, at least for Justin, was simply a position by which Christians would know that there is an unnameable being behind the limiting terms that we have. Justin is telling us that God

---

47. Justin, *First Apology*, n. 13, in *A Library of the Fathers*, p. 9. For the Greek text, see Migne, *Patrologia Graeca*, vol. 6, col. 348.

remains the unknown. He believed in Jesus and the Holy Spirit, but in the passage above it seems that neither the Logos nor the Holy Spirit is coessential with the ultimate God, the Father.[48]

Clement of Alexandria

Clement of Alexandria (ca. 150–215 CE) was an outstanding intellectual giant. He was probably born in Athens from non-Christian parents. The date of his entry into the Christian community is unknown. In his travels, he visited southern Italy, Syria, and Palestine. He then went to Alexandria and met Pantaenus, a major Christian scholar who was the head of a Christian school in Alexandria. Around 200 CE, Clement became the successor of Pantaenus.

One of his more complicated writings is the *Stromata* (Στρωματεὺς). The title of this work has been translated in many ways: *The Miscellanies, The Patchwork, The Carpets, Die Treppen*, etc. In a non-overly academic way, Clement discusses many sundry issues, particular philosophical issues. Quasten remarks:

> The name, *Carpets*, is similar to others used at the time, like *The Meadow, The Banquets*, and *The Honeycomb*. Such titles indicated a genre favored by philosophers of the day, in which they could discuss most varied questions without strict order or plan and pass from one problem to another without systematic treatment, the different topics being woven together like colors in a carpet.[49]

In the *Stromata*, Clement makes a lengthy statement regarding our human knowledge of God similar to that of Justin, quoted above. Clement writes:

> Since the first principle of everything is difficult to find out, the absolute first and oldest principle, which is the cause of all other

---

48. In a similar way, John Duns Scotus in the late thirteenth and early fourteenth centuries came to the conclusion that the very "essence" of God was infinite and therefore unknowable. However, this infinite and unknowable God was, in Scotus's view, the Trinitarian God, the center of the Christian faith. An infinite God cannot be named, and for Scotus, the naming of the very nature of God is far beyond human intelligence. Scotus writes: "You [God] are infinite and incomprehensible by what is finite." The Latin reads: "Te esse infinitum et incomprehensibilem a finito" (an infinite God is inexpressible). See chapter 7.

49. Quasten, *Patrology*, 2:12. Quasten explains the word "carpet."

things being and having been, is difficult to exhibit.... No one can rightly express Him wholly. For on account of his greatness He is ranked as the All, and is the Father of the universe.[50]

Ἐπεὶ γὰρ ἀρχὴ παντὸς πράγματος δυσεύρετος, πάντως που ἡ πρώτη καὶ πρεσβυτάτη ἀρχὴ δύσδεικτος, ἥτις καὶ τοῖς ἄλλοις ἅπασιν αἰτία τοῦ γενέσθαι καὶ γενομένους εἶναι. ... Οὐχ ἂν δὲ ὅλον εἴποι τις αὐτὸν ὀρθῶς ἐπὶ μεγέθει γὰρ τάττεται τὸ ὅλον, καὶ ἔστι τῶν ὅλων πατήρ.[51]

And if we name it, we do not do so properly, terming it either the One, or the Good, or Mind, or Absolute Being, or Father, or God, or Creator, or Lord. We speak not as supplying his name.[52]

Κἂν ὀναμάξωμεν αὐτό ποτε οὐ κυρίως, καλοῦντες ἤτοι ἕν, ἢ τἀγαθὸν, ἢ νοῦν, ἢ αὐτὸ τὸ ὄν, ἢ Πατέρα, ἢ θεὸν, ἢ Δημιουργὸν, ἢ Κύριον, οὐχ ὡς ὄνομα αὐτοῦ προφερόμενοι λέγομεν, ὑπὸ δὲ ἀπορίας ὀνόμασι καλοῖς προσχρώμεθα.[53]

We use good names, in order that the mind may have these as points of support, so as not to err in other respects. For each one [each name] by itself does not express God; but all together are indicative of the power of the Omnipotent.[54]

Clement, like Justin, provides a list of names for God and then states that these are only "names." Not one of them is a proper name for God, since no human person is capable of knowing the proper name of God. Both of these Christian scholars are considered "Fathers of the Church." Neither of them is considered heretical. Whereas most of the "Fathers of the Church" explained God as "Father, Son, and Holy Spirit," Clement and Justin state that no human person really knows the name of the "Ultimate." This implies that such names as "the One, or the Good, or Mind, or Absolute Being, or Father, or God, or Creator, or Lord" are all human names which do not contain the "essence" of God, but only provide a

---

50. Quasten, *Patrology*, 2:22. English trans.

51. See Clement, Στρωμάτεων, original text in Minge, *Patrologia Graeca*, vol. 9, bk. 5, ch. 12, col. 121.

52. Quasten, *Patrology*, 2:22. English translation.

53. Clement, Στρωμάτεων, original text in Minge, *Patrologia Graeca*, vol. 9, bk. 5, ch. 12, col. 121.

54. Clement, Στρωμάτεων, original text in Minge, *Patrologia Graeca*, vol. 9, bk. 5, ch. 12, col. 121. Tomus IX, 121.

"finite" name for an "infinite and ultimate" unknowable source of all created life.

The name Logos and the name Holy Spirit are also found in the writings of Justin and Clement of Alexandria. These may be the names which we Christians have given them, but we do believe that these names—Father, Logos, and Holy Spirit, in one way or another—help us understand the divinity of God at least to some degree. The closest human name for God, as we shall see later in this volume, is "infinite."

Given the above, I want to state again that the two terms "Father" and "Son" do not express the ultimate essence of God. These two names seem to be merely human terms for the Unknowable. In many ways, the reflections on the naming of God in the writings of both Justin and Clement challenge the usual explanations of a Trinitarian God. If one reviews the Jewish and Christian material in chapters 3 and 4, we find that the term YHWH is used, and yet there is no clear meaning of the term YHWH. Scholars have suggested many meaning for the term YHWH, but most contemporary scholars simply write YHWH and do not offer any translation. Both Justin and Clement, from a different starting point, state that the Ultimate is unnameable and unknowable, and that such terms as the One, or the Good, or the Mind as well as the Absolute Being, the Father, the Creator, and the Lord are all finite terms and none of them provide us with the one and only "true name" of the Ultimate.

I am suggesting that today's religious scholars might begin with the "Unnameable" rather than with the "Nameable." If "God" is unnameable, then the names "Trinity" and the names "Father," "Son," and "Holy Spirit" do not express the nature of the "Divine." God is the unknown and unknowable who cannot be named. This approach would affect every naming of the ultimate as expressed in almost all religions.

Theophilus of Antioch

Theophilus of Antioch (ca. 120–ca. 180) was born near the Euphrates River from pagan parentage. He had an excellent education. It was only after he had studied the Christian biblical data at a mature age that he became a Christian. In 170 CE, he became the bishop of Antioch. He was also the first Christian author who used the word Τριάς for the Trinity, but this word is mentioned only once.

> The three days which were before the luminaries, are types of the Trinity of God, and his word, and his wisdom.⁵⁵
>
> Αἱ τρεῖς ἡμέραι πρὸ τῶν φωστήρων γεγονυῖται τύποι εἰσιν τῆς Τριάδος, τοῦ Θεοῦ καὶ τοῦ Λόγου αὐτοῦ καὶ τῆς Σοφίας αὐτοῦ.⁵⁶

Theophilus, in this statement, simply mentions the Trinity. Theophilus makes a much stronger statement on the nature of God in book 1, n. 4 of *Ad Autolycum*. In this book, he states that God has no beginning and that he is immutable; he is Lord because he has power over all things; and he is Father because he is prior to all.⁵⁷

McGuckin describes the second-century situation in which scholars such as Theophilus took on the role of an "apologist." The opponents were often Jewish sages and religious philosophers and they were formidable opponents to Christian leaders. McGuckin continues:

> For Theophilus, the Father exists as the supreme monad in infinite transcendence. But when he decides to create the material world, he "utters" what he has hitherto kept secret within his own mind. In other words the Father's Wisdom is always co-present and co-eternal, but at a specific moment (purely for the world's making) the Logos is "expressed," and becomes manifest in order to work.⁵⁸

Creation is not immediately connected to God, and therefore human beings come to know God only by means of their apprehension of the invisible Logos, who is made visible indirectly in the humanity of Jesus. He mentions "*Trias*" in his reference to God, but the "*Trias*" in *Ad Autolycum* does not have quite the same meaning as the word Trinity.

Little by little, in the second century, it became clearer and clearer that a "theology" of the Trinity, and not simply a reference to the Trinity, is needed. The next author, Athenagoras of Athens, is perhaps the first Christian scholar who presents at least the beginning of a Trinitarian theology.

---

55. English trans. in Quasten, *Patrology*, 1:239.

56. Theophilus of Antioch, Πρός Αὐτόλυκον, *Patrologia Graeca*, 6:1077. For further information on Theophilus, see Bardy, "Théophile d'Antioche," 1034–35.

57. Theophilus, Πρός Αὐτόλυκον, *PG*, vol. 6, n. 4, col. 1029.

58. See McGucken, "Trinity in the Greek Fathers," in Phan, *Cambridge Companion to the Trinity*, 56. Bardy, "Théophile d'Antioche," provides us (in French) with a detailed section of Theophilus's *Apology to Autolycus*, 508–10.

The Beginning of Trinitarian Theology (100 to 300 CE)

Athenagoras of Athens

Athenagoras was a Greek philosopher who at a later age of his life became a Christian. The dating of his life is ca. 133 to ca. 190 CE. His major writing is *The Supplication for the Christians* (Πρεσβεία περί τῶν Χριστιανῶν), written in 177 CE.[59] This "letter" was addressed to the two emperors, Marcus Aurelius Antoninus and Lucius Aurelius Commodus, and therefore it was held in admiration by the Christian community. In his writings, Athenagoras provides us with a brief presentation on the Christian God. He writes:

> I have given sufficient proof that we are not atheists, but hold God to be one, unbegotten, eternal, invisible, suffering nothing, comprehended by none, circumscribed by none, apprehended by mind and reasoning alone.[60]
>
> Τὸ μὲν οὖν ἄθεοι μὴ εἶναι, ἕνα τὸν ἀγένητον καὶ ἀΐδιον καὶ ἀόρατον καὶ ἀπαθῆ καὶ ἀκατάληπτον, καὶ ἀχώρητον, νῷ μόνῳ καὶ λόγῳ καταλαμβανόμενον.[61]

This passage is similar to the citations of both Justin and Clement regarding the inability to know and name God since God is incomprehensible. Athenagoras clarifies his understanding of the relationship between the Father and the Son:

> But if, in your surpassing intelligence, it occurs to you to inquire what is meant by the Son, I will state briefly that he is the product of the Father, not as having been brought into existence—for from the beginning, God, who is the eternal mind (νοῦς), had the Logos in Himself, being from eternity instinct with Logos— but inasmuch as he came forth to be the idea and energizing power of all material things.[62]

Athenagoras adds another detail to his exposition of the Trinity. He writes:

> That we are not atheists, seeing that we acknowledge one God, I have sufficiently demonstrated. Who then would not be

---

59. Crehan, *Athenagoras*, 21–24. An important source is the Coptic Orthodox Church Network—copticchrch.net.athenagoras.

60. English trans., Crehan, *Athenagoras*, vol. 1, n. 10, p. 40.

61. Athenagoras, Πρεσβεία περί Χριστιανῶν, in Minge, *Patrologia Graeca*, 6:908, n. 10.

62. English trans., Quasten, *Patrology*, 1:232–33.

astonished to hear men who speak of God the Father, and of God the Son, and of God the Holy Spirit, and declare both their power in union and their distinction in order, [so that they can be] called atheists?[63]

Perhaps the entire chapter 10 of his volume should be cited, but it is a long and detailed chapter. The two citations above are simply taken from chapter 10 since theologically their phrasing of the two texts is clear and strong.

These above citations are, for the most part, major statements concerning a "Trinity." Trinitarian writings from the third century onward are far more explanatory of the relationship between Father and Son than between Son and Spirit. However, for a theology of the Trinity in the second century, Athenagoras presents the typology for a deeper theology of a Triune God.

Irenaeus

Irenaeus of Lyon (ca. 125–ca. 200 CE) became a presbyter in the Greek-speaking church in Lyon. He was sent to Rome to obtain toleration for the Montanists. While he was away, a persecution of the Christians took place in Lyon, and the bishop of Lyon, Pothinus, was martyred. When Irenaeus returned to Lyon, he was selected to be the bishop of Lyon. He remained as bishop of Lyon until his death around 200 CE.

Joseph Smith, in his volume *St. Irenaeus: Proof of the Apostolic Preaching*, offers us a lengthy and well-detailed introduction.[64] According to patristic scholars, the Greek text of the *Proof of the Apostolic Preaching* was written sometime between 180 and 200 CE. As of today, Irenaeus's Greek text has not been discovered, but there is an Armenian text from which translations into Latin and English have been made. Without the original Greek text, one cannot be sure that the Armenian text corresponds exactly to the original Greek text. However, contemporary

---

63. The English text is taken from Quasten, *Patrology*, 1:233.

64. Irenaeus, *Proof of the Apostolic Preaching*, English trans. Joseph Smith. See "Introduction," nn. 3–44. Irenaeus's writings were in Greek, but none of them have come down to us. For the "proof" we have an Armenian translation of Irenaeus's Greek text. The Armenian translation probably dates from 570–590 CE, and the Armenian translation is made from an original Greek text. The English translation made by Joseph Smith is from the Armenian text.

The Beginning of Trinitarian Theology (100 to 300 CE)   119

patristic scholars indicate that the Armenian translation of the *Proof* is for the most part fairly exact.[65]

After the introductory paragraphs, Irenaeus presents his understanding of the Trinity for the first time:

> We must keep strictly, without deviation, the rule of faith, and carry out the commands of God, believing in God and fearing Him, because He is Lord, and loving Him because He is Father. ... First of all, it [faith] admonishes us to remember that we have received baptism for remission of sins in the name of God the Father, and in the name of Jesus Christ, the Son of God, who became incarnate and died and was raised, and in the Holy Spirit of God.[66]

Immediately after this reference to baptism, Irenaeus adds a number of phrases describing God: "this baptism is rebirth unto God," "the eternal and everlasting on *is* God," "all things are God's," "God therefore is the almighty."[67] Irenaeus continues: "One must believe that there is one God, the Father, who made and fashioned everything."[68] Again, he writes: "There is declared one God, the Father, [who is] uncreated, invisible, maker of all things, above whom there is no other God whatever, and after whom there is no other God."[69] His description of the one God, "Father," is extremely all-inclusive. He writes:

> God, the Father, uncreated, beyond grasp, invisible, one God the maker of all; this is the first and foremost article of our faith.[70]

Irenaeus then moves to the Logos and to the Holy Spirit: "God is rational, and therefore He produces creatures by his Word, and since God is a spirit, and so fashioned everything by His Spirit."[71] Nonetheless, Irenaeus in a later text speaks strongly on God the Father. He writes:

> Therefore the Father is Lord, and the Son is Lord, and the Father is God and the Son is God; for he who is born of God is God. And thus God is shown to be one according to the essence of

---

65. Joseph Smith (Irenaeus, *Proof*), deals with the state of the text and principles of his translation into English, pp. 10–12.

66. Irenaeus, *Proof*, n. 49.

67. Irenaeus, *Proof*, nn. 49–50.

68. Irenaeus, *Proof*, n. 50.

69. Irenaeus, *Proof*, n. 50.

70. Irenaeus, *Proof*, n. 51.

71. Irenaeus, *Proof*, n. 50.

> His being and power; but, at the same time, as the administrator of the economy of our redemption, He is both Father and Son: since the Father of all is invisible and inaccessible to creatures, it is through the Son that those who are to approach God must have access to the Father.[72]

In some ways, these citations are similar to the citations from Justin and Clement, for Irenaeus states that God the Father is "invisible and inaccessible." As with Justin and Clement, we may call the divine both "God" and "Father," but these are "our" names for a supreme being who is "invisible" and "incomprehensible." Whereas Justin and Clement state this situation clearly, Irenaeus makes no mention of the intricacies which dominate our human understanding of God. For Irenaeus, God is the creator and lord of all men and women, Jew or Gentile. This universal God is eminently just and this universal God is also a loving Father God.[73] In the following passage, the major focus is on the Son of God.

> In the first place . . . the Son of God was preexistent, from the fact that the Father spoke with Him and caused Him to be revealed to men before his birth; and next, that He had become a man, born of mankind, and that the very God Himself forms Him from the womb, that is, that He would be born of the Spirit of God; and that he is Saviour of those who believe in Him.[74]

Smith, in his introduction, informs us that "Irenaeus does not state explicitly the divinity or personality of the Holy Spirit, but there is no reason for describing his theology of God as 'binatarianism.' He enumerates Father, Son, and Holy Spirit as the three articles of the faith."[75] At the very end of his introduction, Smith adds: "The *Proof* must not be supposed to contain a full exposition of what its author regarded as essential to Christian theology and behavior. Its scope is to prove the Church's credentials."[76]

Nonetheless, Irenaeus gives a basic and somewhat detailed notion of the Trinity, as found in nn. 3–10. This is much more than a mere statement that "God is Trinitarian." It may not be totally clear, but Irenaeus does take into account that God the Father is supreme. God the Son and

---

72. Irenaeus, *Proof*, n. 78.
73. Irenaeus, *Proof*, nn. 37–39.
74. Irenaeus, *Proof*, n. 81.
75. Irenaeus, *Proof*, n. 27.
76. Irenaeus, *Proof*, n. 44.

The Beginning of Trinitarian Theology (100 to 300 CE)

God the Holy Spirit are divine, but one might ask Irenaeus whether they are all equally divine. It seems his answer is negative.

The Main Theologians in the Third Century CE Who Either Accepted or Rejected the Divinization of Jesus Christ

Before we consider the remarkable writings of several third-century Christian theologians, we need to consider the political situation in the third century. One of the main issues of the Christian community in the second century CE was the demise of Jewish leadership and the role of Greek leaders and scholars. From the time of Clement of Rome (d. 98 CE), down to the end of the second century, almost all the Christian communities had one leading bishop, and most of these bishops were no longer Jewish Christians. Bishop Simeon of Jerusalem was one of the last Jewish leaders who became a Christian bishop. He was martyred under the emperor Trajan around 107 CE. Cerinthus was a Jew who lived in Egypt. He converted to Christianity, but he founded a Christian group, which was strongly attached to Jewish theology. Fernand Mourret, in volume 1 of his *History of the Catholic Church*, states that Jewish groups who were Christianized in the early second century CE "were devout and austere, and whole-heartedly attached to Christ; but as they had not yet broken sufficiently with Israel's past, they remained almost altogether outside the great movement that would regenerate the world by freeing it from the Law."[77]

Within the Christian church, Montanism also became a prophetic movement which began around 150 CE. It, too, had many affinities with many Jewish Christian scholars. At the end of the second century CE, the leadership of the Christian church at Rome, Constantinople, Alexandria, Antioch, etc., included men of almost every culture in the western and eastern areas of the Roman Empire. In the third century CE, major situations arose which seriously opposed Christian religion.

THE THIRD CENTURY CE: A TIME OF PERSECUTION

In the third century CE, many Christian theologians debated the issue of the divinity of Jesus. The writings of these scholars are cited by Christian authors even in the twenty-first century CE. However, in the third

---

[77]. See Mourret, *History of the Catholic Church*, 1:136.

century, Roman armies and leaders were killing Christians in almost a continuous way. Christians, therefore, lived in fearful danger almost year after year.

In *Christianity: The First Three Thousand Years*, Diarmaid MacCulloch described the second and third centuries of the Christian world in the following way:

> When the Danube froze in the winter of 166–167, it was a particular disaster for the empire, giving thousands of the Langobordi a chance to cross over and devastate Rome's central European provinces. On the eastern Roman frontier, matters became even more serious in the early third century. A new dynasty in Iran, the Sassinans, regained independence from their neighbours, the Parthians, and they were determined to take revenge on the world of Greece and Rome for the humiliations inflicted on Iran.[78]

In 202 CE, the emperor, Septimius Severus, issued an edict forbidding conversions to Judaism and Christianity. If anyone attempted to be a convert, both the person and the spiritual director suffered arrest and even death. Christian and Jewish activities were under severe supervision and missionary Christian work was forbidden.[79]

The successor of Severus was Caracalla (211–217 CE) who provided a short time of religious toleration. After Caracalla, Heliogabalus became emperor (218–222 CE), and he too chose to be religiously tolerant. So too was Severus Alexander (222–235 CE). When Maximinius (235–239 CE) became emperor, things changed, and Maximinius began a ferocious persecution and murdered hundreds of Christians. The emperor Decius (249–251 CE), also persecuted both Jews and Christians. The emperor Valerian (253–260 CE) did the same, and when Diocletian took over the Roman Empire in 284 CE, he issued four edicts of persecution. His sons who succeeded him also displayed their father's ruthless brutality. From 211 to 284, hardly a single emperor had died a natural death. The third century, politically, was in many ways a police state. In the larger cities within the Roman Empire, "archeologists have noted a particularly sinister feature of many of the new schemes of fortification. The officials enclosed only part of the city, the official headquarters and the wealthy

---

78. MacCulloch, *Christianity*, 166. The Sasanian Empire began in 224 CE and lasted to 651 CE when the Islamic armies took over the empire.

79. See Baus, *Handbook of Church History*, 1:217–18. English translation by Hubert Jedin. See also Eberhardt, *Summary of Catholic History*, 1:88–89.

The Beginning of Trinitarian Theology (100 to 300 CE)

areas. The old spirit of civic solidarity had withered."[80] Outside these fortified neighborhoods, poverty and ill health were rampant. Most Christians, therefore, lived outside these barriers and therefore they too shared the degradation of slum-living. In the third century, from 235 CE down to 284 CE—almost fifty years—the Roman Empire was involved in its own civil challenges and the empire itself was almost destroyed.

The third century CE was a difficult century for Christians, since major persecutions took place again and again. However, in the third century CE, five major theologians profoundly enriched the Christian church, namely Tertullian, Origen, Cyprian, Hippolytus of Rome, and Novatian.

The persecutions of the emperor Decius (249–251) were extensive and intensive. His imperial successor, Gallus (251–253), continued the persecution of Christians. The successor of Gallus, Valerian (253–260), martyred numerous Christians. The emperor Gallienus (260–285) finally broke with persecutions. He even issued a *Rescript of Toleration*. However, Christians were not totally free. The succeeding emperors, such as Claudius II (268–270), Aurelian (270–275), Tacitus (275–276), and Probus (276–282), were challenged again and again with revolts and the persecution of Christians. The number of apostates from the Christian church was enormous. When Diocletian became emperor (285–305 CE) his persecutions of Christians were again both extensive and intensive.

Tertullian

Tertullian, a native of Carthage, was born about 155 CE and died about 220 CE. Quasten rightfully states: "Except for St. Augustine, Tertullian is the most important and original ecclesiastical author in Latin. . . . It is in the doctrine of Trinity and the intimately connected Christology that Tertullian made the greatest contribution to theology."[81] Tertullian died around 220 CE.[82] Two of his more important writings on the Trinity are the *Apologeticum*, which he wrote in ca. 197, and *Adversus Praxeam*, which he wrote sometime between 213 and 218. In many ways Tertul-

---

80. MacCulloch, *Christianity*, 168.

81. Quasten, *Patrology*, 2:247 and 324.

82. Tertullian died ca. 220 CE. In *Patrology*, Quasten states: "Between the years 195–220, he [Tertullian] carried on his literary activity" (247). He also states that Tertullian became a Montanist about 207. In 213 he wrote one of his most important books, *Adversus Praxeam*.

lian's theology is partly second century and partly third century. Tertullian was the first Christian scholar to use the Latin term *Trinitas* for the three divine persons.

> Nam et Ecclesia proprie et principaliter ipse est Spiritus in quo est trinitas unius divinitatis, Pater et Filius et Spiritus Sanctus. Illam Ecclesian congregat, quam Dominus in tribus posuit.[83]

In his *Adversus Praxeam*, Tertullian presents his major theology of Trinity. After repeating many questions on the Trinity in which other scholars denied the Trinity, Tertullian concludes: "Ubique teneo unam substantiam in tribus cohaerentibus" (Everywhere [in all of my writings] I maintain that there are three cohering realities in [only] one substance).[84]

Tertullian deserves the praises mentioned above and he has clearly stated his Trinitarian positions. Quasten, however, reminds us that "Tertullian could not shake off entirely the influence of subordinationism. In chapter 7 of *Adversus Praxeam*, Tertullian presents the Father as the one and only true eternal God, and the Son is generated by God, and thus the Son is not eternal."[85] In chapter 8 of *Adversus Praxeam*, Tertullian presents a lengthy and beautiful passage in which he describes the Son's going out from the Father, to a beam of light which comes out from the Father. However, this lengthy passage strongly indicates that the Son is subordinate, not equal, to the Father. Tertullian was also the first Christian scholar to use the Latin term *Persona* to distinguish the Father, Son and Holy Spirit.

> Quaecunqe ergo substantia Sermonic fuit, illam dico personam, et illi nomen Filii vindico; et dum Filium agnosco, secundum a Patre defendo.[86]

The Latin word *persona* is a "speaking through something." God the Father generated the Son through a gradual process, beginning with the emanation (ἐνδιάθητος), the internal development of the Logos, and the utterance (προφορικός), the external development of the Logos which came at the time of the incarnation. Quasten offers several citations in which Tertullian is presenting his theology of Trinity. In some passages,

---

83. Tertullian, *Liber de Pudicitia*, ch. 11; see Migne, *Patrologia Latina*, vol. 2, *Tertulliani Opera Omnia*, 1080.

84. Tertullian, *Liber Adversus Praxeam*, ch. 12; see Migne, *Patrologia Latina*, 2:192.

85. Tertullian, *Liber Adversus Praxeam*, ch. 7, 184–86.

86. Tertullian, *Liber Adversus Praxeam*, ch. 6, 186.

Tertullian seems to say that the three "persons" have only one "nature," while in other passages he seems to say that only the Father is truly God, while the Logos as well as the Spirit emanate from this one God.[87] The subordination of the Son and the Spirit to the Father is a major indication that the divinization of Jesus was not totally accepted by Christian theologians in the third century. However, Tertullian's Trinitarian language was used by the bishops at the Council of Nicea in 325 CE in a major way, and his indecision was set to one side.

Hippolytus of Rome

The life of Hippolytus of Rome (d. 235 CE) is filled with "ups" and "downs." He was a priest in Rome, even though he was probably not of Roman extraction. His Greek writings were unbelievably clear and well-defined. He thought in Greek and spoke in Greek. In his writings on the Trinity, he rejected in a very clear theological way both the modalism and the patri-passionism of Noetus and Sabellius. Vis-à-vis Noetus, he wrote:

> God, subsisting alone, and having nothing contemporaneous with himself, determined to create the world. . . . For us, then, it is sufficient simply to know that there was nothing contemporaneous with God. . . . There appeared another beside Himself. But when I say another (ἕτερος), I do not mean that there are two Gods. There is but one power, which is from the All, from whom cometh this Power, the Word. And this is the mind (λόγος) which came forth into the world and was manifest as the Son (παῖς) of God.[88]

In the above citation one can see that Hyppolitus defended the Logos in a subordinate way. There is only one God. Jesus is indeed holy but not divine. In the text of his *Apostolic Tradition*, which is focused on liturgical worship, Hippolytus gives us a ritual of baptism in great detail. In this ritual, one finds strong belief in a God who loves those who are baptized. He is not presenting a theology per se; rather, in his ritual one sees that baptism is a sacrament which in a secondary way divinizes a person and "christofies" a person. There is a clear sense of spirituality in Hippolytus presentation of baptism.

---

87. Quasten, *Patrology*, 2:324–28.
88. Hippolytus, *Contra Noetus*, 10–11.

Quasten presents an analysis of Hippolytus's Christology, soteriology, ecclesiology, and the remission of sins. Even though, Jesus is not divine, Hippolytus relates in a spiritual way his Christology to ecclesiology, soteriology, and to the remission of sins. Hippolytus, even though rejecting the divinization of Jesus, seems to have returned to the Roman Christian church prior to his death in 236/237 CE. Today, he is called "Saint Hippolytus."

Novatian

Novatian was a Roman presbyter who opposed the election to the episcopacy of Rome in 251 CE. He was also a well-educated individual. He was the first theologian in Rome to write in Latin, and his first Latin work was *De Trinitate*. Quasten describes Novatian's theology of the Trinity as very exact and systematic, and also very complete and extensive.[89] He seems to have written his work on the Trinity prior to his renunciation of the Roman Christian church. Although he never mentions the term Trinity, his entire work deals with the understanding that God is Trinitarian. His treatment of the Trinity is much more complete and extensive than any prior presentation on the Triune God. He emphasizes this issue as follows:

> The rule of truth requires that we believe, first, in God the Father and Lord Almighty, that is to say the most perfect founder of all things.[90]

Novatian emphasizes that the one and only God is the one whom we call "Father," and Novatian presents God as eternal, unbegotten, and unknowable. There is, therefore, only one God. Jesus, the Logos, is in the Father and therefore called son, but the Logos is not the same as the "one God." The Logos comes from the Father but is not the same as the Father. The Logos is not human or angelic; rather, the Logos different from all other creatures and different from the Father. Novatian again and again states that there is only one God, and he also states the Jesus, the Son of God, is in God and from God, but is not the only One God. Again, one sees that Jesus, the Son of God, is subordinate to the God whom we call Father.

---

89. See Quasten, *Patrology*, 2:217.
90. Novatian, *De Trinitate*.

Origen

Origen (ca. 185–ca. 254 CE) became one of the strongest patristic scholars. Quasten's praise for Origen's intellectual talent and his deep faith in Jesus has been repeated by many scholars. He was born in Alexandria, the son of well-to-do Christian parents.[91] In 202 CE, his father, Leonidas, was martyred during the persecution of the emperor Severus. In his teen years, Origen began his academic studies at the school of Alexandria. Bishop Demetrius of Alexandria put the eighteen-year-old Origen into the school as its director, a post he held from 203 to 232. From 234 to 250, Origen was the director of similar school in Caesarea. Origen was a man of spotless character, encyclopedic learning, and one of the most original thinkers the world has ever seen.[92]

In the third century CE, the Trinitarian doctrine was beginning to be organized in a theologically detailed way. Origen's volume *First Principles* (Περὶ ἀρχῶν) was the first manual of Christian theology. In his philosophical themes, Origen used Platonic philosophy and in his theological themes he used Aristotelian writings. His theological teaching on God was similar to that of Justin, namely that the bridge between God and all others is the Logos. Both scholars referred to the Logos as a "second God." Nonetheless, Origen was accused by Jerome of subordinating Jesus to the Father, while Gregory Thaumaturgos and Athanasius cleared him of all suspicion.[93]

In his writings, Origen defended his theological view of the Father-Son relationship. In several places he presented God the Father as superior to both the Son and the Spirit. He writes:

> We, who say that the visible world is under the government of Him who created all things, do thereby declare that the Son is not mightier than the Father, but inferior to him.[94]

---

91. Origen was born ca. 185 CE and his major work, Περὶ ἀρχῶν, was written in 220–230 CE. His writings are influenced strongly by Ammonius Saccas, a late second-century professor and the founder of Neoplatonism. In a strong way, Origen argues his positions on the basis of Platonic philosophy. Quasten summarizes the importance of Περὶ ἀρχῶν in *Patrology*, 2:57–61.

92. Quasten, *Patrology*, 2:37.

93. See Quasten, *Patrology*, 2:77. Quasten also states that both Ferdinand Prat (1857–1938 CE) and Théodore de Régnon (1831–1893 CE) affirm that Origen's theology of the Trinity is not subordinationism.

94. Origen, *Contra Celsum*, ch. 8, 15; for English, see Quasten, *Patrology*, 2:79. For Greek text, see Origen, Κατά Κέλσον, Minge, *Patrologia*, 11:1557.

> Σαφῶς γὰρ ἥμεις, οἱ λέγοντες τοῦ πάντα κτίσαντος καὶ τὸν αἰσθητὸν κόσμον εἶναι, φαμὲν τὸν Υἱὸν οὐκ ἰσχυρότερον τοῦ Πατρὸς ἀλλ᾽ ὑποδεύτερον.

In the *First Principles*, Origen stresses the uniqueness of the Father and at the same time he stresses that the Son of God is the image of God.

> The existence of the Son is generated by Him [the Father]. For this point must above all others be maintained by those who allow nothing to be unbegotten, i.e., unborn, save God the Father only. . . . Our Saviour, therefore, is the image of invisible God, inasmuch as compared with the Father himself He is truth; and as compared with us, to whom He reveals the Father, He is the image by which we come to the knowledge of the Father, whom no one knows save the son, and he to whom the Son is pleased to reveal Him.[95]

In the writings of Origen, the Logos was distinct from the Father, even though the Logos was also eternal. The Arians of his time were saying that "there was a time when he [the Logos-Son] was not" (ἠν ἦ ὅτε οὐκ ἦν) but Origen wrote that there was "no time when He was not" (οὐκ ἔςτιν ὅτε οὐκ ἦν).[96]

Origen also states both the Son of God and the Holy Spirit were divine. Quasten expresses Origen's position on the Trinity as follows:

> From this and similar passages it can be easily be understood why Origen has been accused of subordinationism. It is quite evident that he presupposes a hierarchical order in the Trinity and regards the Holy Spirit as ranking even below the Son.[97]

Origen's understanding of God is based on the absolute and unbegotten Father; God alone is unbegotten ἀγέννητος. Quasten explains this in a clear way: "God the Father is as an absolute being incomprehensible. He becomes comprehensible through the Logos who is Christ."[98] As mentioned above, some patristic scholars have considered Origen's Trinitarian theology as subordinationism while other scholars deny this claim. In Origen's commentary on John's Gospel, he writes:

---

95. Origen, *De Principiis*, I, v. 11.
96. Quasten, *Patrology*, 2:78.
97. Quasten, *Patrology*, 79.
98. Quasten, *Patrology*, 2:75.

> We say that the Savior and the Holy Spirit are without comparison and are very much superior to all things that are made, but also that the Father is even more above them than they are themselves above creatures even the highest.[99]

Other theologians had begun with the Logos, focusing on the relationship of the Logos and the Father. For Origen, God the Father is first. He writes: "God, therefore, is . . . an uncompounded intellectual nature, admitting within Himself no addition of any kind."[100]

Concluding Observations

The "Origenistic Controversy" erupted in the final years of the fourth century, almost one hundred years after Origen's death. Consequently, there is a problem with Origen's own theology and there is a problem with the major theologians in the "Origenistic Controversy." The theology of the divinization of Jesus in the Origenistic writings goes far beyond the writings of Origen himself. During this century, there were Christian bishops and theological scholars who accepted the divinity of Jesus, but there were other Christian bishops and theological scholars who did not accept the divinity of Jesus and/or the Trinitarian God.

1. From the second century CE to the end of the eighth century CE, the theological issues on the divinization of Jesus continued to divide almost all the major Christian churches. In 451 CE, the Council of Chalcedon took place, and at the conclusion of the council, five autocephalous churches removed themselves from all Chalcedonian churches. These five churches came to be called "Oriental Orthodox." The five churches were and are the churches of Egypt, Syria, Armenia, India, and Ethiopia.[101]

---

99. Origen, *In John*, 13, 25, cited by Quasten, *Patrology*, 2:79.

100. Origen, *De Principiis*, I, 1, 6. See also Marguerite Harl, "Recherches sur le Περὶ ἀρχῶν d'Origène en vue d'une nouvelle édition: la division en chapitres," in *Studia Patristica* 3 (1967) 57–67.

101. Pelikan states that with the Council of Chalcedon, the Trinitarian debates had formally ended, but with some remaining questions on the Holy Spirit. He writes: "The climax of the doctrinal development of the early church was the dogma of the Trinity. In this dogma the church vindicated the monotheism that had been at issue in its conflicts with Judaism, and it came to terms with the concept of the Logos, over which it had disputed with paganism." In actuality, the Trinitarian debates have continued down to today, as we have seen in chapters 1 and 2. Pelikan, *Emergence of the Catholic*

2. When the Christian world moved into the second century CE, most Christian leaders did not believe that Jesus was divine. As the second century moved forward, there were a few theological presentations in which the divinity of Jesus was explained. However, there were still many Christian leaders and scholars who did not accept the divinization of Jesus. In the third century CE, the tension between Christians who believed that Jesus was divine and Christians who denied his divinization became very divisive. Throughout the many years when Christians were divided over the issue of the divinity of Jesus, one must realize that the material from both sides presented only "human" discussions on the divinity or non-divinity of Jesus. Whether the nature of God is monotheistic or tri-theistic is a human question. The theological focus in these discussions is not the cause of a Trinitarian God. Rather, it is only a new human theology of the divine nature.[102] In the Jewish world from Moses onward, YHWH was worshiped as the one and only God. The followers of Jesus in the first century CE continued to worship YHWH. A Trinitarian theology, which is a human way of thinking, began to be expressed theologically in the second century CE.

3. None of the authors mentioned above presented a comprehensive "theology" of the Trinity. The authors of the Gospel of John as well as Clement of Rome, Ignatius of Antioch, and Barnabas used the terms "Father" and "Son" but the relationship between Father and Son was not stated in a clear theological way. Both Justin and Clement of Alexandria stated that the essence of God is totally unknown. Marcion simply denied the Christian Trinity but he was not Gnostic. Quasten has a detailed analysis of Marcion's theology of God.[103]

4. I will return to the two positions on the Trinity which are found in Justin and Clement of Alexandria. If, as both of them state, God is totally unknowable, could we today also maintain that God is totally

---

Tradition, 172.

102. The early theologies of the Trinity were developed by Christian scholars who were either Greek or Latin authors. If these authors had been Indian or Chinese scholars, a totally different linguistic theology would have been used. There is a major philosophical and terminological division between the Greek and Latin languages and the Indian and Chinese languages. See the detailed description of both the Indian and Chinese languages as well as their individual difference between these languages and the Greek and Latin languages in the writings of Hajime Nakamura.

103. Quasten, *Patrology*, 1:268–72.

unknowable? If God is infinite, would not God be unknowable? This does not mean that we have no knowledge of God. But it does mean that in faith and only in faith do we believe that there is a God. Denominationally, Christian communities may have "glimpses of God," but no individual religion can claim its "glimpse of God" is the only comprehensive understanding of God.

Various religions, including Christianity and Islam, are described in and through a given language, but the major languages of these human men and women differ in a radical way from each other. This differentiation can be seen in today's contrast of languages.

6

Trinitarian Theologies from the Beginning of the Fourth Century to the End of the Eighth Century

CHAPTER 5 FOCUSED ON the beginning of a Trinitarian theology. This took place during the second and third centuries. During these two hundred years, Christian leaders and scholars presented both a "pro" and a "con" explanation of the triune God.[1] Prior to the second century, there had never been a theology of a Trinitarian God, and as a result in the second and third centuries, there were Christian scholars and leaders who rejected a theology of a Triune God, and there were major Christian scholars and leaders who accepted a theology of a Triune God.[2]

Theological discussions take place within a political framework, and the Christian communities in the second and third centuries lived in a

---

1. MacCulloch's *Christianity*, ch. 4, "Boundaries Defined (50 CE–300)." In this chapter, MacCulloch focuses on the early development of the Christian religion. In these boundaries, the divinity of Jesus was both affirmed and denied, and, as we have seen, Roman rule killed Christians whether they believed in the divinity of Jesus or not. MacCulloch mentions on p. 112 that 85 percent of second-century Christian texts of which today's Christian sources make mention are now missing.

2. Christians, in these centuries, did not deny the existence of God; their belief in God was central to their faith. In the opening decades of the second century CE, the theology of Jesus' divinization was just beginning. The theological divinization of the Holy Spirit began to be included in theological presentations from mid-century onward. The addition of the Holy Spirit is simply mentioned in the final words of the Nicene Creed: καὶ εἰς τὸ ἅγιον πνεῦμα.

time in which the Roman government wanted to exterminate Christians. It is amazing how these early Christian leaders and theologians managed to maintain not only Christian belief but also Christian writings on a theology of God.

The emperor Diocletian (285–305 CE) had divided the Roman Empire into four prefectures, two in the east and two in the west. In the east, Diocletian was the emperor, and Maximian was the "co-augustus" in the west. In the east, Galerius was the co-emperor and Constantius was the co-augustus in the west.

In 321 CE, Constantine became the emperor of the entire Roman Empire. Because the empire was no longer divided into east/west, the Christian church also began a time of unity. However, it was a frail Christian unity since there were several theologies of the Trinity, as well as several theological rejections of a Trinitarian God. This theological disunity continued down to the end of the ninth century CE. In this chapter, I do not go into details. Many other historians and theologians have written lengthy and highly detailed accounts of all the key theological situations which took place during these six hundred years. In chapter 6, my focus is on the writings of important scholars and church leaders, some of whom continued to reject a Trinitarian God, while other important scholars and church leaders maintained a Trinitarian God. I have divided this chapter into nine parts, with a tenth part for concluding thoughts.

THE ROMAN EMPIRE BECAME A UNIFIED EAST-WEST EMPIRE THROUGH THE WARFARE OF CONSTANTINE

Newman Eberhardt, in the first volume of his history of the church *Ancient and Medieval History*, presents the main issues in the warfare of Constantine.[3] In 306 CE, Constantine's father, Constantius, died in York, England. His troops immediately elected Constantine as the western Roman emperor. Diocletian had resigned in 301 CE, and the selection of Constantine as the western emperor was at first disregarded by many others in the tetrarchy. But the military was in favor of Constantine. In 307 CE, Maxentius was chosen to be the western emperor, with Constantine as his second-in-command. Both Constantine and his army refused to accept Maxentius. Constantine and Maxentius met as enemies at the

---

3. Eberhardt, *Summary of Catholic History*, 1:165–70.

Milvian Bridge. In the battle, Maxentius was killed and Constantine became the sole emperor in the western empire.

The eastern emperor was the pagan Licinius, and the two major emperors despised each other. In July 324 CE, two battles took place, one at Adrianople and a second at Chrysopolis. Constantine's army won both. Licinius was later executed due to a conspiracy against the west, and Constantine became the ruler of the entire Roman Empire from 324 to 337 CE.

His openness to Christianity, therefore, was felt in both the west and the east. However, MacCulloch states a very important aspect to Constantine's rule. He writes:

> Constantine has often been seen as undergoing a "conversion" to Christianity. This is an unfortunate word, because it has all sorts of modern overtones that conceal the fact that Constantine's religious experience was like nothing which would today be recognized as a conversion, ... Constantine had learned enough about the jealous nature of this God to make the mistake of trying to merge imperial and divine identities, but their association was still intimate. Most obviously, and for reasons which will probably remain hidden to us, the Emperor associated the Christian God with military successes which had destroyed all his rivals, from Maxentius to Licinius.[4]

MacCulloch challenges those who see Constantine as a devout person on his way to being a Christian. Constantine, MacCulloch states, has something which is more personal. First of all, Jesus was not gentle, nor meek, nor mild. For Constantine, Jesus was not someone who counseled his followers to forgive their enemies seventy times seven. Rather, God, for Constantine, was a God of battles. Constantine was a military leader and a ruthless politician. He moved his central residence out of Rome and he established Constantinople as simply "The City."

In the first two decades of the fourth century, the issue of a divine Trinity became a major source of division within the Christian communities. In 313 CE, Constantine called for a Christian council which was to be held at Rome; however, the Donatists refused to attend. Nonetheless, a small local council was held, even though Constantine was not in attendance.[5] In 314 CE, Constantine called for another Christian

---

4. MacCulloch, *Christianity*, 190–91.

5. The emperor Constantine in 313 CE called upon Miltiades, the bishop of Rome, to preside over a council in Rome. The three-day council began on Oct. 2, 313

council, this time in Arles. This synod was convened on August 1, 314 CE. Constantine, since he was in Thrace with one of his armies, was not at the council. However, he had personally arranged the major details for the council. Thirty-three western bishops were in attendance, but we have no documentary evidence of the proceedings of this council. We can say that the council leaders declared that all Donatist bishops were illegitimate. Constantine called for yet another council, which was to be held in Alexandria in 320 CE,[6] but this council became only a synod of Egyptians. By 324 CE, one could say that there was one emperor, but one also had to say that Christian church remained a strongly divided church.

THE MAIN ISSUE OF THE CHRISTIAN CHURCH FROM THE EARLY FOURTH CENTURY TO THE LATE EIGHTH CENTURY: THE NAMING OF GOD AS "FATHER" AND AS "SON"

In chapters 3, 4, and 5, I have presented in great detail the earliest data in which God has been referred to as "Father." We have seen that in the Jewish religion, God is called Father but only in a poetic, descriptive, and metaphorical way. Even today, in Jewish hymns and prayers, God is still referred to as Father but only in a poetic way. In the Christian religion, the writings of Paul and the Synoptic authors, the name "God" frequently refer to God as "Father" but again only in a poetic, descriptive, and metaphorical way. From the second century CE onward, a movement in the Christian church slowly began to take place. Jesus began to be considered the actual Son of God the Father. This theological view was not poetic. Rather, it was a total revision of these poetic words as found in the second and third chapters of this volume. The "poetic, descriptive, and metaphorical" naming of God as Father and Jesus as His Son slowly became a divisive issue since in the early decades of the second century some Christian leaders and scholars began to speak and write about the divine Sonship of Jesus. They simply stated God the Father had a divine Son. Such a statement was not well theologized until Justin, Clement

---

CE in the Lateran palace. Eighteen bishops attended the council, and Miltiades was the convener. The members of this council declared that the reigning bishop of Carthage, Caecilian, was legitimate, but they also declared that the theology of the Trinity, which the Donatists maintained, was heretical.

6. The dating of this council is not clear. Some authors defend 320, while other scholars defend 321 and even 323 CE.

of Alexandria, and Tertullian began to explain the theology of a Triune God, and they did so in an affirmative and a negative way.

Those who accepted the divinization of Jesus believed that the Father and Son have one and the same nature; and yet the Father and Son are individualized persons. From an intellectual standpoint, second-century CE Christian scholars considered human nature as essentially the same for all human beings, and they also believed that each "person" was singular and unique.

Bruce Metzger has put together a very important essay on "The Language of the New Testament," and he centers on the ways that biblical scholars today should read the Hebrew texts of the *Tanakh* and the Greek text of the New Testament. His views on this issue are really central to my essay which you are now reading.[7] Many words in the *Tanakh* and the New Testament have different meanings from the ordinary modern translations of many passages. Metzger offers us several examples of certain words which have not been well translated into English.

Metzger gives the following answer as regards "Koine Greek" such as the Greek term ἡλικίαν. This Greek word is used in Matt 6:7 and Luke 12:25. In the King James Bible and the English Revised Bible, the word ἡλικίαν is translated as "taller." The true meaning of ἡλικίαν in the first century Jewish world did not refer this word to a person's stature. Rather, Metzger states that in the Hebrew writings of the first century CE, the translation of ἡλικίαν is a reference to one's age.[8] Today, the English translation of ἡλικίαν in Luke 12:25 as found in *The Interpreter's Bible* is a reference to one's age: "Can any of you, however much you worry, add a single cubit to your span of life (ἡλικίαν)?" The word is not about one's height but about the length of one's life.

Metzger clarifies other biblical terms, such as ἀπέχουσιν (Matt 6:2, 5, 16),[9] ἀρραβῶνα (2 Cor 1:22),[10] etc. Metzger offers many examples in which scholars today have restated the original meaning of many terms as they were used in the early Hebraic and Greek biblical texts. These words have one meaning for a New Testament text which was used in the first two centuries. In later centuries, these same words were often translated into

---

7. Metzger, "Language of the New Testament," 7:43–59, esp. sections A, B, and C.

8. New Jerusalem Bible. In the revised New American Bible (Oxford Press, 1995) the translation of Luke 12:25 reads: "Can any of you by worrying add a moment to your life-span?"

9. Metzger, "Language of the New Testament," 54.

10. Metzger, "Language of the New Testament," 54.

English using different meanings. There are contemporary meanings, while in the New Testament we have Greek words which in the first and second centuries had different meaning.

When I read Metzger's essay, my mind went back to the naming of God as "Father" and the naming of Jesus as "Son of God." In the Hebrew world from Exodus down to today, YHWH has been called Father (אָב) but this naming of God is poetic, descriptive, and metaphorical. In the Christian world, from 98 CE onward, God began to be called "Father" but not in a poetic way. This change came about because a few early Christians believed that Jesus was the divine Son of God the Father. At first, a few second-century Christians gave new meanings to the titles "God the Father" and "God the Son." God had been called Father in a poetic way. When Jesus was beginning to be divinized, both names—Father and Son—were no longer poetic. Both Father and Son had one and the same divine nature, and the Father and Son were two divine persons.

Divinizing the very essence of God as "the divine Father" and divinizing the very essence of Jesus as "the divine Son of God" changed the meaning of the term "God." In the *Tanakh*, God was never referred to as a divine Father. Poetically, YHWH was called "Father" but only a few times. In the *Tanakh*, YHWH was also referred to as "Father" indirectly when authors used the phrase "sons of YHWH," but this phrase was also poetic, descriptive, and metaphorical.

In the Pauline letters and in the three Synoptic Gospels, YHWH was called "Father" frequently, and Jesus was called "Son of God" or "Son of the Father." However, Raymond Brown's comment, which was stated above, qualifies the situation when he writes that no New Testament passage states precisely that the Son coexisted from all eternity with the Father.[11]

Some contemporary Christian authors have stated that the doctrine of the Trinity has been defined in the New Testament. For example, in 1964, the Second Vatican Council began, and in the same year, Joseph Dalmau published his essay on the divinity of Jesus in the *Summa Sacra Theologiae*.[12] He writes:

> Trinitatis personarum in unitate divinae essentiae probatur ex N.T.[13]

---

11. Brown, "Aspects of New Testament Thought," 1359n22.
12. Dalmau and Sagüés, "De Deo Uno et Trino," 2:228.
13. Dalmau and Sagüés, "De Deo Uno et Trino," 298.

> The Trinity of persons in the unity of the divine essence has been proved by [texts] in the New Testament.

Dalmau devotes thirty pages to prove his thesis, and in his proof he cites only New Testament passages. Dalmau and Brown are at opposite theological positions, and there are many other Catholic theologians who could be cited as representatives of one or the other side. In Christianity, the use of terms divine Paternity and divine Sonship slowly took place from 200 CE and became more and more divisive down to 800 CE. In these centuries, there were seven ecumenical councils of the Christian church and in each of these councils, the issue of Jesus' divinity was the primary topic for the members of these councils.

The fact that there were seven ecumenical councils indicates that Christians were not unified on the issue of the two names for God: Father and Son. In the following pages, I will present the Trinitarian problem vis-à-vis the names Father and Son which each council seriously considered. The focus of these ecumenical councils was not on the existence of God; rather they were focused on naming God "Father and Son." In each council, the theological explanation of the essence of God as "Father" and as "Son" was questioned. These ecumenical councils did not focus on the existence of God; rather, the bishops focused on the two names for God: Father and Son.

325 CE: THE COUNCIL OF NICEA; THE FIRST ECUMENICAL COUNCIL

Although the emperor Constantine was not a Christian, his position at this first ecumenical council helped in a very strong way to unify in some degree the eastern and western churches. Constantine, who was still nonbaptized, called and convened the council in 325 CE. Bishop Hosius of Cordova was the emperor's advisor, and Constantine asked him to preside over the Council of Nicea. Constantine, however, could take over the presidency whenever he wished.

The divinity of Jesus was the centering theme of the council, and the final conciliar text states the divinity of Jesus as follows:

> We believe in one God, the Father Almighty . . . and in one Lord Jesus Christ, the only begotten Son of the Father that is from the substance of the Father, God from God, Light from Light, true

God from true God, begotten not made, of one substance with the Father.[14]

Πιστεύομεν εἰς ἕνα Θεόν πατέρα παντοχράτορα . . . καὶ εἰς ἕνα κύριον Ἰησοῦν Χριστόν, τὸν υἱὸν τοῦ Θεοῦ . . . ὁμοούσιον τῷ πατρί. [Important Greek passages.]

However, the above conciliar statement of Nicea was not totally clear. The bishops stated that the Father and the Son were of the same nature, "homoousios." What the bishops at the council did not do, however, was to offer an explanation of how the "Father" and the "Son" are different even though they had one and the same nature. Moreover, there was only a single phrase regarding the Holy Spirit, namely "and in the Holy Spirit" (καὶ εἰς τὸ ἅγιον πνεῦμα). After the Council of Nicea, the Arian doctrine continued to have considerable support, especially in Alexandria.[15]

The majority of the Nicene bishops ratified the conciliar statements but some bishops did so in a hesitant way. Many contemporary historians have stated that some of the Arian-minded bishops voted yes for the final statements, but they repudiated their approval when they returned to their episcopal sees. They protested that force had been used to obtain their compliance. Almost all of these Arian bishops denigrated the integrity of the Nicene Council. Because of this, the so-called "Catholic victory" was not totally realized. From 328 CE onward, the conclusions of the Nicene Council were strongly questioned, and because of this questioning, a second ecumenical council, the first Council of Constantinople, was called to clarify the Nicene positions.

381 CE: THE FIRST COUNCIL OF CONSTANTINOPLE; THE SECOND ECUMENICAL COUNCIL

The First Council of Constantinople, which was basically a council of the eastern church, remedied some of the unclear issues of the Nicene Council.[16] The conciliar bishops removed the anathemas at the end of the

---

14. Greek text, Denzinger, *Enchridion Symbolorum*, n. 125, p. 52; English text from the *Catechism of the Catholic Church*, 49. Cf. Dalmau and Sagüés, "De Deo uno et trino," 228–251.

15. Quasten, *Patrology*, 3:20–21.

16. It should be noted that Constantius II, the eastern Roman emperor, held a council in Constantinople in 360 CE. He did this in opposition to the decisions of the Nicene Council. This new council reaffirmed the Arian view that Jesus was only ὅμοιος

Nicene Creed. They also inserted a lengthy description of the Holy Spirit, who had been simply mentioned by the Nicene bishops, namely: "and [we believe] in the Holy Spirit." Contemporary scholars, such as Robert Krieg, indicate that many changes were made in the Nicene Creed after the council but the names of the people who did this are unknown. Krieg mentions that there are a few scholars today who imply that the entire creed was anonymously written after the council. The historian Newman C. Eberhardt explains the situation as follows:

> The First Council of Constantinople was not ecumenical in its inception; it was intended to be merely the Eastern portion of a general episcopal meeting. . . . The first explicit information available of its acceptance as normative is its confirmation by the general Council of Chalcedon in 451 CE.[17]

The Nicene-Constantinopolitan Creed states, in a very clear way, that Jesus was both divine and human. These councils and their subsequent creeds, however, did not end the differing factions in the Christian church regarding the Trinity.[18] In the latter part of the seventh century CE, Arianism was still a major issue in the early church.

431 CE: THE COUNCIL OF EPHESUS; THE THIRD ECUMENICAL COUNCIL

In 428, the Nestorian crisis took place. The Nestorians believed that there were two distinct persons in Jesus, one divine and the other human. This twofold understanding of person contradicted the teaching of the fourth-century church regarding three issues. First, if there are two persons in Jesus, then the human person has no ability at all to be the savior of the world. Like all other humans, the human person of Jesus could not accomplish divine actions. Second, if there are two persons, the human

---

and not ὁμοούσιος. The conciliar bishops were almost all from the east. The council was also deemed heretical by many other Christian churches. It reminds us, however, that Arianism was a very strong theological movement and it remained so down to the seventh century.

17. Eberhardt, *Summary of Catholic History*, 1:203–4.

18. In the fourth century, several major theologians wrote on the Trinity: St. Athanasius (ca. 295–373 CE); St. Hilary (ca. 315–ca. 367 CE); St. Basil the Great (ca. 330–379 CE); St. Gregory Nanzianzen (ca. 330–ca. 390 CE); St. Gregory of Nyssa (ca. 335–ca. 390 CE); and St. John Chrysostom (ca. 349–407). The Trinitarian theologies of these scholars are still part of today's Christian theology.

person of Jesus is not present in the Eucharist. Third, if there are two persons in Jesus, Mary was not the mother of God; she was simply the mother of the human Jesus.

The Council of Ephesus denounced all three opinions. The Council of Ephesus had been summoned by the Emperor Theodosius II to settle the problems between the Alexandrian and Antiochene scholars vis-à-vis Christology. Nestorius, the bishop of Constantinople, did not attend the council; rather he was eventually exiled to the Great Oasis of Upper Egypt.

451 CE: THE COUNCIL OF CHALCEDON; THE FOURTH ECUMENICAL COUNCIL

The Council of Chalcedon was convoked by the emperor Marcian (450–457), in an effort to unite the eastern and western churches.[19] The immediate cause for calling the council was the theological positions presented by Eutyches (d. 454 CE). Eutyches taught that there was only one nature in the incarnate Jesus, the divine nature. The divine nature had "swallowed up" the human nature of Jesus. The emperor Marcian insisted that the bishops convoke a council against the teachings of Eutyches. At the council, the bishops declared that Christ was to be known as one person or hypostasis, and was "to be known in two natures, without division or separation, confusion or change." The phrase "to be known" was ambiguous. Are the two natures only to be "known"? The text does not say that the two natures "act" in two different ways. The conciliar decision, therefore, could be interpreted in a dyophysite way (two natures) or in a monophysite way (one nature). This left the church open to further theological divisions.

Once again, we can see that in these early centuries the church's teaching was not unified. The Chalcedonian doctrine could be interpreted in a strongly dyophysite way which was central to Roman and Antiochene theological teaching. But it also could be interpreted through an emphasis on the one person, the Logos, which was central to most eastern church communities.

In the Western, or Roman, Church today, many leaders and scholars may think that "their" church is the only correct Catholic Church.

---

19. Pope Leo I was not in favor of a church council but he acquiesced to Emperor Marcian's summons for a council at Ephesus in 451 CE.

However, even though there were several acceptable theologies in the early centuries, the Roman Church at that time may have been considered the major church, but other churches maintained their own theologies, and especially their own Christologies.[20]

553 CE: THE SECOND COUNCIL OF CONSTANTINOPLE; THE FIFTH ECUMENICAL COUNCIL

The second Council of Constantinople centered on the Nestorian position of "Mary as the mother of the human Jesus, but not the mother of God." This council was convened by the emperor Justinian. The council condemned Theodore of Mopsuestia, Theodoret of Cyrrhus, and Ibas of Edessa. It affirmed that Mary was the mother of the human Jesus and also the mother of the divine Logos. In many ways, the position of Mary simply complicated the meaning of the two natures of Jesus, but it also embellished human life, especially the lives of women.

Raymond Brown has written a book on the virginal conception of Jesus. He is a biblical scholar, and he focuses on the biblical data which is found in the Gospels of Luke and Matthew.[21] The position of Theodore of Mopsuestia, Theodoret of Cyrrhus, and Ibas of Edessa was based on Nestorianism. Pope Vigilius (537–555 CE) tended to agree with this position, but slightly before his death he accepted the condemnation of the three men just mentioned. In the fifth century, the Christian church was theologically divided, and in many ways it has remained divided down to today.

In this dispute on the virginity of Mary, it is the divinization of Jesus which is central. Is Jesus truly God or is he truly God and Man or is he only human?

---

20. See Eugene TeSelle, "Council of Chalcedon," in Patte, *Cambridge Dictionary of Christianity*, 183.

21. Brown, *Virginal Conception*; also appendix 4 in *Birth of the Messiah*, 517–33. In this second book, there is a lengthy bibliography in which many books on this subject are listed.

680–681 CE: THE THIRD COUNCIL OF CONSTANTINOPLE; THE SIXTH ECUMENICAL COUNCIL

The Third Council of Constantinople was convoked by the emperor Constantine IV in 680 CE. It centered on the issue of "two wills" in Jesus, the divine will and the human will. In 638 CE, Heraclius had promulgated an Ἐκθεσίς in which he stated that Jesus had only one will, namely a divine will. His followers were called Monothelitists, which means that Jesus had only one will. In 638 and 639 CE, the episcopal synods in Constantinople accepted the position of the emperor. In the sixth ecumenical council, which was held at Constantinople in 680–681 CE, the bishops condemned Monotheletism and they declared that Jesus had two wills, one divine and one human, as well as two natures, one divine and one human. Four Patriarchs of Constantinople and one former Roman pope, Honorius, were condemned for their teaching that Jesus had only one will, a divine will.

Once again, we see that the Catholic Church remained divided, particularly in and through theological positions, national positions, and episcopal positions. Many Catholics today might say that "there is only one holy catholic Church." From the above brief listing of the early church's ecumenical councils, one could state that from 325 CE down to 681 CE both the Trinitarian issue and the issue of the divinity of Jesus continued to cause serious and major divisions within the Christian churches. In 681 CE, the divinization of Jesus remained center stage. If Jesus had two wills, how can one say that the human Jesus was truly divinized?

OTHER MAJOR CHURCH DOCUMENTS FROM 683 CE TO 800 CE

In the closing years of the seventh century, there were several major instances in which the divinity of Jesus continued to be denied, even though Monothelitism had been condemned by the Second Council of Constantinople (553 CE). The Fourteenth Council of Toledo (684 CE), as well as the Fifteenth Council of Toledo (688 CE) and the Sixteenth Council of Toledo (693 CE) focused clearly on the issue of the two natures and two wills in Christ.[22] In 785 CE, there is a letter of Pope Hadrian I in which he condemned the position that the human Jesus was "adopted" in order to be called the "Son of the Father."[23] In a similar way, in 794 the bishops of Frankfurt and Maine held a synod and the French bishops sent an official letter to the bishops of Spain in which they asserted that Jesus was a "natural Son of God," not an "adopted Son of God."[24] In 796, the bishops at Friuli approved of a conciliar statement on the divine Trinity and on Jesus Christ who was not "an adopted Son of God."[25] From the first decades of 800 CE, the theological issue of the divinity and humanity of Jesus finally became an acceptable and basic issue of the Catholic faith in the Western world.

A major and contemporary source for the divided "church and state" from 300 CE to the end of the seventh century CE is found in MacCulloch's volume *Christianity: The First Three Thousand Years*. Chapter 6 is entitled "The Imperial Church (300–451)," chapter 7 is entitled "Defying Chalcedon: Asia and Africa (451–622)." In these centuries, theologies of the Trinity by and large used the terms: God the Father and God the Son, but in many instances Jesus was not truly God, since he was only united to God in a special way.[26]

In the nineteenth and twentieth centuries, the major theologians of Anglicanism, Protestantism, and Roman Catholicism focused more strongly on the oneness of God rather than on a Trinitarian God. The revival of Trinitarian theology began with Karl Barth and Karl Rahner. Barth edited an eleven-volume work on sacred theology. In these volumes, his Trinitarian theology was lengthy and detailed.

In Karl Rahner's writings, his longest explanation of the Trinity is found in his essay "Bemerkungen zum dogmatischen Traktat '*De Trinitate*,'" in which he devotes thirty-three pages to Trinitarian theology. The

---

22. See Denzinger, *Enchridion Symbolorum*, nn. 564–75, pp. 190–95.

23. Denzinger, *Enchridion Symbolorum*, nn. 610–11, p. 204.

24. Denzinger, *Enchridion Symbolorum*, nn. 612–15, pp. 205–6.

25. Denzinger, *Enchridion Symbolorum*, nn. 616–19, pp. 206–7. The area is called Friuli-Venezia-Giulia.

26. In the fifth century, Theodoret of Cyrrhus (d. 460 CE) accused Cyril of Alexandria (d. 444 CE) of using the term "Filioque" which means that the Son of God played a role in the origin of the Holy Spirit. In the eleventh century, Benedict VIII inserted "Filioque" into the creed and this furthered the schismatic division of the Western and Eastern Churches.

first fifteen pages of this essay focus on the theological history of Trinitarian theology. He then mentions his main position:

> Also eine identität von *ökonomischer* und immanenter
>
> Trinit*ät gegeben ist.*

Phan translates "Rahner's Rule" as follows:

> The "economic" Trinity is the "immanent" Trinity,
>
> and the "immanent" Trinity is the "economic" Trinity.[27]

As we move into the twenty-first century, theological ecumenism has slowly become a major process of theological discourse. In a recent publication, namely *The Cambridge Dictionary of Christianity*, the editor, Daniel Patte, has devoted twenty-four pages to essays by several major Orthodox theologians.[28] The authors of these pages offer us a larger understanding of Christian theology than simply the theology of the Western Catholic Church. Today, many Western Christians say: "Our Western Christian theology is the only true theology." Perhaps we of the Western churches should keep in mind that the Christian church is larger than just the Western churches and that the Eastern churches Christian theologians have outstanding writings on the Trinity.

In *The Cambridge Dictionary of Christianity*, Archbishop Demetrios Trakatellis explains the fundamental approach to theology as follows:

> The spirit of Orthodox theology is epitomized by the maxim: "The theologian is the one who prays, and the one who prays is a theologian." Orthodox theology is experiential and doxological in character, drawing from and leading to the personal encounter of love between God and human kind. Orthodoxy disfavors speculative or scholastic approaches to theology, reserving the title "theologian" for those who have been enlightened by personal experience of God.[29]

---

27. See Phan, "Mystery of Grace and Salvation," in *Cambridge Companion to the Trinity*, 197.

28. See Patte, *Cambridge Dictionary of Christianity*, 892–915.

29. See Patte, *Cambridge Dictionary of Christianity*, 894. Reading the twenty-four pages which contain essays by Orthodox theologians offers us a better understanding of Christian theology. Today, Western Christians should not say "our Christian theology" is the only true theology; rather we of the Western Christian churches should keep in mind that in the Eastern Christian churches there are theological writings in many different languages, e.g., the Christian churches of Russia, Serbia, Czechoslovakia,

In the Orthodox Churches, one starts with the premise that human words and expressions are inadequate when we speak of God. In essence, God is unknowable. Christians cannot grasp intellectually the mysteries of our faith. We "believe in" rather than we "know about" the mysteries of God.[30] This position is referring to the theologies of the Trinity, the incarnation, the church itself, and the sacraments. All of these mysteries cannot be grasped, but they are partially understood through *theosis*.

Harry Pappas presented an essay entitled "Salvation in Christ: Perspectives of the Orthodox Church."[31] In his essay, he states that "*Theosis*" is a "very distinctive feature of the Orthodox Church's vision of salvation in Christ." *Theosis*, is not an absolute bonding but a relative bonding. *Theosis* springs from the core of Christian life. In the Greek Orthodox Church, there is no universal teaching. There is a restrictive view that "one can only be saved by belonging to the Orthodox Church in this life."[32] However, there is also a more liberal Greek Orthodox view:

- one which recognizes the goodness inherent in all human beings;
- another which appreciates love and truth found anywhere in the world;
- which includes the acceptance that the last judgment is in the hands of God.

Pappas concludes these four statements by saying that at the last judgment which is completely in God's hands, "There are going to be a lot of surprises both within the Church and outside of it."[33]

CONCLUDING OBSERVATIONS

1. The Council of Nicea was the first "ecumenical council" of the Christian church. I have stated the major issues of this council as well as its deficiencies. Constantine called for the council, and he was literally in charge of the council. However, he asked Bishop

Romania, Bulgaria, etc.

30. This view of the Orthodox Churches is reminiscent of the insights of Justin and Clement of Alexandria which are mentioned in chapter 2. God is totally other and therefore infinite. No one truly knows God's name.

31. See Pappas, "Salvation in Christ."

32. Pappas, "Salvation in Christ," 258.

33. Pappas, "Salvation in Christ," 259.

Trinitarian Theologies from the 4th Century to the 8th Century

Hosius to be the acting presider. There were few major issues which were either not on the agenda. The text merely states: καὶ εἰς τὸ ἅγιον πνεῦμα (and in the Holy Spirit). A major issue in the Trinity is the role of the Holy Spirit. Nonetheless, the Council of Nicea was only the first Christian council and it stated that Jesus was both human and divine.

2. The divinity of Jesus remained the major issue in all of the above councils. One can say that the divinity of Jesus was not totally approved until the end of the eighth century. Even at this time line, a few Western Christian communities remained anti-Trinitarian, and a few theologians also remained anti-Trinitarian. For instance, Peter Abelard (1079–1142 CE) taught that the doctrine of the Trinity was simply a form of modalism. Gregory of Palamas (1296–1359 CE) taught that the divine essence was and is absolutely unchangeable and transcendent. Only in a secondary way are there three equal hypostases in God.

3. In the Christian world, with the exception of Peter Abelard and Gregory Palamas, a belief in the Trinity has been part of Christian faith. However, from the Council of Trent onward, the theology of Trinity remained simply a part of one's Christian faith, ecclesiology as a belief in the one true church—the Catholic Church—became the central theological issue and all other so-called Christian churches were invalid. Recently, however, there has been a rethinking of the Christian theology of the Trinity in a much wider context. In his essay "Trinity and Hinduism," Francis Clooney draws together the writings of several Hindu scholars who have joined, at least in a beginning way, Hindu religion and Christian Trinitarian religion, namely Keshab Junder Sen, Paramahansa, Yogananda, Jules Monchanin, and Henri Le Saux.[34] Other theologians and scholars today have tried to maintain one God but also there is a "threefold something" which allows one to say that God is Trinitarian. We see this in the writings of Jürgen Moltmann, Wolfhart Panneberg, Sergius Bulgakov, Vladimir Lossky, and John Zizioulos. Heup Young Kim, James Fredericks, Patricia Fox, and Miguel Díaz have reconsidered the standard Christian theology of Trinity and in doing so have "re-theologized" the Trinitarian God. In the writings of these scholars,

---

34. See Clooney, "Trinity and Humanism," in Phan, *Cambridge Companion to the Trinity*, 309–24.

there is an attempt to go beyond the common Trinitarian theology of Christians which is basically expressed in early Greek philosophy and also in Latin philosophy.

4. Another issue which needs to be considered is the use of the terms "Father" and "Son." In today's world, we know much more on the structured nature of fatherhood and son-hood. God is by no means a "Father" in the current understanding in all languages vis-à-vis the meaning of "father." Likewise God is by no means a "Son" in the current understanding in all languages vis-à-vis the meaning of "son." We have seen in many of the above religious explanations that God was called "Father" in a poetic, descriptive, and metaphorical way. In the writings of Paul, Mark, Luke, and Matthew, God—YHWH—is also called "Father" but once again in a poetic, descriptive, and metaphorical way. The same can be said of the New Testament authors in their referral to Jesus as the "Son" of God. Calling Jesus "Son" of God is also only a poetic, descriptive, and metaphorical description. Only in earliest years of the second century CE, did major changes take place. Theologians and major prelates began to speak of Jesus as a true son of God. This step changed the meaning of Father for God and the meaning of Son of God for Jesus. In 1964, Joseph Dalmau published in Latin a lengthy passage on the Trinity.[35] He states that human procreation of a father son is merely analogical. Only the relationship of God the Father and God the Son is truly a relationship. This is putting the cart before the horse. Father, in whatever language, is basically a human name and son, in whatever language, is basically a human name. In the earliest stages when God was called "Father," it was basically poetic, descriptive, and metaphorical. In the writings of Paul, Mark, Luke, and Matthew, the authors refer to Jesus as "Son of God," but only in a poetic, descriptive, and metaphorical way. Only in the early decades did some writers begin to refer to Jesus as the "Divine Son" of God.

---

35. Joseph Dalmau published a theological text book in which he dealt with the divinity of Jesus. He writes: "Generatio divina ineffabilis est, et analogice tantum convenit cum generatiionibus creatis." Dalmau and Sagüés, *De Deo uno et trino,* 2:302. In this statement Dalmau claims that in the divine generation by God the Father of God the Son is the truest meaning of a Father-Son relationship. The multiple realities of a generation by a human father and his human son is merely analogical. I find this totally unacceptable.

5. I realize that the reference to God as "Father-Son" is a time-honored description of God. However, I also realize that in the last two centuries, the relationship of father to son has been developed scientifically in a way quite different from earlier times. Paternity DNA testing is a very modern process, but the test indicates in a clear way whether this man or that man is one's father. Physically, contemporary science can tell whether or not a certain male individual is the father of a particular child. From a legal standpoint, one can determine the responsibility of a man for a child. From an emotional standpoint, there is or at least can be a strong relationship between the father and mother for a specific child. There is an economic relationship, since a father and mother can be held responsible for any monetary situation in which an infant or child needs payment. There is or there can be a religious relationship between a father-mother baptized child. The list could go on, but in today's world fathers and mothers have clear relationships to their children. God's relationship to human men and women is not based on chromosomes, etc. Consequently, the relationship of a father to a son or daughter is totally different from the religious teaching that there is a "Father-God" and a "Son-God" but the meaning of a divine Father-Son relationship is totally different from a human relationship of a father and son. In today's religious world, I am suggesting that leaders and scholars of the Christian church might begin to find other words than "father-son" for God. If we look at all religions, there could be one "Infinite God" and all finite religious people would therefore have limited insights into the meaning of God. The naming and explanation of God varies from one religion to another. God as "Trinity" is not an acceptable name for God vis-a-vis all human beings. With all of this in mind, let us turn to the final chapter of this book which focuses primarily on the issue of divine infinity.

7

An Infinite God: A Name Which Transcends All Other Names for God

This final chapter is centered on an infinite God, but I want to begin by restating the three issues which are foundational for this volume and which were already presented in the introduction.

PART ONE: THE THREE FOUNDATIONAL ISSUES

The First Foundational Issue

The historical use of the term "Father" for God is found abundantly in both Judaism and Christianity. In Judaism, the use of the word "Father" has been and still is a poetic name for God. In Christianity, from the second century CE onward, the use of the word "Father" for God gradually ceased to be poetic. This took place when Christians began to divinize Jesus as the Son of God.

Today, there are serious questions regarding the title "Father God." The name "Father," when used for God, can be poetic, descriptive, and metaphorical. A poetic use of the term Father for God has been frequently used in Judaism from its earliest beginnings down to today. However, at the very end of the first century and into the early decades of the second century CE, a few Christian leaders began to call Jesus the "divine" Son of

God. In their view, the human Jesus remained human but Jesus was also divine since he was the Son of God.

My question is this: In Judaism, the word "Father" has been and still is used as a name for God but only in a poetic, descriptive, and metaphorical way. Did not Jesus himself during his lifetime use the term "Father" (in Aramaic: אבבא) in a poetical way, and did not his close Jewish followers also use the Aramaic term for "Father" in a metaphorical way? If this is the case, why did the followers of Jesus only at the very end of the first century CE begin to speak of Jesus as the "true Son of the Father"?

The Second Foundational Issue

From the second century CE down to the ninth century CE, there was a major division in Christian theology. There were Christian scholars who upheld the two natures of Jesus, but they also upheld that there was only one person in Jesus, namely the second person of the Holy Trinity. During these same centuries, there were also well-educated Christians who believed that there was only one God, namely God the Father. These Christian scholars stated that Jesus might be called "God's Son," but his Sonship was not divine in the sense that it was equally one and the same nature as that of the Father.[1]

My question is this: How can one call the Christian God both a "Father God" and at the same time call a human being, Jesus, a "Son God"?

The Third Foundational Issue

> If Christians use of the term "infinite" as an essential aspect of their God, then the Christian Church can call their God: "The One and Only God." All other so-called gods are not infinite, and therefore they are not truly divine.

The issue of infinity was first referred to by two Greek philosophers, Anaximander (ca. 609–547 BCE) and Anaxagoras (ca. 500–437 BCE). Historically, the issue of infinity has had many differing meanings. Today

---

1. In the second century CE, the divinity of the Holy Spirit was mentioned here and there, but a theology of the Holy Spirit as the third person of the Trinity began in the late decades of the third century. The ecumenical council of Nicea held in 325 CE simply mentions the Holy Spirit—καὶ εἰς τὸ ἅγιον πνεῦμα—at the very end of the main statement.

the word is used in mathematics, physics, metaphysics, psychology, religion, and the arts. In religious writings, many theologians state that God is infinite, but "infinite" is not the primal issue. In the *Catechism of the Catholic Church*, the authors state the following:

> God is the Father Almighty, whose fatherhood and power shed light on one another: God reveals his fatherly omnipotence by the way he takes care of our needs; by the filial adoption he gives us; ... finally by his infinite mercy he displays his power at its height by freely forgiving sins.[2]

In the *Catechism*, the infinity of God is not presented as the basic essence of God's nature. It seems that divine omnipotence is far more ultimate in God than divine infinity. Only once do the authors refer to the "infinity" of God (n. 270). Throughout the *Catechism*, the authors describe many aspects of God in a generous way. A single mention of divine infinity seems to lack the same generosity.

My question is this: How can a finite and limited human mind come to an understanding of an infinite being? If God is infinite, and most Christians refer to God as infinite, is not the term "infinite" used in an incorrect way?

PART TWO: THE ISSUE OF DIVINE INFINITY

In the above paragraphs—part 1—the adjective "infinite" is connected to the "mercy" of God. Over many centuries, other Christian theologians have used the term infinite for God in a similar way such as God is infinitely holy, is infinitely loving, is infinitely just, etc. In my volume *The Infinity of God and a Finite World*, chapter 1 presents in some detail the history of the terms infinite and infinity as found in religious literature.[3] The term "infinity" in a religious sense is usually called a "metaphysical infinity" signifying that God is essentially without limit. But this raises some questions as to its centrality in our discourse about God. For example, the Roman Catholic bishops state that Catholics must believe in one, true, and living God. They then describe this one God: namely, God is creator, lord of heaven and earth, omnipotent, eternal, immense, etc. In these descriptions, one finds the adjective "infinite" only in a very limited

---

2. Catholic Church, *Catechism of the Catholic Church*, n. 270, p. 71. See also the *Catechism*'s citation of Gregory of Nazianzus, n. 256, p. 67.

3. Osborne, *Infinity of God*, 1–19.

way. In the preface of my volume, I mention that the majority of theologians from various religions seem to reject a "univocal God." In these various religions, many scholars state that their God is the one and true God. Religions, however, are not the center of our faith; rather, religions contain different ways of honoring God. It is my view that one of the key issues regarding God and the multiplicity of religions does not lie in their diverse theologies, but in their diverse ways of presenting, at least to some extent, the infinite nature of God. To date, however, the infinity of God has not been presented as the major theme for interreligious dialogues.

Belief in God—not knowledge of God—is the only way through which we can have some apprehension of God. If, on the other hand, I believe that there is only one infinite God—and infinitely speaking there can only be one God—then my way of believing might be different from the way others believe in God. Nonetheless, there is only one, and this one God is an infinite God and remains the same. The center of all religions is one's faith in God. It is the various "ways of faith in God" that separate us from each other. Jürgen Moltmann explains and evaluates the threefold *Self-Communication of God*, which Karl Rahner presents in some detail.[4] Moltmann writes:

> On the basis of the modern, changed concept of the person, we ought no longer to talk about una substantia—tres personae, but about a single divine subject in three "distinct modes of subsistence."[5]

PART THREE: THE INFINITY OF GOD; A THEOLOGICAL ISSUE WHICH HAS BEEN ALMOST A SECONDARY ISSUE IN THE HISTORY OF CHRISTIAN THEOLOGY

In the Old Testament and in the New Testament, the term "infinite" is not used at all. The first time that the word "infinite" appears in a major church document is in the final statements of the Lateran Council in 649 CE. In the Latin text of the conciliar council, the authors use the phrase "sine initio" (without beginning) for the first time in a conciliar text. In

---

4. Moltmann, *Trinity and the Kingdom*, 144–48. Moltmann explains in detail what Rahner presents in his article. See also Phan, "Mystery of Grace and Salvation," in *Cambridge Companion to the Trinity*, 192–207.

5. Moltmann, *Trinity and the Kingdom*, 144.

the Greek text of the Lateran document, one reads "ἄπειρον." This Greek word means "without beginning" or "without ending."

The second time that church officials used the term "infinite" was in their letter to a French theological professor, Louis de Bautain, in which they condemned his teaching as "fideism." He was teaching that the human intellect could not prove with certainty either the existence of God or the infinite perfection of God. His position was condemned as heretical.

Third, the early theologians of the Christian church—from Augustine to the twelfth century—used the term infinity infrequently. These scholars did not provide their readership with any detailed information vis-à-vis divine infinity.

Fourth, the major Christian theologians from the thirteenth century down to the end of the fifteenth century, used the two words "infinite" and "infinity" abundantly. We find this abundance in the writings of Alexander of Hales, Thomas Aquinas, Bonaventure, and John Duns Scotus.

Fifth, in the sixteenth century the Protestant Reformation took place, and from the sixteenth century down to the early decades of the twentieth century, the main theological issue in the Western Christian world was ecclesiology. In 1870, the first Vatican Council took place, and in the dogmatic constitution *Dei Filius*, the word infinite appears once. The bishops state that there is one God and then they add a descriptive list of divine attributes: "true, living, creator and lord of heaven and of earth, omnipotent, eternal, immense, incomprehensible, infinite in every perfection."[6] In this document, the term "infinite" along with other qualities is used in a descriptive way.

In the middle of the twentieth century down to today, the theology of infinity has once again become center stage. In the documents of Vatican II, the adjective infinite appears only once. As the Christian issue of Trinity moved into the twenty-first century CE, another focus emerged, namely the infinity of God. The infinity of God is an issue which far surpasses our limited understanding and yet contemporary scholars have focused in a major way on the meaning of infinity. In 2006 CE, a conference was held in San Marino, California, in which a group of contemporary scholars centered on the issue of infinity in all its major fields today: mathematics, physics, metaphysics, theology, and psychology. After the conference, a book was published which included a slightly

---

6. Vatican I, *Dei Filius*, ch. 1; Latin text in Denzinger, *Enchridion Symbolorum*, 587.

revised edition of their presentations. Each of the authors of this volume present in great detail both the important aspects as well as the limiting aspects of mathematical, physical, metaphysical, theological, and psychological infinities. It is at this point that I am calling for theologians to reconsider the term "infinity" in our discourse about God.

PART FOUR: THE BEGINNING OF HUMAN LIFE; BASED ON NASA, ON THE HUBBLE SPACE TELESCOPE, ON THE MAX PLANK INSTITUTE, AND ON NEW RELIGIOUS TEACHING ON SALVATION

Contemporary science has provided us with a very careful and a very detailed history of human life. The term "human life" for many scientists has two different references. Some scientists use the term *Homo sapiens* for a certain animal species which began centuries ago. These living creatures were not yet human beings in our sense of the term, but they were the ancestors from which contemporary human life came into being. Consequently most contemporary scientists use a different phrase for a human being, namely *Homo sapiens sapiens*.

The Smithsonian Institute provides us with an explanation of human evolution.[7] NASA also has studied the origins of human life.[8] Moreover, the Hubble Space Telescope, as well as scientists connected to the Max Plank Institute, have provided today's world with the age of the universe, roughly 3.7 billion years. In 2006 CE, Bernard Carr, a professor of mathematics and astronomy at Queen Mary College, London, published an article entitled "Cosmology and Religion." He states that today there are three issues regarding the cosmos which question certain religious positions.

> First, the expanding vistas opened up by cosmological progress have come at a price: the bigger the universe has grown, the more insignificant humans have become. Second, the heavens have been progressively stripped of their divinity, so we can no longer delude ourselves into thinking that we have some special or singular connection with a Creator. Third, cosmology has

---

7. See humanorigins.si.edu/research.
8. See astrobiology.nasa.gov.

had to strive constantly to maintain its scientific respectability, battling not only religious but also scientific orthodoxy.[9]

In *The Oxford Handbook of Religion and Science*, published in 2006, there is a plethora of essays written by well-known scientists and well-known theologians.[10] These essays explain the positions on the ways in which contemporary religious aspects of human life relate to contemporary scientific aspects of human life and vice versa. Moreover, the current scientific dating of the first appearance of *Homo sapiens sapiens* varies in highly differing ways.[11] Generally speaking, I will use one of the datings of *Homo sapiens sapiens* which is fairly well accepted, namely 10,000 years ago.

During the earliest centuries of human life, writing did not exist, and therefore scientists have had to use differing items such as bones, spears, foundations of a building, etc., to describe the origin and the earliest ages of *Homo sapiens sapiens*. Jack Finegan, in his volume *Myth and Mystery: An Introduction to the Pagan Religions of the Biblical World*, states that the beginnings of Sumerian civilization took place between the Euphrates and Tigris Rivers in the southern par of Mesopotamia. This occurred around the middle of the sixth millennium BCE. The Sumerians in the fourth millennium "invented cuneiform, the wedge-shaped form of writing which remained in use thereafter for some three thousand years."[12] This was the beginning of what we know today as "human writing."

From 4000 BCE to 2000 CE, human beings have developed many languages. In those same years the population of humankind increased in an overwhelming way. If one posits the beginning of human life from 10,000 years ago down to 4000 BCE—a time when human beings did not write—we have no written material on human life.

9. See Bernard Carr, "Cosmology and Religion," in Clayton and Simpson, *Oxford Handbook of Religion and Science*, 139–55.

10. Clayton and Simpson, *Oxford Handbook of Religion and Science*: in this volume, which is roughly a thousand pages, various contemporary experts in both science and theology have presented major essays on both current scientific and religious issues. In a clear way they indicate how today's science questions today's religions and vice versa.

11. In the *New York Times*, Feb. 26, 2002, John Noble Wilford presented a lengthy article entitled "When Human Beings Became Human." See www.nytimes.com/2002/02/26. Today, it is somewhat dated, but the article presents a readable review of the emergence of contemporary human life. In 2018, the Northern Kalahari human beings are still examples of human life and they have a history which goes back thousands of years and are still primitive in their way of life.

12. Finegan, *Myth and Mystery*, 19.

During this lengthy period of time, there were thousands of husbands and wives, fathers and mothers, sons and daughters. I find it puzzling that in today's Christian theological writers there is no mention of these human beings who were created by God. They were neither Christians nor members of any religion. An example of this silence can be found in a statement made by Catholic bishops at Vatican II, in *Gaudium et Spes*:

> Human dignity rests above all on the fact that humanity is called to communion with God. The invitation to converse with God is addressed to men and women as soon as they are born. (n. 19)

The phrase—"The invitation to converse with God is addressed to men and women as soon as they are born"—would seem to imply that the men and women who belonged to those earliest of centuries in which there was no writing are also included with those who converse with God as soon as they are born. There is, however, no data of any kind which might indicate that the earliest *Homo sapiens sapiens* "conversed with God as soon as they were born." This same issue is found in the *Catechism of the Catholic Church*:

> The desire for God is written in the human heart, because man [and woman] is created by God and for God; and God never ceases to draw man [and woman] to himself.[13]

Did the first human beings—the earliest *Homo sapiens sapiens*—have a desire for God which was written in their hearts from the various moments right after birth? As far as we can tell, they knew absolutely nothing about a Christian Trinitarian God or about the economy of the Word incarnate, or about the Christian economy of salvation for all men and women. However, the first human beings, which contemporary scientists describe as *Homo sapiens sapiens*, and who were also "created" by God, apparently have no connection to the salvific life of Jesus and the salvific existence of the Christian church. Nor did they have any connection to Judaism, to Buddhism, to Hinduism, to Confucianism, etc. We have no idea if the earliest human beings had any religion at all or had a name for "God."

The Fourth Lateran Council took place in 1215 CE, and in chapter 1, entitled "De Fide Catholica," one reads: "Una vero est fidelium Ecclesia, extra quam nullus omnino salvatur" (However, there is one church

---

13. See Catholic Church, *Catechism of the Catholic Church*, n. 27, p. 13.

of the faithful, beyond which there is no salvation at all). In the documents of Vatican II and in several major essays after Vatican II, the issue of "salvation outside the Catholic Church" is stated in a more comprehensive way, but there is no mention of the issue regarding the first human beings.[14] In 1951, the anniversary of the Council of Chalcedon was celebrated by many church theological groups. In many of these celebrations, some theologians pointed out that today Christians need to expand the theological meaning of salvation. However, even in these Christian discussions, the earliest humans, *Home sapiens sapiens*, were not even mentioned. In the essays in the volume *World Christianity: Perspectives and Insights*, the authors open up today's religious borders.[15] The authors move beyond today's religious understandings of God and they begin to move toward an "Infinite God" who is the God of every human being. On November 21, 1964, the bishops at Vatican Council II published their first document, *Lumen Gentium*. In their opening statement, one reads:

> The eternal Father, in accordance with the utterly free and mysterious design of his wisdom and goodness, created the entire universe. He chose to raise up men and women to share in his own divine life, and when they had fallen in Adam, he did not abandon them, but at all times offered them the means of salvation, bestowed in consideration Christ, the Redeemer, who is the image of the invisible God, the firstborn of all creation.[16]

---

14. Denzinger, *Enchridion Symbolorum*, n. 800, p. 259. For an updating of this position, see *Vatican II: An Interfaith Appraisal* (University of Notre Dame Press, 1966), 232, 355–94. Rabbi Marc Tannenbaum and Fr. Thomas Stransky are the two major speakers, but in the Q&A sections there are several other theological scholars.

15. See Tan and Tran, *World Christianity*. The essays of the many authors in this volume looked to the present and to the future of world Christianity. I am adding to their vision the human beings who have been overlooked since they were the first human beings and for centuries they lacked the ability to write. They were not Christians nor did they belong to any religion as far as we know. As yet, no contemporary religious scholars have included these millions of people into the later millions of people who belong to a variety of religions. Did God create them? Did Jesus redeem them? They are as much *Homo sapiens sapiens* as we are but theologians and religious leaders simply ignore them. Think, for a moment, how many hundreds and thousands of years they were the only human beings on planet earth. They have absolutely no connection to Judaism, Hinduism, Christianity, Islam, etc., and yet many Christians state that Jesus is the redeemer for every human being.

16. *Lumen Gentium*, n. 2. http://www.vatican.va/archive/hist_councils/ii_vatican_council/documents/vat-ii_const_19641121_lumen-gentium_en.html

In this passage, the bishops focus on the salvation of all men and women which, they say, took place in and through Jesus Christ. Does this statement include all men and women ca. 100,000 or 50,000 years ago? None of these men and women knew anything about a Triune God or about an Incarnate Jesus. Christian doctrine, as yet, has not been interrelated with this scientific data. The number of human beings from the beginning of human life—namely from *Homo sapiens sapiens*—down to today could be almost a "quintillion." In the United States and France, "quintillion" means the number "1" followed by eighteen zeroes. In Great Britain and Germany, "quintillion" means number "1" followed by thirty zeroes. How many fathers, mothers, daughters, and sons have been born and have lived on planet earth? The answer could be: "in the quintillions!"

In the citations from the *Catechism*, the authors state, "By natural reason man can know God with certainty."[17] We also read: "The desire for God is written in the human heart, because man [and woman] is created by God and for God; and God never ceases to draw man [and woman] to himself."[18] If these statements are theologically correct, then church teaching could state that there is indeed salvation outside the Christian church, including the salvation of the earliest human generations of *Homo sapiens sapiens*. If this is not possible, then these first human beings had no way of being saved. If the leaders and theologians of the Catholic Church do not include these thousands or millions of human beings, then there is a serious challenge to the integrity of their teaching.

Contemporary scholars in the religious communities mentioned above would be very helpful if they explained why they do not face up to the "salvation" of the men and women who lived for centuries prior the first appearance of any and all religious denominations. I suggest that we consider the infinity of God as the most important aspect of God, since God is not limited by anything human, and this unlimitedness of God incudes the religious communities of every denomination. An infinite God has two major factors: first of all, God is infinite in a way that is different from all other forms of infinity (scientific infinity, philosophical infinity, mathematical infinity, etc.), and since the major focus is on the divine, then the divinity of God is a position of faith and not of reason. In an analogous area, the scientific evidence also has implications for how we interpret God in the light of world religions.

---

17. Catholic Church, *Catechism of the Catholic Church*, n. 50, p. 19.
18. Catholic Church, *Catechism of the Catholic Church*, n. 27, p. 13.

PART FIVE: THE INFINITY OF GOD AND THE CURRENT MULTIPLICITY OF RELIGIONS

To some degree, Christian theologians during and after Vatican II have begun to reconsider the theological meaning of God's infinity. We see this in such books as *Reforming the Doctrine of God*, by LeRon Schults, and also *Rediscovering the Triune God: The Trinity in Contemporary Theology*, by Stanley Grenz. These books speak to the contemporary, multicultural, and multireligious world.[19] In 2011 CE, Yujin Nagasawa, a senior lecturer at the University of Birmingham, UK, stated the following in his book *The Existence of God: A Philosophical Introduction*:

> Infinity is an intractable concept; it could well be beyond our full comprehension. Yet, it underlies some of the most profound philosophical problems, such as the existence of God, the origin of the universe, and the meaning of life.[20]

At the same time, in the religious writings of various world religions, some authors have maintained that "their God" is the one and only true God. These religious authors also make no mention of the thousands of human beings who lived prior to appearance of Sumerian writing. In the Jewish-Christian tradition, the book of Genesis begins with creation, especially the creation of Adam and Eve, the first human beings. Modern science has rendered the Genesis account as a "story" rather than a "history." Likewise, the entire *Tanakh* has no reference at all to the thousands of sons and daughters who have existed in our world. How does this traditional position interface with modern scientific discovery?

As one example, it is clear that contemporary scientists have proposed many dates when human life occurred. No matter which date is chosen, there have been countless fathers and mothers as well as sons and daughters who have existed long before any written historical data has appeared. These early human beings spoke different languages and these thousands of people had different names for a father, mother, son, and daughter. But the meaning of these terms is the same for all languages, for instance a "father" is father even though the naming is Père,

---

19. Shults, *Reforming the Doctrine of God*; Grenz, *Rediscovering the Triune God*.
20. Nagasawa, *Existence of God*, 152. Nagasawa's book centers on three major issues: (1) an armchair proof of the existence of God; (2) evolution vs. intelligent design; and (3) the big bang, infinity, and the meaning of life.

Padre, Πατήρ, etc. The same listing could be made for "mother," "son," and "daughter."

The contemporary data on the beginning of religious practices, which are generally presented by scientists, can be stated in the following way:

- The first written data regarding Sumerian-Akkadian religion is dated ca. 3,500 BCE. Christian religion begins in the first century CE.
- The first written data regarding Egyptian religion is dated ca. 3,000 BCE. Christian religion begins in the first century CE.
- The first appearance of Hindu religion in India is usually dated ca. 2,000 BCE. However, there were several more localized religions in India prior to 2000 BCE and these earlier religions came to be called "Hinduism." Christian religion begins in the first century CE.[21]
- The first appearance of possible data regarding Chinese religion is found in Banpo near Xian. Most scientists refer to the people in Banpo as Neolithic. The dating is ca. 6,700 to 5,600 years ago. In these findings, religious relics are minimal.

No matter which scientific dating is accepted as regards the origins of religions, we can state today that from the dating of the first *Homo sapiens sapiens* down to the Sumerian-Akkadian writings around 3,500 BCE, there were thousands of human fathers, mothers, daughters, and brothers. During those many years there was no mention of Jesus, the Trinity, or the Christian religion. In the *Catechism of the Catholic Church*, one reads: "All men [and women] are called to this Catholic unity of the people of God" (n. 836). The authors then describe the relationship of the Christian church with the Jewish people (nn. 839–40); then the relationship of the Christian church with the Muslim community (n. 841); and finally the relationship of the Christian church with all non-Christian religions (nn. 842–44). These writers do not even mention *Homo sapiens sapiens*, even though they were human beings whose numbering is in the thousands, even millions, or even trillions. The fact is that these first human beings, *Homo sapiens sapiens*, whose beginnings might have begun thousands and thousands of years ago, are never mentioned in contemporary theology, especially in Jewish, Christian, Islamic, Hindu, and even Chinese theology. One cannot help but question the validity of these religions that

21. An unknown author has indicated that in Banpo, China, there were some religious relics. See "Eternal Symbols," https://www.eternalsymbols.com/china/banpo.

simply ignore the earliest *Homo sapiens sapiens,* and yet many religious leaders and scholars trace their origin to the divinity of God.

My theological interest in the origins of *Homo sapiens sapiens* can be stated as follows. These early fathers, mother, and children are never mentioned in Christian theology or in the theologies of other denominations. Christian theologians maintain that Jesus is the savior of the world, but in this Jesus-world the earliest human beings are not included. Given these thousands of years of historical silence, I cannot help but question the validity of a statement made by the bishops at Vatican II. On November 21, 1964, the bishops published their first document, entitled *Lumen Gentium*. In their opening statement, one reads:

> The eternal Father, in accordance with the utterly free and mysterious design of his wisdom and goodness, created the entire universe. He chose to raise up men and women to share in his own divine life, and when they had fallen in Adam, God did not abandon them, but at all times offered them the means of salvation, bestowed in consideration of Christ, the Redeemer, who is the image of the invisible God, the firstborn of all creation.[22]

The phrase, "God did not abandon them, but at all times offered them the means of salvation, bestowed in consideration of Christ, the Redeemer, who is the image of the invisible God, the firstborn of all creation." The emergence of *Homo sapiens sapiens* seems to place Christianity as an essential part of the first-ever human beings. Even the bishops at Vatican II did not have *Homo sapiens sapiens* in mind. We see this in the following citation from *Gaudium et Spes*:

> The dignity of man [and woman] rests above all on the fact that he [she] is called to communion with God. This invitation to converse with God is addressed to man [and woman] as soon as he [she] comes into being. For if man exists, it is because God has created him through love, and through love continues to hold him in existence. He cannot live fully according to truth unless he [she] freely acknowledges that love and entrusts himself [herself] to the creator.[23]

---

22. *Lumen Gentium*, n. 2. Latin text in *Constitutiones, Decreta. Declarationes* (Rome: Typis Polyglottis Vaticanis, 1966), 94.

23. *Gaudium et Spes*, n. 19. The above English text is taken from Catholic Church, *Catechism of the Catholic Church*, n. 27, p. 13.

> *Dignitatis humanae eximia ratio in vocatione hominis ad communionem cum Deo consistit. Ad colloquium cum Deo iam inde ab ortu suo invitatur homo; non enim existit, nisi quia, a Deo ex amore creatus, semper ex amore conservatur; nec plene secundum veritatem vivit, nisi amorem illum libere agnoscat et Creatori suo se committat.*[24]

There seems to be no relationship between Adam and Eve on the one hand, and these earliest human beings who lived prior to the ability of writing on the other hand. Nor is there any relationship between the millions of these families and the Jewish religion, the Hindu religion, the Buddhist religion, and the Islamic religion. This means that God created thousands of people who lived on earth for thousands of years before humans began to write. No major contemporary religion was a part of their culture. In other words, contemporary theologians from any of the above religious groups cannot claim that their religious beliefs have a history that goes back to the historical beginning of *Homo sapiens sapiens*. I do not have answers to any of these situations. I simply want to state that contemporary science on human nature raises serious questions on the biblical data concerning human life and on the traditional position with respect to salvation.

My central question is the following:

> If every *Homo sapiens sapiens* is truly a human being, have each one of them been saved by the life, death, and resurrection of Jesus? In the Christian faith, there is a belief that all men and women have been created by God and all human beings have but one savior, Jesus Christ.[25]

PART SIX: THE INFINITY OF GOD AND TODAY'S MULTIPLE THEOLOGIES OF GOD

The philosophical history of the word "infinite" is of major interest, since the meaning of infinite began in a negative way. Anaxagoras (ca. 500 BCE–436/437 BCE) denied divine things and taught that all things

---

24. *Constitutiones, Decreta, Declarationes, Vatican II Council* (Vatican: Typis Polyglottis, 1966), 704.

25. A lengthy but carefully written article on *Homo sapiens sapiens* is Fran Dorey, "*Homo Sapiens*—Modern Humans," Australian Museum website: https://australian-museum.net.au/learn/science/human-evolution/homo-sapiens-modern-humans/.

remained finite. He struggled against superstition and against religious superstition. "Since all things were together, nothing within was clear because of smallness."²⁶ Both Parmenides and Plato had negative views of τὸ ἄπειρον. Aristotle, however, presented in detail a positive understanding of τὸ ἄπειρον, but he did not argue that something active could be infinite forever. Wolfgang Achtner, in his chapter "Infinity as a Transformative Concept in Science and Theology," argues that religious, scientific, and mathematical concepts of infinite are deeply intertwined. He presents the positions on infinity as found in Anaximander, Aristotle, Plotinus, Gregory of Nyssa, Nicholas of Cusa, and George Cantor. In the twentieth century, several major scholars delved into the issue of infinity and contemporary science. Edward Nelson raises the question regarding actual infinity in mathematics and he also rejects an infinite God as presented in today's religious world.²⁷ W. Hugh Woodin, in his essay "The Realm of the Infinite," examines the "set theory," and concludes that there are major weaknesses in the set theory. In his second essay on determinism and non-determinism, Woodin explains what he means by a *Turing Program*, "*eo*" which is based on the inclusion of infinity.²⁸ In the same volume, *Infinity: New Research Frontiers*, there are essays by Carlo Ravalli, a scientist at the Academic Institute of France who considers the role of infinity in physics, in his essay "Some Consideration on Infinity in Physics."²⁹ Likewise, Anthony Aguirre, a scientist at the University of California in Santa Cruz, has an essay on *Cosmological Intimations of Infinity*.³⁰ Professor Robert Russell, from Berkeley, California, presents an essay in *Infinity: New Research Frontiers* entitled "God and Infinity: Theological Insights

---

26. The English translation is taken from the essay on Anaxagoras written in French by André Laks, in *A Guide to Greek Thought*, English translation by Rita Guerlac and Anne Slack. On p. 4 there is a citation from *Die Fragmente der Vorsokratier*, vol. 1, compiled in 1903 by Hermann Diels and edited by Walther Kranz. In this citation, Socrates is stating that "all things were together, infinite in regard both to number and to smallness, for the small too was infinite."

27. Edward Nelson, "Warning Signs of a Possible Collapse of Contemporary Mathematics," in Heller and Woodin, *Infinity*, 76–85.

28. Woodin, "Realm of the Infinite" and "A Potential Subtlety concerning the Distinction between Determinism and Nondeterminism," in Heller and Woodin, *Infinity*, 89–129.

29. Rovelli, "Some Considerations on Infinity in Physics," in Heller and Woodin, *Infinity*, 167–75.

30. Aguirre, "Cosmological Intimations of Infinity," in Heller and Woodin, *Infinity*, 176–92.

from *Cantor's Mathematics*."[31] The term infinite is used by scholars from differing foci: mathematics and infinity, physics and infinity, metaphysics and infinity, psychology and infinity, and to some degree the fine arts and infinity. In some religions, there is also a description of an infinite God.[32]

I mentioned that in 2006, all of these outstanding authors gathered for a meeting in San Marino, California, on the issue of "infinity" in today's scientific and religious world. Their starting point is science and their questions are on the relationship of science to religion. After reading all of these essays, I asked myself, "Is there an agreement between Christian scholars on the one hand and scientific scholars on the other hand regarding the issue of the infinity of God?" Are there Christians today who continue to believe in God, and do so without using the terms "Father" and "Son"? Many Christian Scripture scholars would be totally against this omission. There is no problem with the meaning of the term "Father" for God, if it is used as a poetic or descriptive name for God. Both the Old Testament and the New Testament, as I have documented in chapters 3 and 4, have many citations in which God is referred to as "Father." The nature of God can be described as "Father," but this description is poetic descriptive, and metaphorical.

In the Christian community, the divinization of Jesus changed the theological nature of God. When Christian writers began to divinize Jesus, the nature of God was no longer described poetically, descriptively or metaphorically as Father, since God's nature itself had become a Father-Son nature. A divine Father and a divine Son, share one and the same nature. Every human father is totally different than a divine Father and every human son is totally different than a divine Son. The following paragraphs describe the inadequacy of the terms "father and son" when applied to God.

1. The naming of someone who is only an "honorary father" or a "founding father" or a "father confessor," or a "father-in-law" or a "god-father," etc., is done so in a metaphorical way. Even when we use the phrase "God the Father," we are not describing God in the same sense as "father" in human life.

2. The divinizing of Jesus as the actual "Son of God" began in the early decades of the second century CE onward. From 100 to 800 CE, many Christian writers strongly rejected the divinity of Jesus as the

---

31. Russell, "God and Infinity," in Heller and Woodin, *Infinity*, 278–89.
32. Rucker, introduction to Heller and Woodin, *Infinity*, 1–15.

Son of God the Father, while many Christians maintained the divinity Jesus as the Son of God the Father. The main divisive point was the following: either Jesus is divine, or Jesus is not divine.

3. The focus has been on the divine nature. Is the divine nature found only in God "the Father," or is the divine nature found also in Jesus, "the Son of God"? During the seven centuries mentioned above, the very nature of God was the center of the debate. Did the nature of God allow two divine persons? Did the nature of God allow three divine persons? In many ways, the use of the term "person" complicates the true meaning of God. We are taking a human term and applying it to divinity. When we say that God is infinite, we have moved beyond the use of the term "infinite" as found in whatever language and for whatever reality.

In the recent *Catechism of the Catholic Church*, God is described as transcending all creatures. "We must therefore continually purify our language of everything in it that is limited, image-bound or imperfect, if we are not to confuse our image of God—'the inexpressible, the incomprehensible, the invisible, and the ungraspable'—with our human representations. Our human words always fall short of the mystery of God."[33] Actually, one cannot define God or even describe God. We can only believe that there is a divine reality. The names for God are "our" names. We are praying to an unnamed God or more clearly expressed, an unnameable God, and we do so as a matter of belief, not as a matter of human intellectual intelligence.

The infinite is unnameable

If God is truly infinite, then no finite creature, ourselves included, can truly know what God's divinity entails. God may manifest goodness and love, but God is more than goodness and love. When we call God loving and good, we are using terms as we know them in our finite lives. Infinite love and infinite goodness are far beyond our comprehension.

I am not concluding that I have presented the infinite God in the clearest way. I am simply asking theologians and church leaders to focus more deeply on the issue of infinity as far as God is concerned. Divine

---

33. See Catholic Church, *Catechism of the Catholic Church*, n. 42. In the footnote for this statement, the authors refer to the "*Liturgy of St. John Chrysostom*, Anaphora." See www.saintelias.com/ca/liturgy/anaphora/php.

infinity in many ways simply negates all intellectual human efforts to understand God, whereas theologians and religious leaders too often "explain" who and what an infinite God is all about. My hope would be that all religions would see that their respective understandings of God are fundamentally limited, but each of their different understandings of God, though highly limited, helps religious people see each other not as opponents but as co-witnesses to the one and only infinite God.

PART SEVEN: CONCLUDING OBSERVATIONS

In chapter 7, I have suggested that contemporary theological scholars might focus more deeply on the infinity of God. If God is infinite, then all religious groups would be focused on one and the same God, rather than focusing only on "their God." The following conclusions might be the beginning of a clearer understand of human life as well as divine life:

1. In the *Tanakh*, the words infinite and infinity are not used in reference to anything. Yehezkel Kaufmann states that YHWH is the universal God of all men and women.[34] He does not state that God is "infinite," but he does state that there is only "one God." He adds that we need to distinguish between the various meanings of religious universalism. He mentions that monotheism implies that there is only one creator and ruler of the entire universe and YHWH is the one God for all creation. Kaufmann adds "that there is no inner necessity that compels us to distribute the favor of one God equally among all men. . . . Nothing prohibits that the choice of a particular group is His elect."[35] Kaufmann states that the Israelites are God's "special elect." The favor of this one God, YHWH, is not found equally in all men and women, but YHWH is the one and only God who is found in all religions. However, outside of Israel, the elect of YHWH, "there is no sacrifice and no festival, but only impure ground where idols are worshipped."[36] In other words, YHWH is infinite, but only worshiped in a true way by his elect, the Jewish nation. In some ways, Christianity is similar. There is only one God, the Trinity, and Christians are the only people who worship this one Trinitarian God in a true way.

34. Kaufmann, *History of Israelite Religion*, 127.
35. Kaufmann, *History of Israelite Religion*, 127.
36. Kaufmann, *History of Israelite Religion*, 128.

2. In *The Catechism of the Catholic Church*, the authors have a section entitled "Outside the Church There Is No Salvation."[37] The authors then state this conclusion in a more positive way: "All salvation comes from Christ ... through the Church." However, the authors add a passage from the Vatican II document, *Ad Gentes*:

> Although in ways known to himself, God can lead those who, through no fault of their own, are ignorant of the gospel, without which it is impossible to please him (Heb. 11,6), the church, nevertheless, still has the obligation and also the sacred right to evangelize.[38]

In this passage the focus is on non-Catholics and non-Christians today. The authors, however, do write: "The Father willed to call the whole of humanity together into his Son's Church."[39] This statement needs to be revised, in some way or another, when contemporary Catholic leaders and theologians take into account the nature of God. If God's nature is infinite, God is incomprehensible. Whenever one says that God is "incomprehensible," then the terms "Father" and "Son" become metaphorical.

3. Does this same passage from *Ad Gentes* include the many men and women, sons and daughters of the initial generations of *Homo sapiens sapiens*, that is, those men and women, boys and girls who over thousands of years did not leave anything in writing? During those thousands of years, Jesus was totally unknown, the Christian church was totally unknown, and the Trinitarian God was totally unknown. If we today want to speak of God, we should try to include all of God's creatures. These early human beings were, according to scientists, essentially human men and women just as we are. Therefore,

---

37. *Catechism of the Catholic Church*, nn. 846–56.

38. *Ad Gentes*, n. 7. http://www.vatican.va/archive/hist_councils/ii_vatican_council/documents/vat-ii_decree_19651207_ad-gentes_en.html

39. "The whole of humanity" would include the initial *Homo sapiens sapiens*, but Jesus was totally unknown during those earliest centuries prior to his birth and he could not be known prior to the Sumerian men and women of the fourth century BCE, when writing was yet totally unknown. In 2013, I delivered a series of lectures in Seoul, Korea and two of these lectures were on John Duns Scotus. In the final chapter of his final book, *De Primo Principio*, Scotus states: "Te esse infinitum et incomprehensibilem a finito" (You are infinite and [you are] incomprehensible to a finite being). God is infinite which means that God in his essence cannot be known. This includes that we cannot say that essence of God is the Trinity. God's essence is unknowable and all religions, therefore, express only an "attribute" of God.

instead of referring to God as the Triune God, as the Christian God, as the Jewish God, or as the God of any other group of human beings, we should refer to an "Infinite God." An Infinite God is unnameable but this unnameable God created the earliest *Homo sapiens sapiens*, just as he has created the contemporary *Homo sapiens sapiens*. All religious groups honor the same Infinite God, whether or not these groups are called Christians, Jews, Hindus, Buddhists, etc. If an Infinite God is the one and only God, then this one and only God has created every man and woman, and every son and daughter. Many created human beings honor God in one way or another. However, none of the earliest *Homo sapiens sapiens* belonged to any of today's various religions. When the leaders and members of any contemporary religious group state that their "religion" is the one and only valid religion—and Christians, Jews, and Muslims certainly state this—a major issue arises.

To summarize, there are three foundational issues which have dominated my thinking throughout this book:

The Use of the Term "Father"

The first issue was the use of the name "Father." A change will not happen immediately, but since we know much more about the physical, sexual, social, emotional, etc., characteristics of the term "father." I believe that calling God "Father" is meaningful only when it is used in a poetic, descriptive, and metaphorical way. Calling God "Father" expresses one's love for God, who has loved us in a profound way. I believe I have covered this issue adequately throughout the book. It is related to my second foundational issue.

The Divinization of Jesus

My second foundational issue, which has also dominated my book, is the divinization of Jesus. Theologians describe the union of the divine nature to a human nature. Jesus has two natures, one is divine and one is human. Every human being is also a person. In our Western world, one cannot describe the essence of a human individual without using the words "nature" and "person." I myself am a human person and I also have a human nature. If I would only be a human nature and not a human person, I would be nonexistent. In the Christian theology of the Trinitarian God, there is only one nature, but there are three distinct persons. It is obvious that the words "person" and "nature" are defined in a totally different way when used for human beings and also when used for the one divine nature of God and the three divine persons in this one divine nature. The question remains: how can three "persons" exist in "one" nature?

When you and I in our human natures are radically weakened, we could be emotionally challenged in a profound way. An example might involve losing one's sight, one's hearing, or one's consciousness. If this happened to me, my human nature would go through hours and days of self-pity, or I might have good reason to blame others who have physically molested me. My human person would be profoundly part of my distress. A human person and a human nature go together. In God, there are three different persons who share one nature. One can see that the roots of this way of thinking came from early Greek philosophy. The word "nature" in Greek is φύσις and is used for the nature of things. For the outward appearance of human nature, the more common word is τό εἶδον, since in its many forms things change exteriorly.

In the divinization of the human Jesus, Christians slowly began to see how Jesus relates to the Father. Most Christians believe that "the Trinity has always existed." However, when men and women began to believe in God, they did not have a clear understanding of their God. The historian MacCulloch states: "Altogether, the chronology of the book of Genesis simply does not add up as an historical narrative when it is placed in a reliably historical context."[40] He goes on to state that "at the heart of the Egypt and Exodus story there is something which no subsequent Israelite fantasist would have wished to make up, because it is an embarrassment: the hero and leader of the Exodus, the man presented as writing the Pentateuch itself, has a name which is not only non-Jewish but actually Egyptian: Moses."[41] This position vis-à-vis the nationality of Moses has been a major biblical issue for at least the past twenty-five years. The usual history of Judaism is similar to almost all other religions including Christianity, namely: if God is infinite, one must say that each

---

40. MacCulloch, *Christianity*, 51.

41. MacCulloch, *Christianity*, 52. Naturally, the issue of Moses' nationality is divisive. Two lengthy essays give in a detailed way the reasons why Moses was Egyptian rather than Jewish: www.Biblehistory.net/newsletter/Moses.htm; and Transmissionsnedia.cora/was-moses-an-egyptian-priest.

religion reflects only some aspect of God.[42] We have seen such a situation in Judaism, especially in the description of YHWH as explained by Ringgren.

In Shintoism, God is usually referred to as Kami, meaning the One Above or the Superior Power, or Eminence. Almost all who are eminent and majestic can be referred to as Kami. In Hinduism, there are many different names for God, such as Ātman, which can be stated in a negative way, "neti neti" (not so-not so). In Buddhism, there are negative names as well, such as śūnyatā, which indicates a void. In the void, there is rūpa and parāmarthatā. "Thus, the ultimate Absolute presumed by the people of India is not a personal god but an impersonal and metaphysical Principle. Here we can see the impersonal character of the absolute thought in Indian thought."[43] However, one of the most difficult themes in theology is the union of the human nature of Jesus to the divine nature of the Trinity. Christians basically come up with name "person," but each human person together with his or her nature is distinct. Perhaps, we might find a better word than "person" since we understand the human person to some extent in his or her gender. The majority of human beings perceive that human nature and human person are indivisible. I have no clear conclusion for the Christian "three-in-one" aspect of God. Of course, the divine triplicity is basically an issue between almost all Asian countries and the West. In its own multiplicity, the Asian world has its own way of considering a two-some. I have already mentioned that the yin-yang is basically not yin-and-yang, but only yin-yang. Perhaps what we need today is an international meeting on the meaning of the "supreme." The East has much to tell the West about "the supreme" which is somewhat related to "Kami." And the West has a need to clarify the one divine nature and the three divine persons, since it is a position which remains unclear. How can three persons exist in one nature?

THE ISSUE OF INFINITY

My third fundamental issue is infinity. As mentioned above, divine infinity is totally different from mathematical infinity, physical infinity,

---

42. In my volume *New Being*, chs. 4–6, I explain how Tillich unites old being to new being in Jesus. "Old being" includes the entire universe; "new being" includes the union of old being to new being. Chapter 5 is central to this interrelationship.

43. See Nakamura, *Ways of Thinking of Eastern Peoples*, 57. Nakamura explains this negativity in ch. 3, "Preference for the Negative," 52–59.

cosmological infinity, philosophical infinity, psychological infinity, and artistic infinity. The major difference in my view is the following. We humans often speak of divine infinity, we do so as a matter of religious faith and not as a matter of a rational conclusion. We believe that God is infinite. However, there is a major factor in this belief. If God is infinite, no religious community can say that "our God" is the only one and true God. In my study on *Homo sapiens sapiens*, I can believe in a loving and guiding God who infinitely cares for all these early humans. On the other hand, no human religious scholar that I know of has presented any mention of the early *Homo sapiens sapiens*. Even though they are truly my own human brothers and sisters, I would like to find in some way or another as to how they can be related to God. In our Christian tradition, they are not presented as human beings related to a Trinitarian God. Nor are they presented as human beings related to Allah, or Yahweh, or Kami. Scientifically, these human beings might be mentioned, but there is no written data regarding these early human beings and so we have no clear data on their connection to us. Are they human? Yes. Are they the same as the human beings who have left written documents on their life? The answer is yes. Did they believe in God? The answer is: we have no idea about their culture, their religion, their family life, etc. Their "Creator God" seems to be unknown and unmentioned by all religious leaders and scholars. To speak of an unknown God, we can only refer to an infinite God, whose infinite nature is totally beyond our human understanding.

The many centuries of human life in our universe can be best understood if we believe that God is infinite. This is my main position in chapter 7. There are no limits to a God who is infinite. However, the infinity of God disallows the integrity of any religious group which claims to have the one and only possible religion. Given the beginning of human life about which we have little to know, the infinity of God seems to be the correct understanding of divine existence. All human beings, from any and all religions, might say that there can only be one God, but that only one God is an infinite God.

I am a Franciscan, that is, a follower of Francis of Assisi. John Duns was also a Franciscan. In 1308, the year of his death, he finally completed his last book, *A Treatise on God as First Principle, 4.46*. In the last pages of his volume Scotus says to God: "Te esse infinitum, et incomprehensibilem a finito" (You are infinite and incomprehensible to every finite person.) In some ways, I have led the readers of this volume to a similar conclusion. God is incomprehensible to every man and woman. Therefore, we can believe in God, but we cannot know God.

Bibliography

Achtner, Wolfgang. "Infinity as a Transformative Concept in Science and Theology." Chapter 1 in *Infinity: New Research Frontiers*, edited by Michael Heller and W. Hugh Woodin, 19–50. Cambridge: Cambridge University Press, 2011.
Adewale, Samuel. "The Names and Concepts of Deity: Our Language about Ultimate Reality." Chapter 4 in *Naming God*, edited by Robert P. Scharlemann. New York: Paragon, 1985.
Albright, W. F. "A Catalogue of Early Hebrew Lyric Poems (Psalm 68)." *Hebrew Union College Annual* 23 (1950–1951) 1–39.
Albright, W.F., and C.S. Mann. *Matthew*. Anchor Bible Series. Garden City, NY: Doubleday, 1971.
Alt, Albrecht. *Essays on Old Testament History and Religion*. Translated by R. A. Wilson. Oxford: Blackwell, 1966. Original text is *Der Gott der Väter*. Stuttgart: Kohlhammer, 1929.
———. "The God of the Fathers." In Alt, *Essays on Old Testament and Religion*, 1–77.
———. *Kleine Schriften zur Geschichte des Volkes Israel*. 3 vols. Munich: Beck'sche Verlagsbuchhandlung, 1953, 1959, and 1964.
Ansah, John K. "The Names and Concepts of God among the Buem and the Akan of Ghana." Chapter 5 in *Naming God*, edited by Robert P. Scharlemann. New York: Paragon, 1985.
Arndt, William, and Wilbur Gingrich. *A Greek-English Lexicon of the New Testament*. Chicago: University of Chicago Press, 1979.
Bardy, G. "Théophile d'Antioche." In *Dictionnaire de Théologie Catholique*, 1034–35. Paris: Libraire Letouzey et Ané, 1946.
Barnes, Michel René. "Latin Trinitarian Theology." Chapter 5 in *The Cambridge Companion to the Trinity*, edited by Peter C. Phan. Cambridge: Cambridge University Press, 2011.
Barnstone, Willis, ed. *The Other Bible*. San Francisco: Harper & Row, 1984.
Barth, Karl. *The Doctrine of Reconciliation*. Vol. 4 of *Church Dogmatics*. Translated by G. W. Bromiley. Edinburgh: T. & T. Clark, 1961.
Bauer, Walter. *A Greek-English Lexicon of the New Testament and Other Early Christian Literature*. Chicago: University of Chicago Press, 1979.
Baus, Karl. *Handbook of Church History*. Vol. 1. New York: Herder and Herder, 1965.
Blenkinsopp, Joseph. "Deuteronomy." Chapter 6 in *The New Jerome Biblical Commentary*, edited by Raymond Brown et al. Englewood Cliffs, NJ: Prentice Hall, 1990.
Bonsirven, Joseph. *Le Judaism Palestinien*. Paris: Beauchesne, 1934.

Bowker, John W. *God: A Brief History*. New York: Dorling Kindersley, 2004.
Bredin, Eamonn. *Rediscovering Jesus*. Mystic, CT: Twenty-Third, 1985.
Bright, John. *Jeremiah*. Anchor Bible 21. Garden City, NY: Doubleday, 1965.
Brown, F., et al. *A Hebrew and English Lexicon of the Old Testament*. Oxford: Clarendon, 1910.
Brown, Raymond. "Aspects of New Testament Thought." Chapter 81 in *The New Jerome Biblical Commentary*, edited by Raymond Brown et al. Englewood Cliffs, NJ: Prentice Hall, 1990.
———. *The Birth of the Messiah*. New York: Doubleday, 1993.
———. "Canonicity." Chapter 66 in *The New Jerome Biblical Commentary*, edited by Raymond Brown et al. Englewood Cliffs, NJ: Prentice Hall 1990.
———. *An Introduction to New Testament Christology*. New York: Paulist, 1994.
———. *An Introduction to the New Testament*. New York: Doubleday, 1966.
———. *Jesus, God and Man*. Milwaukee: Bruce, 1967.
———. *The Virginal Conception and Bodily Resurrection of Jesus*. New York: Paulist, 1973.
Brown, Raymond, et al, eds. *The New Jerome Biblical Commentary*. Englewood Cliffs, NJ: 1968.
Catholic Church. *Catechism of the Catholic Church*. Vatican City: Libreria Editrice Vaticana, 1997.
Cavadini, John. "Jewish Christianity." In *The HarperCollins Encyclopedia of Catholicism*, edited by Richard McBrien, 706. New York: HarperCollins, 1995.
Chan, Wing-tsit. *A Source Book in Chinese Philosophy*. Princeton: Princeton University Press, 1969.
Charles, R. H. *The Apocrypha and Pseudepigrapha of the Old Testament*. London: Oxford University Press, 1913.
Charlesworth, James H. *The Pseudepigrapha of the Old Testament*. 2 vols. Garden City, NY: Doubleday, 1983.
Cheng, Chun-ying. "The Trinity of Cosmology, Ecology, and Ethics in the Confucian Personhood." In *Confucianism and Ecology: The Interrelation of Heaven, Earths and Humans*, edited by Mary Evelyn Tucker and John Berthrong, 211–35. Cambridge, MA: Harvard University Press, 1998.
Childs, Brevard. *The Book of Exodus*. Louisville, KY: Westminster, 1976.
Clayton, Philip, and Zachary Simpson, eds. *Oxford Handbook of Religion and Science*. New York: Oxford University Press, 2006.
Clement of Alexandria. "Stromata, Στρωμάτεων." In *Patrologia Graeca* vols. 8–9, edited by J. P. Migne. 1890–1891.
Clifford, Richard. "Exodus." Chapter 3 in *The New Jerome Biblical Commentary*, edited by Raymond Brown et al. Englewood Cliffs, NJ: Prentice Hall, 1990.
Cohen, A. *The Twelve Prophets: Hebrew Text & English Translation*. Bournemouth, UK: Soncino, 1948.
Constitutiones, Decreta, Declarationes: Concilium Vaticanum II. Vatican City: Typis Polyglottis Vaticanis, 1966.
Crehan, Joseph Hugh. *Athenagoras: Embassy for the Christians*. Westminster, MD: Newman, 1956.
Dalmau, P. Iosepho M., S.I., and P. Iosepho F. Sagüés, S.I. *De Deo uno et trino. De Deo creante e elevante. De peccatis*. Sacrae Theologiae Summa 2. Matriti: Biblioteca de Autores Cristianos, 1964.

Denzinger, Heinrich Joseph. *Enchridion Symbolorum: Definitionem et Declarationum de Rebus Fidei et Morum*. Freiburg: Herder, 1963.
Di Lella, Alexander A. *The Wisdom of Ben Sira*. Translated by Patrick Skehan. New York: Doubleday, 1987.
Dubois, J. A. *Hindu Manners, Customs, and Ceremonies*. Calcutta: Rupa, 1994.
Dupuis, Jacques. *Il christianesimo e le religioni: Dallo scontro all'incontro*. Brescia, Italy: Edizioni Queriniana, 2001. English translation by Phillip Berryman, *Christianity and the Religions: From Confrontation to Dialogue*. Maryknoll, NY: Orbis, 2002.
Eberhardt, Newman. *A Summary of Catholic History*. St. Louis: Herder, 1961.
Eisenmann, Robert H., and Michael Wise. *The Dead Sea Scrolls Uncovered: The First Complete Translation and Interpretation of 50 Key Documents Withheld for Over 35 Years*. Rockport, MA: Element, 1992.
Finegan, Jack. *Myth and Mystery: An Introduction to the Pagan Religions of the Biblical World*. Grand Rapids, MI: Baker, 1989.
Fitzmyer, Joseph. *The Gospel according to Luke*. Vol. 1, *I–IX*. Garden City, NY: Doubleday, 1981.
———. "Pauline Theology." In *The New Jerome Biblical Commentary*, edited by Raymond Brown et al. Englewood Cliffs, NJ: 1968.
Fox, Patricia. "Feminist Theologies and the Trinity." In *The Cambridge Companion to the Trinity*, edited by Peter C. Phan. Cambridge, UK: Cambridge University Press, 2011.
Fredericks, James L. *Buddhists and Christians*. Maryknoll, NY: Orbis, 2004.
Gaillardetz, Richard. *Ecclesiology for a Global Church*. Maryknoll, NY: Orbis, 2008.
Goldman, Shalom. *Samuel*. London: Soncino, 1951.
Goodspeed, Edgar. *The Apostolic Fathers*. New York: Harper, 1950.
Greenberg, Moshe. *The Religion of Israel*. Chicago: University of Chicago Press, 1960.
Gremillion, Joseph, and William Ryan, eds. *World Faiths and the New World Order*. Washington, DC: Interreligious Peace Colloquium, 1978.
Grenz, Stanley J. *Rediscovering the Triune God: The Trinity in Contemporary Theology*. Minneapolis: Fortress, 2004.
Heller, Michael, and W. Hugh Woodin. *Infinity: New Research Frontiers*. New York: Cambridge University Press, 2011.
Heltzel, Peter Goodwin, and Christian T. Collins Winn. "Karl Barth, Reconciliation and the Triune God." Chapter 10 in Phan, *The Cambridge Companion to the Trinity*.
Hertz, J. H. *The Pentateuch and Haftoras*. London: Soncino, 1957.
Holmes, Michael, ed. *The Apostolic Fathers: Greek Texts and English Translations*. Grand Rapids, MI: Baker, 1999.
Howell, F. Clark. *Early Man*. New York: Time-Life, 1965.
Hunt, Anne. *Trinity: Nexus of the Mysteries of Christian Faith*. Maryknoll, NY: Orbis, 2005.
Jenkins, Philip. *Jesus Wars: How Four Patriarchs, Three Queens, and Two Emperors Decided What Christians Would Believe for the Next 1,500 Years*. New York: HarperCollins, 2010.
Jeremias, Joachim. *New Testament Theology*. New York: Scribner, 1971.
Johnson, Timothy. *The Gospel of Luke*. Collegeville, MN: Liturgical, 1991.
Jonas, Hans. *The Gnostic Religion*. Boston: Beacon, 1963.
Justin Martyr. "First Apology, Ἀπολογία I" and "Second Apology, Ἀπολογία II." In *Patrologia Graeca*, edited by J. P. Migne, vol. 6. 1857.

———. *The Works of Justin the Martyr*. Library of the Fathers. Oxford: J. H. and Jas. Parker; London: F. and J. Rivington, 1861.

———. "Προς Τρυφωνα Ιοδαιον Διαλογος." In *Patrologia Graeca*, edited by J. P. Migne, vol. 6. 1857.

Kärkkäinen, Veli-Matti. "The Trinitarian Doctrines of Jürgen Moltmann and Wolfhart Pannenberg in the Context of Contemporary Discussion." Chapter 13 in Phan, *The Cambridge Companion to the Trinity*.

Kaufmann, Yehezkel. *The History of Israelite Religion*. 8 vols. Tel Aviv: Bialik Institute-Dvir, 1937–1956. Translated and abridged by Moshe Greenberg, *The Religion of Israel*. Chicago: University of Chicago Press, 1960.

Kim, Heup Young. *Christ and the Tao*. Hong Kong: Christian Conference of Asia, 2003.

———. "The Tao in Confucianism and Taoism: The Trinity in East Asian Perspective." Chapter 17 in Phan, *The Cambridge Companion to the Trinity*.

Kleist, James. *The Didache, The Epistle of Barnabas, The Epistles and the Martyrdom of St. Polycarp, The Fragments of Papias, and the Epistle to Diognetus*. Westminster, MD: Newman Press, 1948.

———. *The Epistles of St. Clement of Rome and St. Ignatius of Antioch*. Westminster, MD: Newman Bookshop, 1946.

Kloppenburg, Bonaventure. *A Eclesiologia do Vaticano II*. Petropolis, Brazil: Editora Vozes Limitada, 1971.

Knabenbauer, Joseph. *Commentarius in Ecclesiasticum*. Paris: Lethielleux, 1902.

Knitter, Paul. *Introducing Theologies of Religions*. Maryknoll, NY: Orbis, 2002.

Komonchak, Joseph, et al., eds. *New Dictionary of Theology*. Wilmington, DE: Glazier, 1987.

Kraus, Hans-Joachim. *Psalmen*. Vol. 1. Netherlands: Neukirchener Verlag, 1960.

Kselman, John, and Michael Barré. "Psalms." Chapter 34 in *The New Jerome Biblical Commentary*, edited by Raymond Brown et al. Englewood Cliffs, NJ: 1990.

Küng, Hans, and Julia Ching. *Christianity and Chinese Religions*. New York: Doubleday, 1989.

Lacugna, Catherine Mowry. "Fatherhood of God." In *The HarperCollins Encyclopedia of Catholicism*, 520. New York: HarperCollins, 1966.

———. "The Trinitarian Mystery of God." In *Systematic Theology: Roman Catholic Perspectives*, edited by Francis Schlüssler Fiorenza and John P. Galvin, vol. 1. Minneapolis: Fortress, 1991.

Laks, André. "Anaxagoras." In *Greek Thought: A Guide to Classical Knowledge*, edited by Jacques Brunschwig and Geoffrey E. R. Lloyd, translated by Rita Guerlac and Anne Slack, 525–34. Cambridge, MA: Belknap of Harvard University Press, 2003.

Lee, Eun-Bong. "The 'Oriental' View of Nature and God." In *Naming God*, edited by Robert P. Scharlemann, 98–105. New York: Paragon, 1985.

Lee, Jung Young. *The Trinity in Asian Perspective*. Nashville: Abdington, 1996.

Lee, Yongho Francis. "Bonaventure and Chinul: Christian and Buddhist Models for Integration of the Intellectual and Spiritual Life." PhD diss., Notre Dame University, 2017.

Lightfoot, J. B., and J. R. Harmer. *The Apostolic Fathers*. Grand Rapids, MI: Baker, 1989.

MacCulloch, Diarmaid. *Christianity: The First Three Thousand Years*. London: Penguin, 2009.

MacKenzie, R. A. F. *Sirach*. Wilmington, DE: Michael Glazier, 1983.

Maertens, Thierry. *Bible Themes: A Source Book*. Vol. 1. Notre Dame: Fides, 1964.

Marshall, I. Howard. *The Gospel of Luke*. Grand Rapids, MI: Eerdmans, 1978.
McBrien, Richard. *Catholicism*. New York: HarperCollins, 1994.
McKenzie, John. "Aspects of Old Testament Thought." Chapter 77 in *The New Jerome Biblical Commentary*, edited by Raymond Brown et al. Englewood Cliffs, NJ: Prentice Hall, 1990.
McNamara, Martin. *Intertestamental Literature*. Wilmington, DE: Glazier, 1983.
Metzger, Bruce M. "The Language of the New Testament." In *The Interpreter's Bible 7*, 43-59. New York: Abingdon Press, 1951.
Ming, Tu Wei. *New Horizons in Eastern Humanism*. New York: Taurus, 2011.
Moloney, Francis. "Johannine Theology." Chapter 83 in *The New Jerome Biblical Commentary*, edited by Raymond Brown et al. Englewood Cliffs, NJ: Prentice Hall, 1990.
Moltmann, Jürgen. *Trinität und Reich Gottes*. Munich, Germany: Christian Kaiser Verlag, 1980. English translation by Margaret Kohl, *The Trinity and the Kingdom of God*. New York: Harper and Row, 1981.
Montefiore, Claude, and Herbert Loewe. *A Rabbinic Anthology*. New York: Shocken, 1974.
Mourret, Fernand. *A History of the Catholic Church*. Vol. 1. St. Louis: Herder, 1944.
Myers, Jacob. *I and II Esdras*. Anchor Bible. Garden City, NY: Doubleday, 1974.
Nagasawa, Yugin. *The Existence of God: a Philosophical Introduction*. New York: Routeledge, 2011.
Nakamura, Hajime. *Ways of Thinking of Eastern Peoples: India-China-Tibet-Japan*. Translated by Philip Wiener. Honolulu: University Press of Hawaii, 1974.
Nikel, Johannes. *Das Buch Jesus Sirach*. Münster: Aschendorffische Verlagsbuchhandlung, 1913.
Osborne, Kenan. *The Infinity of God and a Finite World*. St. Bonaventure, NY: Franciscan Institute Publications, 2015.
Osborne, Kenan, and Ki Wook Min. *Science and Religion: Fifty Years after Vatican II*. Eugene, OR: Wipf and Stock, 2014.
Pahnoyotav, Alexander, et al. *Old Testament Pseudepigripha*. Grand Rapids, MI: Eerdmans, 2013.
Papanikolaou, Aristotle. "Sophia, Apophasis, and Communion: The Trinity in Contemporary Orthodox Theology." Chapter 14 in Phan, *The Cambridge Companion to the Trinity*.
Pappas, Harry. "Salvation in Christ: Perspectives of the Orthodox Church." In *Salvation in Christ: Comparative Christian Views*, edited by Roger R. Keller and Robert L. Millet, 237–62. Provo, UT: Religious Studies Center, Brigham Young University, 2005.
Patte, Daniel, ed. *Cambridge Dictionary of Christianity*. New York: Cambridge University Press, 2010.
Phan, Peter C. *Being Religious Interreligiously*. Maryknoll, NY: Orbis, 2004.
———, ed. *The Cambridge Companion to the Trinity*. New York: Cambridge University Press, 2011.
Quasten, Johannes. *Patrology*. Vols. 1–3. Westminster, MD: Newman, 1950, 1962, 1963.
Rahner, Karl. "Remarks on the Dogmatic Treatise De Trinitate." In *Theological Investigations*, translated by Kevin Smyth, 4:77–102. New York: Seabury, 1974.
———. *Theological Investigations*. Translated by Kevin Smyth. New York: Seabury, 1974.

———. "Theos in the New Testament." English translation in *Theological Investigations*, translated by Kevin Smyth, vol. 1. London: Darton, Longman, and Todd, 1961.

———. *The Trinity*. New York: Herder and Herder, 1970.

Rayan, Samuel. "Naming the Unnamable." Chapter 1 in *Naming God*, edited by Robert P. Scharlemann. New York: Paragon, 1985.

Ringgren, Helmer. *Israelite Religion*. Translated by David Green. Philadelphia: Fortress, 1966.

Rosenbaum, M., and A. M. Silbarmann. *Hamisha humshe torah: 'im Targum 'Onklos, ha-haftorot ve-hatefilot lkol shebetot ha-shana ve'im perush Rashi*. London: Shapiro, Vallentine, 1946.

Rovelli, Carlo. *Some Considerations on Infinity*. New York: Riverhead, 2014.

Rucker, Rudy. "Introduction." In *Infinity: New Research Frontiers*, edited by Michael Heller and W. Hugh Woodin. New York: Cambridge University Press, 2011.

Russell, D. S. *The Method & Message of Jewish Apocalyptic*. Philadelphia: Westminster, 1964.

Schlatter, Adolph. *Wie sprach Josephus von Gott*. Gütersloh, Germany: Verlag C. Bertelsman, 1910.

Schönmetzer, Adolphus, ed. *Enchiridion Symbolorum*. Vol. 32. Freiburg: Herder, 1963.

Schwöbel, Christoph. "Wolfhart Pannenberg." In *The Modern Theologians: An Introduction in Christian Theology in the Twentieth Century*. Cambridge, MA: Blackwell, 1997.

Shults, F. LeRon. *Reforming the Doctrine of God*. Grand Rapids, MI: Eerdmans, 2005.

Shun, Kwong Loi. *Mencius and Early Chinese Thought*. Stanford: Stanford University Press, 1997.

Slotki, Israel. *Chronicles*. London: Soncino, 1952.

———. *Isaiah*. London: Soncino, 1949.

Snape, R.H., ed. *A Rabbinic Anthology*. New York: Macmillian, 1937.

Speiser, Ephraim A. *Genesis*. Anchor Bible. Garden City, NY: Doubleday, 1964.

Strong, James. *The New Exhaustive Concordance of the Bible*. Nashville: Nelson, 1995.

Tan, Jonathan, and Anh Tran, eds. *World Christianity: Perspective and Insights*. Maryknoll, NY: Orbis, 2016.

Wallace, B. Alan. "Buddhism and Science." Chapter 2 in *The Oxford Handbook of Religion and Science*, edited by Philip Clayton and Zachary Simpson. Oxford: Oxford University Press, 2006.

Wippel, John E. *The Metaphysical Thought of Thomas Aquinas*. Washington, DC: Catholic University of America Press, 2000.

Yu-lan, Fung. *A History of Chinese Philosophy*. Translated by Derk Bodde. 2 vols. Princeton: Princeton University Press, 1983.

www.ingramcontent.com/pod-product-compliance
Lightning Source LLC
Chambersburg PA
CBHW062039220426
43662CB00010B/1565